RURAL LEADERSHIP
Emerging Trends

RURAL LEADERSHIP

Emerging Trends

A.S. MALIK
Professor and Chairman
Department of Public Administration
Kurukshetra University
Kurukshetra (Haryana)

DEEP & DEEP PUBLICATIONS PVT. LTD.
F-159, Rajouri Garden, New Delhi - 110 027

RURAL LEADERSHIP
Emerging Trends

ISBN 978-81-8450-407-1

Printed in India at MAYUR ENTERPRISES
WZ Plot No. 3, Gujjar Market, Tihar Village, New Delhi - 110 018

Published by DEEP & DEEP PUBLICATIONS PVT. LTD.
F-159, Rajouri Garden, New Delhi - 110 027 • Phone : 25435369, 25440916
E-mail : ddpubs@gmail.com • ddpubs@yahoo.com
Showroom :
2/13, Ansari Road, Daryaganj, New Delhi - 110 002 • Telefax : 23245122

Dedicated

To

My Respected Father

SH. R.S. Malik

Who guided me to hard work

Contents

Preface

The term "democracy" designates a government where the people share in directing the activities of the state. It means the government controlled by the people or their representatives not by a single class or a select group of people. The democracy is a way of life and it reflects from the everyday activities we perform to contribute the society in order to make it a better place to live in. It is a philosophy which insists on the rights and the capacity of people acting directly and through representatives, to control their institutions for their own purposes. The philosophy of democracy enshrines on the principles of equality of individuals and as far as possible their freedom from restraints. The restraints if need to be imposed then by the consent of majority and must essentially conform to the principle of equality. This philosophy is decentralized to local level through the Seventy-third Constitutional (Amendment) Act, 1992 especially for the people living in the villages of India.

The constitutional amendment envisages the empowerment of people especially the Scheduled Castes and women in order to attain equality of individuals (reservation provisions), restraints by the consent of majority (provision for Gram Sabha), and direct and indirect control (through Ggram Sabha or elected representatives respectively) of their local institutions. In addition to this, the government has also introduced the measures such as transfer of funds, functions and functionaries to the Panchayati Raj Institutions in order to strengthen them and their leadership. However, the experiences in post amendment period, no doubt, indicates that these institutions are acquiring strength and spirit of democratic decentralization but unfortunately are unable to fulfill the desired expectations especially in terms of empowering the scheduled castes and women leadership.

The traditional and dominant leadership still control the decision making process of these institutions. The analysis of the information pertaining to the effectiveness of castes and its numerical strength, gender, education, economic well-being and reservation provisions has dissimilar level of impact (sometimes significant and at other time not so significant) on the attitudes, competence and performance of scheduled castes, women and general/dominant section of rural leadership.

The author wishes to acknowledge the support of Indian Council of Social Science Research New Delhi, Kurukshetra University Kurukshetra, Mr. Sahib Singh and Deep & Deep Publications (P) Ltd., New Delhi, and he is also thankful to every one of them.

A.S. MALIK

1

Introduction

The 'Local Self Government' refers to administration 'of a locality—a village, a town, a city or any other area smaller than state' by a body representing local inhabitants, enjoying a certain degree of autonomy, raising a part of its revenue through local taxation and spending it on services which are local in character as distinct from the services provided by the state or central agencies.[1] The local-self government has a feature of having an elected body of representatives of local eligible inhabitants and that is entrusted with the responsibilities of governance, obviously, within a limited sphere of freedom and indiscipline. This institution has the ability to provide representative, responsible and accountable government.[2] The normative base of local government lies in its ability to promote participation.[3] It is justified for its virtues as a representative, participatory, responsive, accountable, territorial, and a communitarian institution.[4]

It is believed that elected local government is characterized as an efficient level of government.[5] In other words, the local government acts as an effective and efficient provider of local services to meet local needs.[6] However, the efficient service and discharge of duties and responsibilities in local government also depends on the ability of the institution to raise resources for it. More precisely, the level of performance of services largely influenced by 'a complex mix of social, demographic, political and economical factors which go to make up the environment within which each (local government) has to operate'.[7]

The local self-government system in India particularly at village level had enjoyed a very high level of autonomy for regulating its affairs, for undertaking tasks of social and economic development, and for raising their own resources in ancient times.[8] Thereafter, the position and status of this institution has changed in a significant manner. It has happened, even when 'the powers of governance entrusted to panchayat, in earlier time, by the *tacit* consent of the community were replaced, now by the mechanism of conferring powers through constitutional and legal devices'.

It is stated that the local self governments were 'more widespread, more real and successful' in the ancient times than during the British Rule and during the post-independence period.[9] Thus, the belief that local government everywhere and always is efficient not necessarily true. In reality, the local government system is political-*cum*-representational one. It is continuously going through a process of change and therefore its role efficacy has always been unclear and decided by the contemporary conditions. In other words, the role and nature of local government are contingent on the complex milieu of social, cultural, demographic, political and economic factors prevailing in an area in a particular point of time.

LEADERSHIP—CONCEPT

The important factors that shape the nature and performance of an institution are the culture and the behaviour pattern demonstrated by those who lead and control the said institutions and who lead the institutions or organizations are the leaders. In other words, anybody who has responsibility for the performance of others (in the present study for village community) is a leader. The individuals referred as leaders are power holders, men of power, power centres and power elites. A leader is a person who exerts special influence over a number of people.[10]

Leader or leadership does not exist in a vacuum but prevails in a given framework or context. The contextual conditions like position, nature of task, characteristics of the followers and power influence the nature and effectiveness of a leader or leadership in a community/organization. Gangrade, maintained that a leader can not be conceived of without followers.[11] Thus, leadership is essentially an interaction between the leaders and the followers. The behaviour of one is generally influenced by the behaviour of the other, while the behaviour of both is determined by the nature and structure of social system in which they interact.

In the functional leadership model, one conceives of leadership not as a person but rather as a set of behaviours that help a group to perform their task or reach their goal. The leadership is considered as a function of the group.[12] Therefore, an individual (leader) must exhibit one's personality and character in such a manner that makes him/her different from other members of the group in relation to the capability to perform the function of leadership. Anyone, who has the willingness to be a leader and tries to achieve a common goal, can become a leader. Traits can be changed or reduced by focusing on the more desirable traits and then using them to overpower the unhealthy ones. As every individual have one or more unhealthy traits therefore perfect leader is a dream which can not be realized. But the better leaders concentrate on and grow their desirable traits so that they over-power their weaker traits.

Competence, commitment, equity, courage and judgment are essential for a leader to be successful. Power is essential in a leader, but by itself it is insufficient to permit him to lead society or to set a direction for its progress. Persons holding power in a society or an institution may not be necessarily be leader there. Charisma is a function of follower ship which, in turn, is fashioned by the innate capacity of the leadership to perceive the nature and direction of change, to articulate the dominant—feelings of the followers and to transform the prevailing modes of social behaviour and institutions so that society is carried well near its cherished ideas.[13] Ketter identifies a true leader as one working collaboratively with people rather standing over them.[14]

The leadership organizationally and narrowly defined as 'the ability of an individual to influence, motivate, and enable others to contribute toward the effectiveness and success of the organizations of which they are members'.[15] Literally, leadership means to lead, to excel, to be in advance, to guide others, to be the head of an organization, to hold command etc.

Contrary to popular thinking, the term "leadership" is a recent addition to the English language. In fact, the word did not come into usage until the late 19th century. Although the words "lead" and "leader" have a much longer history, they usually referred only to authority figures. The birth and evolution of the idea of "leadership" focuses on a much more complex concept that reaches beyond the single leader.

Leadership is defined as the exercise of influence or authority within a group by one or more members.[16] It also means the direct, face to face contact between leader and followers; it is personal social control.[17] Leadership is the activity of persuading people to cooperate in the achievement of a common objective.[18] Tead regards it 'as an activity of influencing to cooperate towards some goal which they come to find desirable'[19]. It is the activity of influencing people to strive willingly for mutual objectives.[20]

Leadership means giving direction in time of change, inspiring others, building team work and values and providing an example for others to follow. It calls for personal qualities, knowledge and skills of individual/individuals concerned. Leadership is the act of organizing and directing the interests and the activities of a group of persons as associated in some project or enterprise, by a person who develops the cooperation through securing and maintaining their more or less voluntary approval of ends and methods proposed and adopted in their association.[21]

Leadership is an inter-personal influence exercised in situation and directed, through the communication process towards the attainment of a specified goal or goals.[22] It is not independent of community rather it empowers the culture of community making it more self-sustaining.

Leadership depends on three factors, viz. the individual, the followers and the conditions.[23] It has been observed that the leadership emerges, grows and achieved within the group.[24] In fact, contemporary definitions most often reject the idea that leadership revolves around the leader's ability, behaviour, styles or charisma. According to Max Weber, leadership consists of the possibility of imposing one's will upon the behaviour of others.[25] The essence of leadership consists degree or the extent of influence which one person (leader) has over the behaviour of another. Charisma, power and popularity are the three main attributes associated with the leadership. It (leadership) is constant in any equation of social, economic or political change taking place in a society. Popularity may be a necessary but not a sufficient condition for being an effective leader. Leadership is a talent for transformation, the ability to bring out the best in others for the greater good of all. It means inspiration and illumination. R.T. Lapiere and R.R. Farnsworth define leadership as the behaviour that affects the behaviour of other people more than their behaviour affects that of the leader.[26]

George Terry has defined leadership as: 'the activity of influencing people to strive willingly for group objectives'.[27] Krech and Crutch-field observed that the inter-personal relationships within a group are to a greater extent determined by the structure of group rather than by the personality of the individual.[28]

Leadership is not static but ever-changing phenomenon according to man, milieu and moment.[29] Barnard, Millet, Lasswell and Terry have made efforts to list the qualities of the leadership. They described the qualities of leaders as personal largely shaped by the social, educational, economic, political, cultural factors and endowed by birth.

Today, scholars discuss the basic nature of leadership in terms of the "interaction" among the people involved in the process: both leaders and followers. Thus, leadership is not the work of a single person; rather it can be explained and defined as a "collaborative endeavor" among group members. Therefore, the essence of leadership is not the leader, but the relationship.[30]

Rost says that leadership is an influence relationship among leaders and followers who intend real changes that reflect their mutual purposes.[31] He reminds us that leadership is not what leaders do. Rather, leadership is what leaders and followers do together for the collective good. In today's society, leaders operate in a shared-powered environment with followers. No longer does a single leader have all the answers and the power to make substantial changes. Instead, many people participate in leadership, some as leaders and others as followers. It is only when all work together; only then successful changes for mutual purposes can be ensured in the society.[32]

The leadership when defined in terms of relationships between the leaders and followers is composed of four basic components. Each and every component is essential and must exist in a particular relationship, only then, it is called as leadership. The components are: (1) The relationship is based on influence. This influence is multi-directional, meaning that influence can go any way (not necessarily top-down), and the influence attempts must not be coercive. It means that the relationship is not based on authority, but rather on persuasion. (2) Leaders and followers are the people in this relationship. In other words, both leaders and followers are doing leadership. It does not mean that all players in this relationship are equal, but all active players practice influence. Typically, there is more than one follower and more than one leader in this arrangement. (3) Leaders and followers intend real changes. Intend means that the leaders and followers promote and purposefully seek changes. Real means that the changes intended by the leaders and followers must be substantial. (4) The changes, the leaders and followers intend, reflect their mutual purposes. The key is that the desired changes must not only reflect the wishes of the leader but also the desires of the followers.[33]

The traditional approach (Industrial paradigm) to leadership is characterized by a top-down philosophy, where the leader is decisive, efficient, unemotional and in control. The post-industrial leadership paradigm, on the other hand, is characterized by collaboration, power-sharing facilitation and empowerment.[34] The relationships are ecological and temporal in nature. The ecological conditions in local governments are political, constitutional and social, economic and cultural background of the leaders and the people being led by them. As a result, the rural leadership is different from other leadership mainly because of its setting. It is represented in Panchayat Raj Institutions and has certain specific characteristics—owing to the rural conditions in the country. Therefore, it needs to be studied in holistic perspective.

There is difference between leading and leadership also. The 'leading' is a social phenomenon or effect and defined as determining the time and direction of group movement or—more generally—the time and type of group activity. However, the leadership is an individual trait.[35] Similarly, the leadership and management are not the same things. The two concepts do overlap each other but there are some important differences between them.

Kotter argues that leadership exists among free and equal people. It is about winning the followers to be willing to take a journey and what needs to be done in order to achieve a common purpose or vision. If force of any kind has to be used to get people to do the will of some one else then, it ceases to be leadership.[36]

ROLE OF LEADERSHIP

There is recognition of the importance of leadership—of people who can instill a sense of moral and social responsibility into their every activity and who built communities of common ideas and ideologies. The leadership guides others through personal examples and character and enables the people to reach their goals. Leadership translates vision into reality by inspiring followers who want to experience the change process.

Good leadership and leadership for the good of the people are very vital in a village or community. Change is constantly on the move and the responsibility for bringing change largely depends on the local leadership in a traditional rural society. This need is increasing with the rapid socio-economic change taking place all around the rural areas or the village/s.

Leadership is the critical ingredient in successful regional development. Therefore, it needs to be strengthened, not by using a single strategy, rather adopting different kind of contingent strategies for achieving the desired objectives. The quality of community leadership is critical to the quality of life of people of the said community.

The village leadership is also important in the sense that each society needs an effective leadership at all levels and village constitutes the lowest level which is in direct contact with the village community. If the community (village community) is to be able to act as a unit, it must have leadership which is recognized and has community confidence. Community leaders are necessary to take decisions, to direct community activities, and to speak for the community both in relation to its internal organization and its outside relationships. If there is no leader, no one can speak for the community and the effective community action is aborted.[37] Ashok Mehta Committee appreciated the role of the PRIs for the advancement of the democratization process, the increased development orientation of the people, and the rise of new rural leadership to effectuate rapid development in rural India.

Therefore, for the development of better local leadership, it is essential that there must be adequate and accurate information relating to the leadership qualities, technical and professional skills of the leadership, and inadequacies of skills in the leadership.

There should be a real choice for people about how they are governed locally. The institution of local governance, i.e. the Gram Panchayat can provide this choice as Gram Panchayat be an efficient, transparent and accountable institution and reflective of public confidence and trust. Leadership of PRIs has been recognized to be the most crucial variable determining the quality and level of the realization of the tasks and functions vested in them.

The political system consists of political institutions e.g. government associations, e.g. political parties, and other organizations existing in society and performing various kinds of roles based on set norms and goals. The political institutions and associations collectively administer the affairs of society through power and authority endowed through certain principles and procedures established as per the constitutional and political philosophy of the State. Further, exercising the power by the political and executive authority is also in conformity with the existing system of authority of the state. The political system performs the political functions in a society.[38] It is an organization that successfully claims the monopoly of the legitimate use of physical force within a given territory, i.e. state.[39]

The rural political system which is basic and lowest plank of political life is constituent of the national political system and has its impact on the national political culture of the society. Therefore, it becomes very pertinent and essential to understand who hold the power in the village? Besides this, the development delivery system in the country is effected through PRIs and many kinds of reforms were introduced in past and have been introduced to make a dent in rural society. The 73rd Constitutional Amendment Act 1992 and other related measures might have changed the traditional rural leadership and what kind of this newly emerged power structure is the question which needs to be answered.

In the traditional power system in rural area or villages, the main dimensions of power system were: the zamindari system, the caste system and the village panchayat. The villagers referred their social, economic and other problems either to the landlords/zamindars or to their caste leaders or to the village panchayat. But, after independence, the traditional rural leadership has undergone many changes, particularly because of abolition of 'jagirdari' and 'zamindari' system which were synonymous of traditional power system. The process of replacing hereditary and caste leadership, elected persons with political backing was launched not only to train them as political leaders but also to ensure active and effective people participation essential to execute the rural development programmes in the country. In this new process of change, the individual and his capacities to perform his role does merit much more than the caste or class of the leader.

In other words, the leader must possess the sufficient attributes which can elect him/her to the PRIs and enough politically aware to generate motivation among people to participate in rural development activities in the village taking place on government initiative. Many kinds of reforms, beginning from Balwantrai Mehta Committee Report on Democratic Decentralization, were introduced to strengthen the rural leadership in the country consequently social, economic and political changes have taken place in the rural areas of the country.

The power holders in rural areas are classified as: (a) those who have power based on the ownership and control of land; (b) those who have power based on their caste; (c) those who have powers based on their numerical strength (a dimension introduced by democratic system); and (d) those who have power because of the position they hold (as a result of introduction of democratic and other formal models of governance).[40]

Rural population comprising about 72 per cent of total population lives in villages. Their main occupation is agriculture and thus has plenty of surplus time to indulge in politics or other social and cultural activities. They have close personal ties of kinship and friendship and lay stress on traditions, consensus and informality. The family structure, caste composition, religious variations, economic life, land relations, poverty and the standard of life in the villages are instrumental in shaping the social system and consequently the leadership pattern of ruralities. In other words, rural social life is a set of integrated functional model system in which each unit including local political institutions existing at village functioning in terms of role assigned to it.

STUDIES ON LEADERSHIP IN RURAL AREAS

There have been many research works on leadership in rural areas. The available literature on the rural leadership is given below:

According to a study of the pattern of emerging leadership of Panchayati Raj in Rajasthan, (1961)[41] conducted by the State Government after the Panchayat elections held in 1960, the *sarpanches* belonged to a comparatively younger age group and came from well to do families and were normally more than literate. The findings of this study rejected the pessimistic view that the introduction of Panchayati Raj has failed to bring about a change in the nature of rural power structure in India.

C.V.H. Rao[42] (1965) has noticed that a new cadre of leadership has emerged there. He found that considerable section of members, *sarpanches* and *up-sarpanches* of the panchayats are, from the landlord class or those who had traditionally held the leadership in the villages on the caste basis or those who have the backing of one or other political parties.

In his study of Tamil Nadu, Beteille[43] (1966) has found that the structure of rural power system had undergone some changes. The old basis of power structure such as birth and ritual status have been replaced by numerical support, party membership and contact with government officials. He concluded that a new type of popular leadership has emerged in the rural society in place of tradition elite. The study also found that there has been some divergence between caste, class and power. These categories have acquired some element of autonomy from each other as a result of land reforms, community development programme and the process of modernization and politicization. But despite this there continues a great degree of convergence between caste, class and power in the rural society.

In his work on changing power structure of village community in Eastern U.P. Yogendra Singh[44] (1969) has found that rural elite mostly belonged to the upper castes, which have succeeded in continuing their hold despite competition from lower castes and classes. The study rejected the finding of the studies of Government of Rajasthan (1961) and the conclusion of the inference that the rural power structure continue to be static.

V.M. Sirsikar[45] (1970), in his study conducted in Maharashtra, has concluded on the basis of empirical data that the rich peasantry which has a high traditional social status, wealth and other factors on its side dominates the rural power structure. He has also found the domination of Maratha caste on it. Besides this he noted that the congressmen have monopoly of power at the local level. According to him introduction of Panchayati Raj in Maharashtra has resulted in triple dominance of caste, a class and a party and result in the concentration of power in the hands of those who controlled co-operative institutions. Thus, he has not only highlighted the elitist character of power structure in Maharashtra but also drawn attention towards the fact that Panchayat Raj led to the concentration of power in the hands of upper strata of society instead of its democratic decentralization.

A case study of Rahimbad village of Mehrauli Community Development block of the Union Territory of Delhi conducted by Sushila Mehta[46] (1972) found that social and political consciousness had been created in the peripheral village. As a result the youth of the village revolted against the traditional leadership. This revolt culminated in the emergence of a new set of leadership younger in age and better educated than the traditional leadership.

On the basis of his study of rural power structure in the village of Ropar district of Punjab, S.R. Mehta[47] (1972) found that the villages having predominantly traditional social structure continues to have relatively traditional pattern of leadership. At the same time, he has also noticed a perceptible change in the emerging pattern of leadership in all the villages as young and educated leadership has definitely began to emerge. In his study of a village in South Bihar, N.K. Shukla[48] (1976) made an attempt to examine the characteristic of rural power structure at village panchayat level. The study that factionalism between various social groups affects the pattern of leadership in the political power structure of the village community.

In their study of the rural elite in Rajasthan Iqbal Narain[49] and his associates (1976) found that those who occupy elite status in social structure and economic system of the rural dominate its power structure. The members of the elite groups have more resources than the masses in social, economic and political terms. They are more conscious politically and better placed in terms of political linkages. S.N. Mishra[50] (1977) on the basis of his study of rural elite in Bihar has rejected the view that there has been little change in the nature of community power structure in rural India. He found that the traditional rural leadership based on kinship had been successfully challenged by the young and action-oriented leadership. Ascriptive leadership was being replaced by leadership based on achievement.

Surjan Singh Sharma[51] (1978) studied three village panchayats to analyze and explain the continuity, discontinuity and replacement of power position holders, i.e. village panchayats presidents. The study concluded that the *'ex-zamindar'*, *'Mukhiya'* and *'Lambardars'* tend to decline in power positions. They are being replaced by problem solvers in villages. Resourceful, active and urban-oriented persons are being accepted as leaders. There is discontinuity of individuals in power position but the structural continuity in the sense that the same castes are throwing leaders in each election, persists in the society.

A.Y. Darshankar[52] (1979) in his study of Panchayati Raj leadership in Beed district of Maharashtra concluded that all important leaders in the panchayati raj are indirectly elected. He argued that 'unfair means' can be used more easily election in case of limited electors than in a large diffused electorate. Groupism, kidnapping and use of money and appeal to caste have common in these elections. Social and economic factors played an important role in the selection of leaders. He concluded that the Maratha caste people dominated panchayati raj leadership in the district. It was also noted from the study that rises of women as a leadership was rather slow.

An empirical study of panchayat samities of Jhunjanu, Kota and Banswara districts of Rajasthan, conducted by D.S. Choudhry[53] (1981) revealed that the grassroot level political system is still by and large under the control of a leadership which comes from the larger family, higher castes, higher educated section of the society and from those who are economically well to do and have some record of social services to their credit. The study further concluded that even after democratization, the monopoly in politics of rich and well to do families continues at the grass-root level irrespective of caste, education and age and family. The study also pointed out that the level of awareness and quality of rural leadership at village level institution was by and large, poor.

Partap Singh[54] (1983) in his research paper based on a case study of Safidon block of the Jind district in Haryana state found that caste is no longer the decisive detriment of rural leadership. The middle castes have become dominant caste in village affairs because of their numerical strength. The traditionally dominant castes have lost much of their erstwhile political influence despite the fact that they continue to enjoy a high social status. The political processes and *'sanskritisation'* have enabled the lower castes to increase their influence. The leadership has to a large extent freed itself from the matrix of caste and has, in a manner of speaking, become much free floating than it had been previously. *The leaders of the higher castes put on the appearances if a non-believes in castes while seeking support of the lower castes.* It is found in the study that when there is contest between a high caste and low caste leader they prefer to support the former against the latter.

In his work on rural elite in Haryana, Hargian Singh[55] (1985) found that rural power structure in the state is male dominated. The leadership positions were passing on to the young and educated generations. The rural elites mainly come from high castes which have larger size of land. Most of them are agriculturists but some people from other occupations have also acquired the elite status.

D.C. Miglani[56] (1993), in his case study of village Amupur of Karnal district found that women could have become only token representative in rural power structure. He emphasized in the study that Backward Classes (BCs) and Scheduled Castes (SCs) do not act independently in the rural leadership due to poor economic conditions. The study also found that the trading class and the money lenders lost their hold over rural power structure due to green revolution, thus the power system in rural area is controlled by the sound economic position.

Harbhagwan Bathla[57] (1994) found that Saini, Punjabi Khatri, Rors, Jats and Jat Sikhs are more powerful than Banias and Brahmins in panchayat samities of Kurukshetra district. The scheduled castes got larger representation in these institutions than the backward classes in rural areas of he district. He found that rural power structure dominated by semi-literate and literate people. But Ch. Balaramulu and Raghuvendra Rao[58] (1995) in their study found that the leadership at Mandal Praja Parishad level has emerged from the upper castes (particularly Reddys and Velamas) who are rich. The leaders are middle aged and possessing higher qualifications.

N.R. Inamdar[59] (1991) emphasized for reservation of seats for weaker sections including women as this is the method which can ensure not only greater and wider participation but also be considered as conducive to a more rapid development. It would naturally help to upgrade their participatory capacities also.

M. Sam Roy[60] (1995) reveals that the traditional elite oriented panchayat leadership is slowly shifting in favour of weaker sections. The conclusion is based on the study conducted in Thiruvarangulum Panchayat Union in Pudukatai district in Tamil Nadu. It also concludes that while a number of ward members were elected from lower castes and lower income groups, the panchayats presidents were mostly from economically well to do among the numerically superior backward classes.

G.S. Praharaj[61] opined that the local leaders exercise a great influence on the members of the community with regard to the acceptance of or resistance of new practices advocated. The vital role local leaders can play in the extension work is widely recognized. A study conducted in Bihar concludes that the overall role performance of the developed village leaders group was significantly better than the under-developed village group and this supports an earlier conclusion that a few panchayat leaders were performing their roles better than others. The author found that leaders in developed villages were considerate, maintained effective channel of communication with the community, high degree of involvement with the village activity and also had higher organizing capacity. In addition, rural influential that proved to be intelligent were less authoritarian.

Ghanshyam Shah[62] (2001) observes that *Dalits* have not confined their politics to elections and parliamentary institutions. They also launch direct collective action and organise movements. These movements successfully built-up a good deal of pressure on the ruling classes and compelled them to give concession to *Dalits*. However, the movement, which primarily aims at bringing about revolutionary social transformation, has a long way to go. Perhaps the empowerment of leadership is the answer to this kind of the vision.

Hoshiar Singh and A.S. Malik[63] (2001) found that the process of social change has crept in the scheduled castes communities of the state and has acquired a momentum which can not be stopped now. No doubt, the process is slow and has been facing many difficulties but one must be optimistic about the positive results. In total, the process of societal transformation of scheduled castes communities is going on in the Haryana state.

Rajvir, S. Dhaka[64] (2002) opined that reservation of seats in favour of Scheduled Castes and Scheduled Tribes has made a serious dent in the traditional upper caste leadership. . . . Even though their voice is still feeble, the process of mobilization of weaker section has begun.

Suresh Mishra[65] (2002) in his study of a village panchayat called Ulda (near Allahabad) in UP, concludes that it is essential to have a few people within the community who know a little about outside world. In other words, there is a need of motivated group of people (like in Ulda village in UP) who can act as catalyst. This kind of leadership (composed of catalysts) can act as instrumental in bringing change in rural society.

Mohinder Singh[66] (2002) in an empirical study observes that the reservation of women in PRIs is an appropriate step. The author expects that women performance in managing rural affairs can be enough good if provided with appropriate support. However, the role of women representative has not been found effective because of the fact that they are considered as proxy of their family members. Despite some limitations, it is hoped that active and meaningful participation of women in grass-roots democracy would certainly take place after acquiring adequate and proper understanding of policy, planning and administration by them in the coming years .

Satyakam Joshi[67] (2003) in a study conducted in 1999 concludes that with regular elections, women and dalits gained confidence and learnt the art of parliamentary politics. They have begun to assert their rights, though in a small way. The position of upper castes has been challenged by the middle and Other Backward Classes (OBCs). It is also found that 53 per cent of Zila Parishads leadership in Gujarat constitute the first generation in their families to participate in public life. The percentages of such leaders are 58 and 75 per cent respectively for taluka and gram panchayats. Thus, people themselves are coming forward to participate in Panchayat Raj Institutions

(PRIs). Further, PRIs have been highly influential and governed by political parties. However, at Gram Panchayat (GP) level, elections are not fought on party lines and parties are not active at village level. But a majority of gram panchayat members (55 per cent) are affiliated with one or another political party.

B.B. Mohanty[68] (2003), based on his study concludes that in Maharashtra the members of backward classes and women take part in the decision making process in the Gram Sabha (GS). It is true that the elected representatives of excluded groups were unable to challenge the dominance of privileged groups. In a number of cases the women contest elections to retain the seat for the male members of their families and the local bureaucracy also dominates a scheduled caste or tribal woman sarpanch. Notwithstanding this, the inclusion of hitherto excluded communities has generated a kind of awareness among them on local governance and contributed to their empowerment. In fact, their participation is not only because reservation but also attributed to the impact of their strong movements against the privileged groups. Juxtaposed, with Maharashtra, the nature of participation and empowerment of members of hitherto excluded groups in the local governance in Orissa is the dominance of privileged groups and the dominance of local bureaucracy has still remained unchallenged.

Tina Mathur[69] (2003) observes that the reservation has insured women's access to the political process. But the socio cultural factors, constraining their effective presence and influence in the local institutions. The reservation has created political space for women. But the experience of reservation of seats for women on local bodies in Karnataka state has shown that there remains much to be done to make participation of women more effective.

A.S. Malik[70] (2005) that the gram panchayats established after 73rd amendment are no doubt more empowered but there is an urgent need on the part of polity to devolve the powers to these institutions so that they can be established as the real local self government in the country.

G. Palanthurai[71] (2005) has made an attempt to analyze the performance of women and *Dalit* leadership of Tamil Nadu panchayats. In his study the question how the said reserved classes of leaders (Women and *Dalit*) have performed their roles and responsibilities and how much they have been successful in delivering goods for the women and *Dalits* while discharging the responsibilities in panchayats. The study concludes that these representatives cannot deliver goods as they have to struggle a lot even to stabilize their position in the system.

PANCHAYATI RAJ IN HARYANA STATE

The institution of Gram Panchayat was set up in Punjab state as per the provisions of Punjab Gram Panchayat Act 1952, on mandatory basis. This Act was amended in 1960, and when Haryana became a separate state in 1966, the PRIs were having three tiers structure. These included the Gram Panchayats (under the amended Act), the Panchayat Samities and Zila Parishads established as per the provisions of amended form of Punjab Gram Panchayat Act, 1961 Punjab Panchayat Samities and Zila Parishads Act, 1961 respectively. During those days, the GP was the executive branch of the gram sabha and amendment in 1960 had also made it the agency of the PS for implementing development programmes within their area (sabha area). Further, the PS was composed of 19 primary members of whom 16 were elected by the panches and sarpanches, two were representatives of cooperative societies and one was a nominee of the market committee. These 19 members could co-opt four scheduled castes and two women as members of their Panchayat Samiti (PS). Those Members Legislative Assembly (MLAs) whose constituencies fell within the samiti area were made associated members. The Sub-Divisional Magistrate (SDM) and Block Development and Panchayat Officer (BDPO) (executive officer of PS) were its *ex-officio* members.

Similarly, the zila parishads were having indirectly elected members, two each from each panchayat samiti, chairpersons of all PS of the district and seven coopted members (five from SC and two women), the Members Parliament (MPs) and MLAs representing the district and the Deputy Commissioner from the official side. The PS was the executive agency and the ZP was given the status of a coordinating and supervisory body. Since the creation of Haryana in 1966 till 1993 the Punjab Gram

Panchayat Act, 1961 was amended nineteen times and amendment made in Haryana Act of 1987, made provision for the reservation of seats for the members of backward classes if their population was two per cent or more in the gram sabha area. It also provided for representation of one member of the backward classes in the panchayat samitis. Thus, the representation of different sections and inter-castes both in PS and ZP not only restricted one but also not real and meaningful. Therefore, these were not considered as popular institutions in real sense of the term but continued on this pattern till 1973.

A review committee, headed by Maru Singh in 1970, found the excessive and undue interference of bureaucracy and political elite comprising these institutions. The recommendations of the committee including strengthening of Zila Parishad on Maharashtra model were not accepted rather another ad hoc committee was constituted in 1972, which recommended the abolition of Zila Parishads terming these bodies as superfluous ones. As a result, Zila Parishads were abolished on 13 July 1973 in the state. These could be revived only after the constitutional amendment and enactment Haryana Panchayati Raj Act, 1994.

It is concluded by the study published by the Institute of Social Sciences, New Delhi that 'in spite of its weaknesses and its being dominated by the bureaucracy and politicians, the introduction of Panchayati Raj created greater political awareness in rural society and provided the rural masses increased opportunities for political participation. The women, the scheduled castes and the backward classes had been able to get some representation in gram panchayats and panchayat samities'.[72]

The post 73rd constitutional amendment which in turn resulted in the enactment of new Haryana Panchayat Raj Act 1994 and subsequent amendments in this Act have not only restored three-tier structure of panchayati raj in the state but also provided for reservation of seats for women, SCs and backward classes in all the three levels of these institutions.

This provision for the reservation of seats of members and chairpersons for women led to their being elected in one-third of the gram panchayats, panchayat samities and zila parishads led the scheduled castes to elect the candidates from their communities in the proportion to their population in the state. The backward class candidates succeeded to elect their caste's representatives not only from the seats reserved for them but also won the election on the open seats where either they were numerically strong or where they could take the advantage of factionalism among the dominant castes. Thus, the reservation provision for those that many remained unrepresented earlier has become an important political resource to be in rural local politics for reserved classes of people.

Therefore, the present study is an effort to understand the influence of various socio-cultural and economic factors in general and reservation provisions in particular on the rural local leadership of the state.

Population and Research Methods

The study of emerging patterns of rural leadership is quite complex in nature. It involves the culture, traditions, attitudes and interactions of the people with the modern democratic value system. A suitable methodology which can provide insights with the emerging patterns of leadership specifically in the field of social and economic background of rural leaders; their political background and political awareness; traits and characteristics of women and scheduled castes leaders, role perception, etc., need to be employed in such study. Therefore, keeping in view the nature and objectives of the study, the survey method was employed to obtain information relating to the above stated aspects of village level leaders and leadership.

Population of the Study

The present study pertains to Haryana state. The various panchayat samities and gram panchayats constitute the universe of this research study. Since whole of the State is divided into four sub-divisions, therefore, four districts were sampled out on random basis to conduct the field survey. The districts are Ambala, Karnal, Rewari and Jind. Further, since study pertains to the PS and GPs, therefore, panchayat samities and GP were selected on a specific criterion to make it representative one.

The criterion adopted to select panchayat samities was: (i) one of the PS must be headed by the woman, (ii) another must be headed by a person belonging to the scheduled caste, (iii) the chairperson of third PS was a person belonging to general castes, and (iv) the selection of fourth panchayat samiti i.e. Shahazadpur was made on the suggestion of the Director (Panchayats and Development), Government of Haryana Chandigarh. She (Director of Panchayats and Development) insisted to include this block in the study because: (i) it is a newly created block, and (ii) a scheduled caste woman Sarpanch from Rajpura village (elected during second election in post amendment period) had pleaded her suspension case before the Director (also woman) in a very intelligent and confident manner. Therefore, she made suggestion for including that village panchayat in the sample and naturally that made to include the Shahazadpur in Ambala district. Based on this criterion, the panchayat samities, namely, Shahazadpur (Ambala), Nilokheri (Karnal), Bawal (Rewari) and Julana (Jind) were sampled to conduct the present study.

The population of the study comprises of the elected leaders of gram panchayats and panchayat samities and officials associated with Panchayati Raj in the state. The elected leaders selected for this study are those who were elected before and after 73rd Constitutional Amendment Act, 1992. Further, the rural leaders sampled for the present study are both chairpersons and members of panchayat samities and sarpanches and panches of gram panchayats. The members of the youth organizations of the villages were also intended to be selected for obtaining information but such youth associations were not found in the sampled villages selected for the present study.

It is important to mention here that the base of selecting PS and GP was the second election held in post Amendment period. However, the leaders elected during the third elections were also included to make the study more inclusive and representative one.

The distribution of number of respondents from various districts/panchayat samities included in the study is given in the Table 1.1.

The selection of gram panchayats from the sampled panchayat samities was done purely on purposive basis and to ensure adequate representation to women, scheduled castes and

TABLE 1.1
Districts/Panchayat Samities

District/Panchayat Samities		*Frequency*	*Percent*
Ambala	Shahazadpur	81	25.3
Karnal	Nilokheri	96	30.0
Rewari	Bawal	89	27.8
Jind	Julana	54	16.9
		320	100.0

general castes panches and sarpanches. The sampled gram panchayats and number of sarpanches/panches selected for field survey is tabulated in Table 1.2.

TABLE 1.2
Sampled Villages

Villages	*Frequency*	*Valid Percent*	*Cumulative Percent*
Dhanana	34	10.6	10.6
Rajpura	20	6.3	16.9
Vir Badalwa	30	9.4	26.3
Karsa	30	9.4	35.6
Banipur	19	5.9	41.6
Nangal Teju	27	8.4	50.0
Malwi	17	5.3	55.3
Shadipur	16	5.0	60.3
Other villages*	127	39.7	100.0
Total	320	100.0	

* Other villages means the villages of the sampled chairman/members of various PS included in the study.

The study is based upon 320 PS and GP leaders and 18 officials who were contacted during the field survey to elicit relevant information. The data in Tables 1.1 and 1.2 exhibits that almost each GP and PS has been more or less similarly represented in the population. The less coverage of the Julana panchayat samiti and Malwi and Shadipur villages of this block are attributed to the fact that the PS and GP leaders elected during 3rd post-amendment election could not be contacted due to some unavoidable reasons.

It is also evident from the information presented in the Table 1.3 given below that the population of the study comprises of 215 (67.2 per cent) male and 105 (32.8 per cent) female PS and GP leaders.

TABLE 1.3

Rural Leaders Classified on Gender Basis

	Frequency	*Percent*	*Cumulative Percent*
Male	215	67.2	67.2
Female	105	32.8	100.0
Total	320	100.0	

The information reveals that the proportion of male and female leader is incidentally in proportion to the reservation provision made for women in the constitutional enactment. Thus, the sample is truly representative in relation to the proportion of women leaders in the total population of the study.

The another important characteristic of the study is the representation of castes in the sample as the present research study is primarily intended to differentiate between traditional dominant caste leadership and reserved class (which also include women) leadership in the post amendment period (See Table 2.8 in Chapter 2 of the book).

Another important aspect of the study is that this study intending to find out the variability of various characteristics associated with PR leadership of pre and post constitutional amendment period. Therefore, an earnest attempt has been made to include the leaders of pre-73rd Constitutional Amendment Act and post-amendment period. The post-amendment is further classified as PR leaders elected during first (December 1994), second (March 2000) and recently held third (April 2005) election. The data in Table 1.4 presents a picture of this kind of distribution of the sampled leadership.

TABLE 1.4

Rural Leaders Classified on the Basis of their Terms for which they were Elected in PRIs

	Frequency	*Percent*	*Cumulative Percent*
PS leaders before 73rd amendment	4	1.3	1.3
PS leaders after 73rd amendment (1st election)	30	9.4	10.6
PS leaders after 73rd amendment (2nd election)	63	19.7	30.3
PS leaders after 73rd amendment (3rd election)	30	9.4	39.7
GP leaders before 73rd amendment	27	8.4	48.1
GP leaders after 73rd amendment (1st election)	49	15.3	63.4
GP leaders after 73rd amendment (2nd election)	71	22.2	85.6
GP leaders after 73rd amendment (3rd election)	46	14.4	100.0
Total	320	100.0	

The information in the table 1.5 reveals that 39.7 per cent of the respondents are PS leaders and 60.3 per cent are sarpanches/panches of various gram panchayat. Further, it indicates that maximum percentage of respondents is those who were holding the office during the field survey i.e. the second election. The percentage of respondents (particularly belonging to PS) of pre-amendment period is only 1.3 per cent and 8.4 per cent for PS and GP respectively. It is limitation of this study as PS in Haryana has largely remained suspended during pre-amendment period.

PROCEDURE

(a) Tools and Techniques

In order to collect information from the respondents, i.e. gram panchayats leaders, panchayat samities leaders and panchayati raj officials, two set of schedules were prepared and used by the investigators to conduct the survey. Keeping in view, the nature of the sampled subjects, the interview method was considered as most appropriate tool for the collection of data.

In addition to this, the discussion method was also utilized to ascertain the opinions and perceptions of the officials, right from Director (Panchayats), Government of Haryana to village level officials, i.e. Gram Sachiv. The institution of youth associations could not be found in the villages sampled for the present study. Therefore, their view point could not be incorporated in the study. It means that the PS and GP leaders constitute the core population of the study and perceptions elicited from them are utilized to reach the conclusions of the present study.

(b) Construction of Interview Schedule

On the basis of the study of literature, information collected during pre-testing and experiences of some of the officers with panchayati raj, an exhaustive list of items pertaining to the research problem in hand was prepared. While framing questions of non-directive interview schedule for this purpose, suggestions given by scholars about language, frame of reference, levels of information, social acceptance, form of statement, etc. were also taken into consideration. The interview schedule was discussed with language expert and other fellow researchers to modify these in the light of suggestions made by them.

(c) Pre-Testing the Tool

The interview schedule prepared to conduct the survey of the elected village leaders was pre-tested in the village Malwi (Julana) and BDPO office Julana (where contact with a few of PS members could be made after a meeting) mainly to find out the efficacy of schedule framed for the purpose. The pre-testing of the second interview schedule meant for officials could not be made considering that only a few questions are asked in framed reference and the discussion method is utilized for eliciting pertinent information. The pre-testing has enabled the research team in discerning the relevant information from the actual field setting and helped in exploring the diverse issues or aspects for preparing the tool for the study. The interview schedules were also pre-tested to ascertain whether the questions are properly communicated and understood by the respondents in the same spirit with which it was included in the schedules.

(d) Analysis of Data

The collected data was tabulated and analyzed with the help of SPSS 11.5. The sampled leaders were classified on the basis of age, castes, education level, position held in panchayati raj etc., as differently designated broad categories. Simple tabular technique and chi-square method was employed (to differentiate the reserved and non reserved classes of leadership) for analyzing the data and to draw the inferences.

(e) Interpretation of Results

The results were discussed in the light of the overall objectives of the research work. The explanatory variables responsible for the research findings had been diagnosed and discussed through the field assessment and the findings of focus group discussions. The findings of the study were supported through the similar type of studies conducted in other parts of the country. The hypothesis and sub-hypothesis laid in the study had also been decisively analyzed in the light of research findings.

Notes and References

1. Venkatangaiya, M. and Parttabhiram, M. Local Government in India; Select Readings, p. 3, quoted in Srivastava, T.N. (2002). Local 'Self' Government and the Constitution. *Economic and Political Weekly*, July 27, p. 3191.
2. Mill, J.S. (1931). Representative Government, London: Everyman, Wilson, E.H. (1948). Essays in Local Government, Oxford: Blackwell. Jones, G. and Stewart, J. (1985). The case for Local Government, London: Allen and Unwin. Quoted in Goldsmith, Mike (1992) Local Government, *Urban Studies*, 29 (3-4), p. 394.
3. Syed, A. (1966). The Political Theory in American Local Government. New York: Random House and Dahl, R.A. (1967). The city in the future of democracy, *American Political Science Review*, 61(4), pp. 953-70, quoted in *Ibid*., p. 393.
4. *Ibid*., p. 394.
5. Sharpe, I. J. (1970). Theories of Local Government, *Political Studies*; 18, pp. 153-74 quoted in *Ibid*.

6. Goldsmith, Mike (1992). *op. cit.*, p. 394.
7. Goldsmith, Mike (1990). Local Autonomy—Theory and Practice in King, D. and Pierre, J. (eds.). Challenges of Local Government, London: Sage, p. 20.
8. Srivastava, T.N. (2002). *op. cit.*, p. 3191.
9. *Ibid.*
10. See, Atkinson, Philip (1999). Without leadership there is no change. Management Services, August, p. 9.
11. Gangrade, K.D. (1974). Emerging Patterns of Leadership: Comparative Study of Leadership and Social Structure, Delhi; Rachna Publications, p. 6.
12. See http://en.wikipedia.org
13. See Khatkhate, Deena R. (1990). Profile of Leadership in a Developing Society, *Economic and Political Weekly*, Nov. 24, p. 2596.
14. See Ketter, J.P. (1996). *Leading Change.;* Harvard Business School Press, pp. 25-158.
15. House, R.J. (2004). Culture, Leadership and Organizations—The GLOBE study of 62 societies. Thousand Oaks: SAGE Publications, p. 15.
16. Doob, C.B. (1988). Sociology: An Introduction, New York: Holt, Rinehart and Winston.
17. Allport, F.H. (1924). Social Psychology, Boston Houghton: Miffin, p. 41.
18. See Koontz, H. and O'Donnel, G. (1955) Principles of Management, New York, McGraw Hill, p. 69, quoted in Srivastava, R.S. (January-June 1996). *Prashasnika*, 28, (1), p. 39.
19. Tead, Ordway (1935). The Art of Leadership, New York: McGraw Hill, p. 20.
20. Terry, George (1956). Principles of Management. Illinois: Richard D. Irwin quoted in Srivastava, R.S. *op. cit.*
21. See, http://en.wikipedia.org/wiki/Path-goal_model.
22. Tannerbaum, Robert Weschler Irving R. and Massarik Fred (1961). Leadership and Organisation. New York, McGraw Hill, p. 24.
23. Barnard, C.L. (1948). Organization and Management, Cambridge Mass: Harvard University Press.
24. Ross, M.G. and Hendry, C.E. (1957) New Understandings of Leadership, New York: Association Press, p. 28.
25. See Weber, Max (1947). The Theory of Social and Economic Organization, New York, The Free Press.
26. La Piere, R.T. and Farnsworth, R.R. (1936). Social Psychology, New York: McGraw Hill Book Company.
27. Terry, George (1960). The Principles of Management, Homewood Ill: Richard Irwin Inc, p. 5.
28. Krech, David and Crutch-field, Richard, S. (1948). Theory and Problems of Social Psychology, New York, McGraw Hill, p. 401.
29. Likert, R. (1967). The Human Organization: Its Management and Value. New York: McGraw Hill.
30. See Rost, J.C. (1993). Leadership Development in the New Millennium, *The Journal of Leadership Studies*, November, pp. 91-110.
31. See *Ibid.*
32. See *Ibid.*

33. See Rost, J.C. (1991). Leadership in the 21st Century, New York: Praeger.
34. See Rogers, J.L. (Summer 1992). Leadership Development for the 90's: Incorporating Emergent Paradigm Perspectives, *NASPA Journal*, pp. 243-51.
35. Lamprecht, Jurg (Dec. 1996). What an individual a leader of its group? An evolutionary concept of distance regulation and leadership, *Social Science Information*, 35 (4), p. 597.
36. Kotter, John P. (1996). Leading Change, Boston: Harvard Business School Press, p. 25.
37. Sanderson and Palson (1939). p. 85.
38. Almond, Gabriel and Coleman, James, S. (1960). The Politics of Developing Areas, Princeton: Princeton University Press.
39. Weber Max (1947). *op. cit.*
40. Ahuja, Ram (1999). Society in India, Jaipur, Rawat Publications.
41. Quoted in Singh, Surat and Rahim, C.A. (1989), *Journal of Rural Development*, 8(4), p. 420.
42. Rao, C.V.H. (1965). Emerging Leadership in Panchayati Raj, *Kurukshetra*, 13, pp. 64-65.
43. Beteille, Andre (1965). Caste, Class and Power: Changing Pattern of Stratification in a Tanjore village, Berkeley: University of California Press.
44. Singh, Yogendra (1969). Changing Power Structure of Village Community: A Case Study of Six Villages in Eastern U.P. in Desai, A.R. (ed.). Rural Sociology in India, Bombay: Popular Prakashan.
45. Sirsikar, V.M. (1970). The Rural Elite in a Developing Society—A Study in Political Sociology, New Delhi, Orient Longman.
46. Mehta, Sushila (1971). Social Conflict in Village Communities, Delhi: S. Chand.
47. Mehta, S.R. (1972). Emerging Pattern of Rural Leadership, New Delhi: Wiley Eastern.
48. Shukla, N.K. (1976). Social Structure of an Indian Village, New Delhi. Cosmo Publications.
49. Narain, Iqbal and Pande, K.C. and Sharma, Mohan Lal (1976). The Rural Elite in Indian State: A Case Study of Rajasthan, New Delhi: Manohar Book Depot.
50. Mishra, S.N. (1977). Pattern of Emerging Leadership in Rural India; Patna: Ashish Publications.
51. Sharma, Surjan Singh (1979). Rural Elites in India, New Delhi: Sterling Publishers.
52. Darshankar, A.Y. (1979). Leadership in Panchayat Raj, Panchsheel Prakashan: Jaipur.
53. Choudhry, D.S. (1981). Emerging Rural Leadership in an Indian State: A Case Study of Rajasthan. Rohtak, Manthan Publications.
54. Singh, Partap (July 1983). Caste as Determinant of Rural Leadership: A Case Study of Haryana, *The Indian Political Science Review*, 17(2), pp. 157-62.
55. Singh, Hargian (1985). Panchayati Raj Administration in Haryana, Gurgaon: Indira Publications.
56. Miglani, D.C. (1993). Politics and Rural Power Structure: Emerging Trends, New Delhi: Deep & Deep Publications

57. Bathla, Harbhagwan (1994) Panchayati Raj and Political Parties—An Empirical Study of Grass-root Level in Haryana, Kurukshetra: Nirmal Book Agency.
58. Balaramulu, Ch. and Rao, Raghuvendra (Jan.-June 1995). Political Leadership in Panchayati Raj: A Study of Mandal Praja Parishad Leadership in Andhra Pradesh, *Administrative Change*, 22(2), pp. 168-76.
59. Inamdar, N.R. (1991). Panchayati Raj Leadership: Emerging Dimensions, *Journal of Rural Development*, 10(5), pp. 561-73.
60. Roy, M. Sam (1995). Emerging Panchayat Leadership and Polarisation of Political Power at Grassroot Level, *Journal of Rural Development*, Vol. 14(4), pp. 341-56.
61. Praharaj, G.S., Dimensional Role of the Rural Leaders in Relation to their Socio-Psychological Characteristics, pp. 139-45.
62. Shah, Ghanshyam (2001). Introduction: Dalit Politics in Shah, Ghanshyam (ed.) *Dalit Identity and Politics*, New Delhi, Sage Publications, pp. 17-43.
63. Singh, Hoshiar and Malik, A.S. (2001). Socio-Economic Development of Scheduled Castes in India, Jaipur, Aalekh Publishers.
64. Dhaka, Rajvir S. (Jan. 2002). Panchayat Raj Institutions in Haryana: A Field Study, *Kurukshetra*, pp. 46-48.
65. Mishra, Suresh (2002). New Trends in Community Initiatives: Panchayats in Action, *Journal of Rural Development*, 21(3), pp. 395-410.
66. Singh, Mohinder (2002). Role of Chairpersons of Samities: A Study in Haryana, *Dynamics of Public Administration*, 11-12, (1-2), pp. 1-7.
67. Joshi, Satyakam (2003). Panchayat Raj Leadership in Gujarat, *IASSI Quarterly*, 21 (3 & 4), pp. 79-91.
68. Mohanty, B.B. (2003). Panchayat Raj in Maharashtra and Orissa: An Overview, *IASSI Quarterly*, 21(3&4), pp. 92-125.
69. Mathur, Tina (2003). Women in Panchayati Raj Institutions: Reservation and Participation, *Dynamics of Public Administration*, 13-14(1-2), pp. 86-95.
70. Malik, A.S. (2005). Local Self Government at Village Level—An Assessment, *The Indian Journal of Political Science*, 66(4), pp. 773-92.
71. Palanithurai, G. (2005). Process and Performance of Gram Panchayat Women and Dalit Presidents, New Delhi: Concept Publishing Company.
72. Singh, Ranbir (2002). Haryana Panchayati Raj—Creating Political Awareness, *Kurukshetra*, Jan., p. 44.

Social and Economic Profile of Rural Leaders

The socio-economic background of leaders and particularly their age, castes, family sizes, educational achievements, occupations and land holdings, incomes, etc. have a significant impact in shaping the role and behaviour of the community leaders. The social and economic conditions decide the orientation of local leaders towards participative democratic life at local level. Many scholars[1] have found that there exist a positive relationship between the rural leadership and their social and economic background. Therefore, an effort is made to study the social and economic characteristics of the PR leaders of both pre-73rd amendment and post-73rd amendment period.

AGE

Age has always been an important variable for depicting social background of a group of persons in the society. The age influences the perceptions, orientations and behaviour pattern of the leaders particularly in the traditional society residing in the rural areas of the country. The authority of decision-making in the traditional rural society vests in the heads of the joint families and these heads are naturally of the elder age group. That is why, the institution of GP since its inception, irrespective the manner, in which it was composed, and what and how it delivered its responsibilities, its authority has always been monopolized by it (elder age group). Therefore, the age (elder age) has always been an important characteristic in traditional rural society for acquiring elite status not only at GP level but in each sphere of political activities and at all levels of political processes and phenomena. Therefore, scholars hypothesized that upper age groups dominate rural leadership and there is great respect for age in the village community.

S.P Jain[2] in his study conducted in Assam revealed that about 45 per cent of the leaders were in the middle age group of 36-55 years closely followed by 41.9 per cent in the younger age group of 25-35 years. Those who belonged to the old age group of 56 years and above accounted for 12.9 per cent only. Similarly, B.S. Bhargava[3] in a study conducted in Rajasthan found that out of the 51 leaders of a panchayat, 33.3 per cent were in the age group of 20-44 years. Forty-five per cent were in the age group of 45-54 years and 21.5 per cent in the age group of 55 to 74 years. Thus, the maximum percentages of leaders fall in the combined age group of 45-74 years.

The Indian Institute of Public Opinion conducted an All India Rural Survey in 1964 found that more than 50 per cent of the elected representatives were in the age group of 26-40 years. Only one-fifth belonged to the older generation (50 years), whereas the 40-50 age group shared nearly 30 per cent of the elected persons. The Bougirwar Committee (1971) presented the SES (socio-economic survey) of the office-bearers falling in age group of 26 to 45 years were 70 per cent whereas those above 45 years constituted 29 per cent. The percentage of elderly persons above 50 years was five only.[4]

M. Shiviah[5] in a study conducted in West Bengal reported that a majority of elected leaders of PRIs (51 per cent) were in the age group of 21-35 years, and a substantial number (31 per cent) in the age group of 36-45 years. In one another study, conducted in Andhra Pradesh. M. Shiviah[6] (1986) concludes that new leaders are relatively younger and better educated. Forty per cent of the new *sarpanches* belong to the age group of 21-35 years and 26 per cent to that of 36-55 years (in all 66 per cent). Surat Singh and C.A. Rahim[7] found that a majority of rural leaders belong to the middle age group though a considerable number of them belong to the younger age group also. This indicates that now the villagers have readily accepted the active leadership of the middle and younger age groups.

B.K. Chandrasekhar and Anand Ibanathan[8] found that there is a predominance of younger members in Zila Parishads and Mandal Panchayats. The data in the study indicates that more than three-fourths of women ZP members were below 45 years of age and more than one-half of them were in the age group of 25-35 years (the minimum age for contesting the elections is 25 years). Almost similar pattern of age was there in the mandal panchayats of the state. About 78.4 per cent women in these panchayats were below 45 years of age, and the single largest group was the age group of 25-35 years (44.3 per cent). In another study, M. Sam Roy[9] found that 33.2 per cent the panchayat presidents and 32.8 per cent ward members are in the age group of 41 to 50 years. The study inferred that most of the panchayat leaders are young and middle aged. The study also concludes that panchayat presidents are middle aged but ward members are of younger age.

In Haryana, D.C. Miglani[10] found that the voters tend to elect middle age people (31-40 years). He concludes that people in the village under study (Amupur village in Karnal district) indicate their favourable choice as middle-aged persons. Similarly, Subhash Chander[11] in his study in Haryana based on empirical evidences confirmed that the hold of village elders on rural power structure is declining but young leadership is also not emerging in the rural power structure. The failure of the youth to find favour with the electorate attribute to the fact that the villagers continue to consider maturity in age as an essential qualification for leadership role. According to this study, the majority of members (54.67 per cent) in the panchayat samities of the sub-division (Thanesar) belong to this group. It also states that the representation of eldest age group (61-70 years) remains marginal (1.33 per cent). However, in of elder age group (50-60 years) it is 21.33 per cent. Thus, the study confirmed the hypothesis that 'to a great extent rural power structure is dominated by upper middle age groups (41-50 years).'

The explanation of declining percentage of elder people in rural local institution is that their active period of life ends and they could not win against the more active and relatively younger leaders in the competition for power. However, it is also believed that the younger generation voters prefer relatively young leaders, as they possess similar social, cultural and political values, which are different from the elder leaders. The opportunity and possibility of younger person to be in state politics or to be an active worker of a political party is another important inducement, favouring young leadership at village level. However, it is, not a rule rather the conditions, more important in deciding such preferences.

The discussion on the variable of age reveals that there is an absence of standard to classify the age of people while describing them in the role of panchayat raj leaders. Some studies made the groups of leaders of 5 years and others of 10 years. Further, there is a lack of standardization/uniformity of standards who are young, middle aged and elder ones. It is obstructing the efforts to conduct scientific study on the theme to denote the real relationship of age with the nature of rural leadership in village panchayats or other local institutions.

Therefore, to make the study more scientific, a pattern of classification is suggested here as: younger people are those who are in the age group of up to 35 years; middle aged people 36-50 years; and elders above 50 years. These groups may be, further, categorized as: very young, younger and younger but mature; initial level of middle age, middle age and upper middle age; and elders, upper age elders and eldest. In other words, there should be three groups and further each sub-group should have three bands comprising each of 5 years age group as is given in Table 2.1.

The data in Table 2.1 reveals that 29.1 per cent of leaders are young and 46.6 per cent are in the middle age group (out of which maximum 19.4 per cent are in the age group of 36-40 years followed by 15 percent (41-45 years) and 12.2 per cent in the age group of 46-50 years. The remaining, 24.4 per cent of leaders constitute the age group of elders and about half of them are in between 51-60 years and another half above 60 years in age. Thus, the percentage of younger and middle aged leaders is quite significant and elders constitutes only one-

TABLE 2.1

Classification of PR leaders based on their age

Groups	*Age*	*Frequency*	*Percent*	*Cumulative Percent*
Young	Up to 25 years	7	2.2	2.2
	26-30 years	30	9.4	11.6
	31-35 years	56	17.5	29.1
Middle Age	36-40 years	62	19.4	48.4
	41-45 years	48	15.0	63.4
	46-50 years	39	12.2	75.6
Elders	51-55 years	22	6.9	82.5
	56-60 years	18	5.6	88.1
	Above 60 years	38	11.9	100.0
Total		320	100.0	

fourth of them. Thus, it is concluded that the young people have started to dominate the rural political life.

Further, the gender and age based classification of the sampled leaders is tabulated in Table 2.2.

TABLE 2.2

Classification of PR leaders based on their age and gender

		Gender		*Total*
Age groups		*Male*	*Female*	
Age	Young	56 26.0%	37 35.2%	93 29.1%
	Middle Age	97 45.1%	52 49.5%	149 46.6%
	Elders	62 28.8%	16 15.2%	78 24.4%
Total		215 100.0%	105 100.0%	320 100.0%

Pearson chi-square 7.698*.

The data in Table 2.2 makes it evident that the percentage of younger and middle age male leaders is lesser (26 per cent and 45.1 per cent respectively) in comparison to female leaders (35.2 per cent and 49.6 per cent respectively). The chi-square value (7.698) confirms the difference in age of male and female leaders constituting the sample. Therefore, the data in table lead to conclude that the female leaders are younger than the male leaders.

The information about the age of panchayati raj leaders is also classified with reference to their castes and data is tabulated in Table 2.3.

TABLE 2.3

Classification of PR leaders based on their age and castes

Age Groups	*Castes*						*Total*
	Farming castes	*Upper castes*	*Backward castes (A)*	*Backward castes (B)*	*Scheduled castes (A)*	*Scheduled castes (B)*	
Young	34 34.3%	10 25.0%	5 17.2%	11 29.7%	10 19.6%	23 35.9%	93 29.1%
Middle Age	41 41.4%	22 55.0%	12 41.4%	16 43.2%	27 52.9%	31 48.4%	149 46.6%
Elders	24 24.2%	8 20.0%	12 41.4%	10 27.0%	14 27.5%	10 15.6%	78 24.4%
Total	99 100.0%	40 100.0%	29 100.0%	37 100.0%	51 100.0%	64 100.0%	320 100.0%

Pearson chi-square 13.181.

The data presented in Table 2.3 shows that the percentage of younger leaders are the highest among scheduled castes-B (35.9 per cent) followed by farming castes (34.3 per cent) and least among backward castes-A (17.2 per cent). Further, the inter-caste composition of middle-aged leaders (maximum proportion of rural leadership) varies in between 41.4 per cent (among farming castes) to 55 per cent (among upper castes). However, the percentage of leaders to their castes' total in the elder age group varies from 15.6 per cent (scheduled castes-B) to 41.4 per cent (backward castes-A). The elders' average of all castes is about 24.4 per cent. In case of backward castes-A, the proportion of elders is again high, i.e. 41.4 per cent. Thus, the leaders belonging to backward castes-A are very traditional in electing their leaders, as the younger leaders are least and middle aged and elder aged constitute 82.7 per cent of them. Other castes which have more than 80 per cent of such leaders are scheduled castes-A. The chi square value 13.181 indicates that the election of a particular age group's leader does not vary with his/her caste in significant manner.

The age of the sampled leaders is also studied with reference to the terms for which the leaders were elected. (The term position is used in this report for the term for which PS or GP leaders have been elected in the gram panchayats and panchayat samities hereafter will be termed as PRIs). The information is tabulated in Table 2.4.

The data in Table 2.4 reveals that the percentage of young and middle aged group of PR leaders, before 73rd amendment act, is zero. It simply means that the PR leaders elected before 73rd amendment are now in the elder age group. Further, it is evident from the data that from first election onwards after 73rd amendment, the percentage of younger leaders has gone upwards. The chi-square value (65.121) also supports that the percentage of younger people in PR leadership is significantly different from the other leaders elected during earlier terms. In other words, the proportion of younger people is increasing in the PR leadership.

The data pertaining to age and family sizes of the sampled leaders is also interacted and pertinent information is tabulated in Table 2.5.

The data in Table 2.5 illustrates that there is significant difference among the leaders of different age groups with reference to their family sizes (chi-square value 45.367). The data in table reveals an interesting pattern. The pattern is that the middle-aged leaders are from all kinds of families, i.e. small, average and big families. They are also from very large families. However, maximum percentages (45.5 per cent) of leaders are from smaller families but elder leaders are from relatively large families. Thus, it is concluded that the family sizes in villages are decreasing owing to social transformation taking place there and leaders from those small families are joining local panchayat politics.

TABLE 2.4

Classification of PR leaders based on of their age and positions

Age Groups	*Positions (Terms for which elected)*								*Total*
	PS leaders before 73rd amendment	*PS leaders after 73rd amendment (1st election)*	*PS leaders after 73rd amendment (2nd election)*	*PS leaders after 73rd amendment (3rd election)*	*GP leaders before 73rd amendment*	*GP leaders after 73rd amendment (1st election)*	*GP leaders after 73rd amendment (2nd election)*	*GP leaders after 73rd amendment (3rd election)*	
(1)	*(2)*	*(3)*	*(4)*	*(5)*	*(6)*	*(7)*	*(8)*	*(9)*	*(10)*
Young	0 .0%	2 6.7%	20 31.7%	16 53.3%	0 .0%	7 14.3%	27 38.0%	21 45.7%	93 29.1%
Middle Age	0 .0%	19 63.3%	33 52.4%	8 26.7%	12 44.4%	27 55.1%	32 45.1%	18 39.1%	149 46.6%
Elders	4 100.0%	9 30.0%	10 15.9%	6 20.0%	15 55.6%	15 30.6%	12 16.9%	7 15.2%	78 24.4%
Total	4 100.0%	30 100.0%	63 100.0%	30 100.0%	27 100.0%	49 100.0%	71 100.0%	46 100.0%	320 100.0%

Pearson chi-square 65.121.

TABLE 2.5

Classification of PR leaders based on their age and family sizes

Age Groups	*Family sizes*					*Total*
	Up to 2 members	*3-4 members*	*5-6 members*	*9-10 members*	*Above 10 members*	
Young	0 .0%	25 45.5%	27 22.0%	32 30.5%	9 25.0%	93 29.1%
Middle Age	1 100.0%	26 47.3%	66 53.7%	51 48.6%	5 13.9%	149 46.6%
Elders	0 .0%	4 7.3%	30 24.4%	22 21.0%	22 61.1%	78 24.4%
Total	1 100.0%	55 100.0%	123 100.0%	105 100.0%	36 100.0%	320 100.0%

Pearson chi-square 45.367.

The data pertaining to the age is also classified based on the educational qualifications of the sampled leaders and presented in Table 2.6.

It is evident from the data in Table 2.6 that about one-third of leaders are illiterate and 11.6 per cent are educated up to primary level. About one third of them (29.1 per cent) are middle passed and 19.4 per cent have achieved the level of matriculation. The proportion of those who are more than matriculate is only 15.3 per cent of the total sampled leaders and many of them are at PS level instead of GP level.

Further, the proportion of leaders having educational level (above matriculation) is relatively higher in the younger age groups. The chi square value (34.391) indicates that different age groups of sampled leaders are significantly different from each other when classified on educational achievements.

The educational level of villagers in Haryana is increasing despite the migration of educated villagers to the urban settlements. Therefore; there is an expectation that in future many people that are more educated may join rural local politics at village or PS level. Naturally, higher educational level of leaders will definitely contribute to the real empowerment of the leadership at village level.

TABLE 2.6

Classification of PR leaders based on their age and educational levels

Age Groups	*Education Levels*								*Total*
	Illiterate	*Literate*	*Primary*	*Middle*	*Matriculation*	*Senior secondary*	*Graduate*	*Other*	
(1)	(2)	(3)	(4)	(5)	(6)	(7)	(8)	(9)	(10)
Young	17 18.3%	8 32.0%	10 27.0%	14 25.9%	23 37.1%	9 60.0%	7 29.2%	5 50.0%	93 29.1%
Middle Age	39 41.9%	9 36.0%	18 48.6%	33 61.1%	31 50.0%	4 26.7%	11 45.8%	4 40.0%	149 46.6%
Elders	37 39.8%	8 32.0%	9 24.3%	7 13.0%	8 12.9%	2 13.3%	6 25.0%	1 10.0%	78 24.4%
Total	93 100.0%	25 100.0%	37 100.0%	54 100.0%	62 100.0%	15 100.0%	24 100.0%	10 100.0%	320 100.0%

Pearson chi-square 34.391.

Lastly, the information on age is examined with reference to the estimated incomes of the sampled leaders. The data obtained is tabulated in Table 2.7.

The data in Table 2.7 clearly indicates the leaders age groups are not significantly differentiated on the basis of their estimated annual incomes (chi square 12.187). The leaders of all age groups have come from the families having different income levels.

CASTE

The institution of caste* is a unique social feature of Indian society*. Its role in politics particularly at local level is well established and widely recognized. The caste continues to be a very important factor in the local political system and it has a greater influence in rural areas.[12] A.P. Barnabas,[13] Orenstein,[14] Yogender Singh,[15] S.K. Srivastava,[16] Nagesh Jha,[17] are some of the scholars who evaluated the role of caste in panchayati raj institutions.

The political leaders, in the past and present, have utilized this social institution to mobilize support in their favour. It is evident from the fact that the elected representatives who come from rural masses belong to the dominant castes.[18] Other scholars[19] also established that socially influential actors often stem from higher castes that are ritually superior and economically better-off than the vast majority of middle and lower classes. It is also believed that 'belonging to a higher caste immediately establishes a power advantage for the leader over non-leader, an advantage that is ritualized and legitimized by custom', still has its significance.[20] S.S. Sharma[21] in his study of western UP found that landlords and cultivators were dominating the panchayat raj and ex-lambardars were found to

* The system of classification of castes in a traditional society was as per the Varna system. However, the constitutional and legal system of the country has recognized the castes as general castes, backward castes and scheduled castes and scheduled tribes. The phenomenon of progress has made the state to take steps to classify the backward and scheduled castes as backward classes (A) and backward classes (B) and scheduled castes (A) and Scheduled castes (B). However, it does not have constitutional valid therefore not utilised now for classifying the scheduled castes. The backward classes are also treated by Union Government as other backward castes (OBCs).

TABLE 2.7

Classification of PR leaders based on their age and incomes

Age Groups	Incomes							Total
	Up to 12,500	12,501-25,000	25,001-50,000	50,001-1,00,000	1,00,001-2,00,000	2,00,001-4,00,000	Above 4,00,000	
(1)	(2)	(3)	(4)	(5)	(6)	(7)	(8)	(9)
Young	18 42.9%	15 25.4%	20 27.8%	12 28.6%	14 28.6%	7 21.9%	7 29.2%	93 29.1%
Middle Age	16 38.1%	35 59.3%	29 40.3%	18 42.9%	22 44.9%	17 53.1%	12 50.0%	149 46.6%
Elders	8 19.0%	9 15.3%	23 31.9%	12 28.6%	13 26.5%	8 25.0%	5 20.8%	78 24.4%
Total	42 100.0%	59 100.0%	72 100.0%	42 100.0%	49 100.0%	32 100.0%	24 100.0%	320 100.0%

Pearson chi-square 12.187.

be losing position. The significance of caste in local politics was re-confirmed and found that the power in Indian village tends to be vested in the hands of the higher castes who have been dominating the key decisions in rural community.[22] Alternatively, powers in Indian villages tend to be vested in the hands of higher castes who have been dominating the key decisions in rural community.[23]

B.K. Chandershekhar and Anand Inbanathan[24] found the upper caste dominance in the political process holds good for women representation too. They also concluded in their study that caste distribution of women members is in proportion to the concentration and distribution of these castes in different region of the Karnataka state.

The introduction of universal adult franchise has also enabled the numerically dominant castes to acquire political power whereas the numerically weak castes failed to do so in the changed conditions introduced by popular democracy. Sivalinga Prasad's[25] study indicates that the representation of forward castes has come down. Hargian Singh's study in Haryana [26] reflects that although factors like honesty, integrity, reputation and popularity help a great deal in the achievement of leadership but position in villages, economic status, power determinants and affiliation to party in power are more important for the achievement of power positions in rural areas. Thus, the study pointed out the dilution of the role of numerical strength and caste in local politics. In other words, caste has not remained the only determinant of politics in rural India. Shiviah[27] also concluded that 58 per cent of local leaders still belong to upper castes, chiefly the dominant ones but of the impact of remaining 42 per cent can hardly be regarded as minor, especially when a substantial segment of 58 per cent reflect the shared perspectives.

M. Sam Roy[28] in his study found that the numerical strength of a caste plays a pivotal role in determining panchayat leadership. The study also states that all castes had adequate representation in the panchayat as people belonging different castes are distributed in the wards in such a way that a single caste numerically dominated over the other castes in the earmarked wards of the village. Thus, the caste, numerical strength and ward system play relatively more significant role in comparison to other social, economic and political variables in ensuring representation at local levels.

The process of social and economic transformation has diluted the social differentiation among different castes as higher castes, middle castes and lower castes. Not only this, the erstwhile upper castes have become numerically weak in the villages of Haryana state. The distinction as upper castes and middle castes in the state has also lost its significance in terms of their social, economic and political status. Further, both the scheduled castes and backward castes are categorized into Group (A) and Group (B) castes. The inclusion of caste in a specific group of scheduled caste or backward class is based on social, education and economic backwardness level of the said caste as a whole in the state and appropriate guidelines are there for this purpose. Therefore, a different approach of caste classification is adopted for studying the local leadership in the state.

The castes classification used in this study is as under: Farming Castes;[#] Upper Castes;[€] Backward Castes,[£] and Scheduled Castes. The suggested approach of caste classification is evident from the Table 2.8.

The data obtained from field survey presented in Table 2.8 reveals that 30.9 per cent of the sampled leaders are from farming castes which in real sense, have been asserting to dominate village affairs since past. These castes are Rajput, Jat, and Jat Sikhs in the present study. These are land-owning castes and therefore control the agriculture production system, i.e. main economic activity of the village. These castes are relatively at higher level of economic hierarchy in comparison to other non-land owning castes in the village. Therefore, they are more powerful and dominating ones. Their social position in caste

---

The farming castes are defined here those castes who are not backward or scheduled castes or upper castes, having agricultural land and professing agriculture as their primary profession. These castes in this study are Jat, Jat Sikhs, Rajputs, etc.

€ Brahmins, Banias, etc. who are earlier considered as upper castes and may or may not possess agricultural land or have business including money lending/artihas, etc.

£ There have been some backward castes like Ahirs, Sainis, Bishnoi, etc., which are having farming as their occupations and possess agricultural lands but included in backward classes.

TABLE 2.8

Caste composition of the sampled PR leaders

Castes	*Frequency*	*Percent*	*Cumulative Percent*
Farming castes	99	30.9	30.9
Upper castes	40	12.5	43.4
Backward castes (A)	29	9.1	52.5
Backward castes (B)	37	11.6	64.1
Scheduled castes (A)	51	15.9	80.0
Scheduled castes (B)	64	20.0	100.0
Total	320	100.0	

hierarchy and numerical strength are other factors, which make them more effective in gram panchayats.

They (leaders from farming castes) have a little bit higher proportion of representation in panchayats in comparison to their population in the village. The demography pattern also favoured their dominance as most of the villages in the state are inhabited by either one or two farming caste/s or which is/are numerically the largest group of population of the village. Even if there is more than one/two farming caste/s in a village then these castes usually form a combination of farming and land owning backward caste. This combination usually constitutes a unified socially cohesive group which has common interests and behaves in similar fashion in village politics, i.e. attempt to keep dominance over other marginal and non-land owning castes.

The Brahmins and Banias, etc. are taken into upper castes in a village society and constitute 12.5 per cent of the sample. They are loosing numerical dominance with some exceptions. Their dominance in village politics is largely depending on their land possession, economic strength and numerical strength of their caste fellows in the village.

The representation of backward classes in the sample is 20.7 per cent. As already indicated that this group of caste is divided into two groups, i.e. backward castes-A and backward castes-B. The proportions of these two sub-groups in the sampled leaders are 9.1 and 11.6 percent respectively. It is not as per the population of these castes in the state. The castes like Ahirs, Sainis, Kamboj of backward castes (B) constitutes majority-farming caste in many villages of the sample and of state. Hence, the village leaders from these castes are higher in proportion to their numerical strength of the total population.

The representation of backward castes (A) (9.1 per cent) is not adequate even in spite of reservation. The numerical strength (first and foremost) and economic condition (another factor) are the reasons attributed to it. The backward castes because of their low proportion in the total population of the village attempts to group themselves with another caste of their ward and in such kind of cooperation they may not be able to lead the ward. In fact, the polity realized the marginalization of backward castes (A) in village politics and reservation to that effect, was made for them in the Haryana Panchayat Raj Act, 1994.[29]

The representation of scheduled castes in the sample is 15.9 per cent for category A and 20.0 per cent for category B. It is incidental again, the village panchayat Rajpura has the majority of *panches* belonging SCs and BCs. As a result, the percentages of these castes in the sample have become higher than actual proportion in state's population. There exists a strong caste consciousness among the various castes of the village to make sincere efforts to send their representatives to the GP. In other words, it is an established fact that individuals of a particular caste people in the village first attempt to find its leader in its own caste. The reservation provision, made there in new enactment, has strengthened this feeling in a significant sense.

Thus, the castes of the sampled representatives are quite diverse and it is due to the reservation provisions, numerical strength and delimitation of wards. The data and discussion with the leaders and officials lead to conclude that every caste having enough electors, has been able to send its representative to GP. However, it is not true in case of Panchayat Samities.

The data about the castes of the sampled PR leaders tabulated in Table 2.8 is studied with reference to their gender, age, educational levels and incomes and the related statistical information is presented in Tables 2.9 to 2.13.

The data in Table 2.9 clearly indicates that there is not any significant variation between male and female leaders of

TABLE 2.9
Classification of PR leaders based on their castes and gender

Castes	*Gender*		*Total*
	Male	*Female*	
Farming castes	70 32.6%	29 27.6%	99 30.9%
Upper castes	25 11.6%	15 14.3%	40 12.5%
Backward castes (A)	19 8.8%	10 9.5%	29 9.1%
Backward castes (B)	26 12.1%	11 10.5%	37 11.6%
Scheduled castes (A)	36 16.7%	15 14.3%	51 15.9%
Scheduled castes (B)	39 18.1%	25 23.8%	64 20.0%
Total	215 100.0%	105 100.0%	320 100.0%

Pearson chi-square 2.553.

various caste groups (chi square 2.553). In other words, the women from all castes are represented in PRIs but due to reservation alone. The socio-economic and attitudinal characteristics might have not influenced their election in PRIs.

The data in Table 2.10, however, reveals that there is variation of proportion of representation of leaders belonging different family sizes. The proportion of upper castes and farming castes leaders belonging smaller families is higher in comparison to other castes. In average sized families, the backward castes (A), backward castes (B), scheduled castes (A) and scheduled castes (B) lead over other castes in this context. However, in case of big families the castes having larger proportion are backward castes (B), scheduled castes (A) and scheduled castes (B). The farming castes and scheduled castes are ahead of others in case of large families. Nevertheless, the chi-square value is 22.455, which means that there is not any significant difference between castes in terms of their family sizes.

TABLE 2.10

Classification of PR leaders based on their castes and family sizes

Castes	*Family sizes*					*Total*
	Upto 2 members	*3-4 members*	*5-6 members*	*9-10 members*	*Above 10 members*	
Farming castes	0 .0%	22 40.0%	35 28.5%	26 24.8%	16 44.4%	99 30.9%
Upper castes	0 .0%	11 20.0%	13 10.6%	12 11.4%	4 11.1%	40 12.5%
Backward castes (A)	0 .0%	3 5.5%	15 12.2%	8 7.6%	3 8.3%	29 9.1%
Backward castes (B)	0 .0%	6 10.9%	15 12.2%	13 12.4%	3 8.3%	37 11.6%
Scheduled castes (A)	1 100.0%	4 7.3%	20 16.3%	20 19.0%	6 16.7%	51 15.9%
Scheduled castes (B)	0 .0%	9 16.4%	25 20.3%	26 24.8%	4 11.1%	64 20.0%
Total	1 100.0%	55 100.0%	123 100.0%	105 100.0%	36 100.0%	320 100.0%

Pearson chi-square 22.455.

The relationship between the variable of caste and education level is evident from the data given in Table 2.11. The data indicates that the upper castes, farming castes, and backward castes (B) leaders are relatively higher in their education level. The sampled PR leaders belonging backward castes (A) and scheduled castes (A) are on the least side of the continuum. The chi-square value 55.772 confirms the significant difference among the leaders of various castes in terms of their educational achievement in a significant manner. Thus, based on the data it is concluded that the upper castes, farming castes, and backward castes (B) leaders are relatively better educated than the others.

The variable of caste is also analyzed with reference to the land holdings possessed by the sampled leaders (Table 2.12). The data shows that a large number of scheduled castes (both groups) and backward castes (A) are landless or having smaller landholdings. The farming castes, upper castes and backward

TABLE 2.11

Classification of PR leaders based on their castes and educational level

Castes	Education Levels								Total
	Illiterate	*Literate*	*Primary*	*Middle*	*Matri-culation*	*Senior secondary*	*Graduate*	*Other*	
(1)	(2)	(3)	(4)	(5)	(6)	(7)	(8)	(9)	(10)
Farming castes	27 29.0%	7 28.0%	7 18.9%	17 31.5%	27 43.5%	4 26.7%	6 25.0%	4 40.0%	99 30.9%
Upper castes	5 5.4%	5 20.0%	4 10.8%	4 7.4%	9 14.5%	4 26.7%	8 33.3%	1 10.0%	40 12.5%
Backward castes (A)	14 15.1%	1 4.0%	4 10.8%	6 11.1%	2 3.2%	0 .0%	2 8.3%	0 .0%	29 9.1%
Backward castes (B)	6 6.5%	4 16.0%	4 10.8%	9 16.7%	6 9.7%	3 20.0%	4 16.7%	1 10.0%	37 11.6%
Scheduled castes (A)	21 22.6%	5 20.0%	8 21.6%	4 7.4%	7 11.3%	3 20.0%	3 12.5%	0 .0%	51 15.9%
Scheduled castes (B)	20 21.5%	3 12.0%	10 27.0%	14 25.9%	11 17.7%	1 6.7%	1 4.2%	4 40.0%	64 20.0%
Total	93 100.0%	25 100.0%	37 100.0%	54 100.0%	62 100.0%	15 100.0%	24 100.0%	10 100.0%	320 100.0%

Pearson chi-Square 55.722.

TABLE 2.12

Classification of PR leaders based on their castes and land holdings

Castes	Land-holdings							Total
	Nil	*Up to 1.25 acres*	*1.25-2.5 acres*	*2.5-5.0 acre*	*5.0-12.5 acres*	*12.5-25 acres*	*Above 25 acres*	
(1)	(2)	(3)	(4)	(5)	(6)	(7)	(8)	(9)
Farming castes	2 1.5%	4 28.6%	7 33.3%	20 44.4%	31 50.8%	20 66.7%	15 93.8%	99 30.9%
Upper castes	10 7.5%	4 28.6%	3 14.3%	8 17.8%	10 16.4%	4 13.3%	1 6.3%	40 12.5%
Backward castes (A)	23 17.3%	1 7.1%	1 4.8%	1 2.2%	3 4.9%	0 .0%	0 .0%	29 9.1%
Backward castes (B)	1 .8%	2 14.3%	2 9.5%	11 24.4%	15 24.6%	6 20.0%	0 .0%	37 11.6%
Scheduled castes (A)	39 29.3%	2 14.3%	7 33.3%	1 2.2%	2 3.3%	0 .0%	0 .0%	51 15.9%
Scheduled castes (B)	58 43.6%	1 7.1%	1 4.8%	4 8.9%	0 .0%	0 .0%	0 .0%	64 20.0%
Total	133 100.0%	14 100.0%	21 100.0%	45 100.0%	61 100.0%	30 100.0%	16 100.0%	320 100.0%

Pearson chi-square 241.758.

castes (B) are having relatively larger landholdings. The chi-square value (241.758) confirms that the leaders belonging different castes significantly differ in terms of land possession as a few groups of castes have the land holdings and other castes' leaders either do not have or possess very small land holdings.

Many leaders do not possess the land holdings; therefore, the variable of income is analyzed with the leaders' castes and information is tabulated in Table 2.13. The data in indicates that the leaders belonging different castes have different levels of annual incomes and proportion of leaders having annual incomes above Rs. 50,000 is higher among farming castes, upper castes and backward classes (A). These are land owning castes and naturally having higher levels of incomes. The chi square value (151.918) clearly establishes that the leaders from various castes' groups differ significantly when compared based on their estimated annual incomes. In other words, the income variable very much differentiate the leadership in conformity to castes' classification and the leaders belonging farming castes, followed by upper castes, and backward castes (B) are relatively well off in economic sense unlike scheduled castes and other castes.

EDUCATION

Education facilitates progress to an individual. It brings modernity in the personality of a person. Its need particularly in village leadership is essentially significant as the rural society is characterized with illiteracy and social backwardness. The education develops progressive attitude in individuals towards social and economic problems. The leader at local level is not only a representative but also act as buffer between the rural people and local bureaucracy. Therefore, the educated persons are considered to be more suitable than the illiterates for leading traditional village society.

Some scholars found that literacy or education contributes positively in establishing a person as local leader in rural areas of the country.[30] The findings of some of the studies are presented here to have an idea of educational level of PR leadership in the country.

M. Shiviah[31] in Andhra Pradesh concludes that new leaders are relatively younger and better educated. B.K. Chandrasekhar

TABLE 2.13

Classification of PR leaders based on their castes and estimated annual incomes

Castes	*Incomes*							*Total*
	Up to 12500	*12,501-25,000*	*25,001-50,000*	*50,001-1,00,000*	*1,00,001-2,00,000*	*2,00,001-4,00,000*	*Above 4,00,000*	
(1)	*(2)*	*(3)*	*(4)*	*(5)*	*(6)*	*(7)*	*(8)*	*(9)*
Farming castes	2 4.8%	6 10.2%	21 29.2%	15 35.7%	20 40.8%	21 65.6%	14 58.3%	99 30.9%
Upper castes	1 2.4%	4 6.8%	9 12.5%	4 9.5%	10 20.4%	4 12.5%	8 33.3%	40 12.5%
Backward castes (A)	6 14.3%	9 15.3%	7 9.7%	2 4.8%	2 4.1%	2 6.3%	1 4.2%	29 9.1%
Backward castes (B)	0 .0%	1 1.7%	15 20.8%	4 9.5%	12 24.5%	4 12.5%	1 4.2%	37 11.6%
Scheduled castes (A)	12 28.6%	18 30.5%	9 12.5%	9 21.4%	2 4.1%	1 3.1%	0 .0%	51 15.9%
Scheduled castes (B)	21 50.0%	21 35.6%	11 15.3%	8 19.0%	3 6.1%	0 .0%	0 .0%	64 20.0%
Total	42 100.0%	59 100.0%	72 100.0%	42 100.0%	49 100.0%	32 100.0%	24 100.0%	320 100.0%

Pearson chi-square 151.918.

and Anand Inbanathan[32] in their study found that women elected members lagged behind men in educational levels, in both ZPs and Mandal Panchayats (MPs). It states that 'among ZP members, while there were a substantial proportion of men who had professional and post-graduate education and degrees, among the women those with such educational qualifications were just five per cent. It is not surprising that only a small proportion of women members of ZP had professional or post-graduate education. Among women mandal panchayat members, the educational levels were not only lower than that of men, but even independently could be considered as very low indeed (37.2 per cent of the sample were illiterate, 45.6 per cent were literate with primary education). Among SCs and STs the situation was even poorer'. M. Sam Roy[33] in his study in Tamil Nadu concludes that there is . . . inequality among the rural poor, ward members and panchayat presidents in terms of their level of education . . . the panchayat presidents are better educated than the ward members whose educational qualification is better than the rural poor.

The information pertaining to educational level of sampled leadership of the present study is tabulated in the Table 2.14.

TABLE 2.14

Educational levels of sampled panchayat raj leaders

Educational Levels	*Frequency*	*Percent*	*Cumulative Percent*
Illiterate	93	29.1	29.1
Literate	25	7.8	36.9
Primary	37	11.6	48.4
Middle	54	16.9	65.3
Matriculation	62	19.4	84.7
Senior secondary	15	4.7	89.4
Graduate	24	7.5	96.9
Other	10	3.1	100.0
Total	320	100.0	

The data in Table 2.14 indicates that the largest chunk of the sampled leaders (29.1 per cent) are illiterate, followed by matriculates (19.4 per cent), middle pass (16.9 per cent) and the leaders possessing primary level education (11.6 per cent). The percentages of leaders who are senior secondary pass, graduates and higher qualified are 4.7, 7.5 and 3.1 per cent respectively.

Thus, an overwhelming majority (84.7 per cent) is either illiterate or educated up to matriculation level. Therefore, it is very difficult to expect that in near future they will constitute an empowered leadership at GP and PS if education is an instrument of empowerment for village people of the state. In other words, educated leadership at panchayat level is a goal, which is not likely to be achieved in near future.

The level of educational achievement is higher among male in comparison to female leaders as is evident from the data in Table 2.15.

TABLE 2.15
Classification of PR leaders based on their educational levels and gender

	Gender		*Total*
Education Levels	*Male*	*Female*	
Illiterate	38 17.7%	55 52.4%	93 29.1%
Literate	14 6.5%	11 10.5%	25 7.8%
Primary	22 10.2%	15 14.3%	37 11.6%
Middle	44 20.5%	10 9.5%	54 16.9%
Matriculation	53 24.7%	9 8.6%	62 19.4%
Senior secondary	13 6.0%	2 1.9%	15 4.7%
Graduate	22 10.2%	2 1.9%	24 7.5%
Other	9 4.2%	1 1.0%	10 3.1%
Total	215 100.0%	105 100.0%	320 100.0%

Pearson chi-square 57.546.

The data in Table 2.15 indicates that a pattern of rising percentage of male leaders as one move up across the educational levels. In other words higher the educational level, lesser the percentage of women leaders. More specifically, there are only five women in the sample strength of 105 women leaders, who are educated higher than the matriculation level. The chi-square value (57.546) makes clear that the difference between male and female leaders is very significant as 17.7 per cent male and 52.4 per cent female are illiterates.

The variable of educational achievements of PR leaders is examined with reference to their (sampled leaders) castes.

The data in Table 2.16 stands for evidence that the scheduled castes (both groups) and backward castes (A) are having larger percentages (more than their caste groups' average) of illiterate. However, in case of upper castes and backward castes (B), this percentage is 5.4 and 6.5 per cent of the total illiterate in the sample, respectively. Further, the educational levels of the leaders belonging the upper castes, backward castes (B) and scheduled castes is relatively showing an upward trend. It is attributed mainly to the disinterest on the part of educated candidates belonging farming castes to contest GP election, tendency for searching educated leaders within the caste by the scheduled castes particularly and above all the rising educational levels of rural people as a whole. The chi-square value is (55.722) confirms the significant difference among the leaders of various castes in terms of their educational levels.

The educational level of the sampled leaders is also studied with reference to their family sizes. The data in this regard presented in Table 2.17 makes it clear that the family sizes are independent of educational achievements of the PR leadership as is evident from chi square value (20.572) which is not significant.

Further, the educational level of the sampled leaders is examined with reference to their estimated annual income.

It is evident from the data in Table 2.18 that although the leaders of a particular educational level are more or less evenly distributed among all castes but higher educated people (more than graduation) is not found in the lower income ranges of less than Rs. 50,000 per annum. The data also reveals that the percentage of leaders who are higher educated decreases with the increase in income range. The leaders who are matriculate or more are higher in the income range of Rs. 25,001 to 50,000 and

TABLE 2.16

Classification of PR leaders based on their educational levels and castes

Education Levels	*Castes*						*Total*
	Farming castes	*Upper castes*	*Backward castes (A)*	*Backward castes (B)*	*Scheduled castes (A)*	*Scheduled castes (B)*	
(1)	*(2)*	*(3)*	*(4)*	*(5)*	*(6)*	*(7)*	*(8)*
Illiterate	27 27.3%	5 12.5%	14 48.3%	6 16.2%	21 41.2%	20 31.3%	93 29.1%
Literate	7 7.1%	5 12.5%	1 3.4%	4 10.8%	5 9.8%	3 4.7%	25 7.8%
Primary	7 7.1%	4 10.0%	4 13.8%	4 10.8%	8 15.7%	10 15.6%	37 11.6%
Middle	17 17.2%	4 10.0%	6 20.7%	9 24.3%	4 7.8%	14 21.9%	54 16.9%
Matriculation	27 27.3%	9 22.5%	2 6.9%	6 16.2%	7 13.7%	11 17.2%	62 19.4%
Senior secondary	4 4.0%	4 10.0%	0 .0%	3 8.1%	3 5.9%	1 1.6%	15 4.7%
Graduate	6 6.1%	8 20.0%	2 6.9%	4 10.8%	3 5.9%	1 1.6%	24 7.5%
Other	4 4.0%	1 2.5%	0 .0%	1 2.7%	0 .0%	4 6.3%	10 3.1%
Total	99 100.0%	40 100.0%	29 100.0%	37 100.0%	51 100.0%	64 100.0%	320 100.0%

Pearson chi-Square 55.722.

TABLE 2.17

Classification of PR leaders based on educational levels and family sizes

Education Levels	*Family sizes*					*Total*
	Upto 2 members	*3-4 members members*	*5-6 members*	*9-10 members*	*Above 10 members*	
(1)	(2)	(3)	(4)	(5)	(6)	(7)
Illiterate	1 100.0%	12 21.8%	38 30.9%	29 27.6%	13 36.1%	93 29.1%
Literate	0 .0%	5 9.1%	11 8.9%	6 5.7%	3 8.3%	25 7.8%
Primary	0 .0%	9 16.4%	10 8.1%	15 14.3%	3 8.3%	37 11.6%
Middle	0 .0%	7 12.7%	20 16.3%	24 22.9%	3 8.3%	54 16.9%
Matriculation	0 .0%	11 20.0%	27 22.0%	16 15.2%	8 22.2%	62 19.4%
Senior secondary	0 .0%	4 7.3%	4 3.3%	5 4.8%	2 5.6%	15 4.7%
Graduate	0 .0%	6 10.9%	7 5.7%	7 6.7%	4 11.1%	24 7.5%
Other	0 .0%	1 1.8%	6 4.9%	3 2.9%	0 .0%	10 3.1%
Total	1 100.0%	55 100.0%	123 100.0%	105 100.0%	36 100.0%	320 100.0%

Pearson chi-square 20.572.

TABLE 2.18

Classification of PR leaders based on educational levels and incomes

Education Levels	*Incomes*							*Total*
	Up to 12,500	*12,501-25,000*	*25,001-50,000*	*50,001-1,00,000*	*1,00,001-2,00,000*	*2,00,001-4,00,000*	*Above 4,00,000*	
(1)	(2)	(3)	(4)	(5)	(6)	(7)	(8)	(9)
Illiterate	21 50.0%	23 39.0%	18 25.0%	9 21.4%	14 28.6%	4 12.5%	4 16.7%	93 29.1%
Literate	2 4.8%	3 5.1%	7 9.7%	2 4.8%	6 12.2%	3 9.4%	2 8.3%	25 7.8%
Primary	4 9.5%	8 13.6%	11 15.3%	4 9.5%	6 12.2%	2 6.3%	2 8.3%	37 11.6%
Middle	5 11.9%	13 22.0%	8 11.1%	5 11.9%	7 14.3%	12 37.5%	4 16.7%	54 16.9%
Matriculation	6 14.3%	11 18.6%	16 22.2%	10 23.8%	8 16.3%	5 15.6%	6 25.0%	62 19.4%
Senior secondary	1 2.4%	0 .0%	4 5.6%	4 9.5%	3 6.1%	1 3.1%	2 8.3%	15 4.7%
Graduate	3 7.1%	1 1.7%	8 11.1%	5 11.9%	2 4.1%	3 9.4%	2 8.3%	24 7.5%
Other	0 .0%	0 .0%	0 .0%	3 7.1%	3 6.1%	2 6.3%	2 8.3%	10 3.1%
Total	42 100.0%	59 100.0%	72 100.0%	42 100.0%	49 100.0%	32 100.0%	24 100.0%	320 100.0%

Pearson chi-square 58.029.

it deceases with the increase in income. The reason is poor people are not much educated and if educated they find an employment for their livelihood and did not contest PR elections. On the other hand, some of the higher income groups either did not find a suitable job or not interested in finding a job and prefer to join rural politics

The chi-square value (58.029) also confirms that there is not any significant difference of educational achievements based on income levels of PR leaders. In other words, the educational achievements of PR leaders are independent of their income levels.

MARITAL STATUS

The marital status of the leader has always been an important factor in rural society of Haryana state. The married persons are preferred as leaders in the traditional village society. Nevertheless, it does not mean that unmarried persons are not elected; they are definitely elected, however, very rarely. The married persons are considered mature and responsible in their behaviour and people prefer them. The information in the present study also testifies it, as all of the sampled PR leaders (both male and female) are married.

SIZE OF THE FAMILY

Earlier studies on the rural local leadership has emphasized that size of family is an important factor in establishing a person as PR leader. Dhillon[34] found in his study that all the families having 12 members or more have; leadership positions. On the other hand, none of the 55 families with less than five members has any leadership status. Chaudhary[35] also found a positive correlation between the family size and leadership. The large family size facilitates more votes, resources and muscle power required for this job of panchayat leadership. Sirsikar[36] observed, 'Inclination towards the large families among the leaders might be explained in terms of better economic ability of the leaders to bear the burden of leadership. Atmosphere in large family is such that it helps to develop the leadership qualities. It provides free time to some of its members to devote themselves to political activities.'

In this context, the data pertaining to family sizes of the sampled PR leaders was collected and given here in Table 2.19.

TABLE 2.19

Family sizes of the sampled PR leaders

Family Sizes	*Frequency*	*Percent*	*Cumulative Percent*
Up to 2 members	1	.3	.3
3-4 members	55	17.2	17.5
5-6 members	123	38.4	55.9
9-10 members	105	32.8	88.8
Above 10 members	36	11.3	100.0
Total	320	100.0	

The data in Table 2.19 clearly indicates that a majority of families (55.9 per cent) are having up to six members in their families. Further, 17.2 per cent of these have even smaller families of 3-4 members. It means that the conclusion of earlier studies is not valid now.

The very large families comprises more than ten members are 11.3 per cent of the total sampled families. The leaders whose families are big and consisted of 9-10 members are 32.8 percent.

Naturally, the question arises, how it happened?. The reasons are disintegration of joint families, population control measures, two children norm to contest election, social and educational progress and reservation provisions. In real sense, the above stated factors nullified the importance of economic security, number of votes and free time provided by the big joint families. Now, the *'Kunba'* or caste provides votes to the leader in a ward/class fellows. The need of economic security and availability of free time are compensated by the economic progress and introduction of technology in the farm and farm-related activities. However, the data also point out to the fact that the large families still provide better prospects to send their nominee to the PRIs if they desire so, particularly at GP level.

The family sizes of the sampled leaders are also studied with reference to their gender and pertinent data is presented in Table 2.20.

TABLE 2.20

Classification of PR leaders based on their family sizes and gender

Family sizes	Gender		Total
	Male	Female	
Up to 2 members	1 .5%	0 .0%	1 .3%
3-4 members	35 16.3%	20 19.0%	55 17.2%
5-6 members	81 37.7%	42 40.0%	123 38.4%
9-10 members	68 31.6%	37 35.2%	105 32.8%
Above 10 members	30 14.0%	6 5.7%	36 11.3%
Total	215 100.0%	105 100.0%	320 100.0%

Pearson chi-square 5.439.

The data in the Table 2.20 and chi square value 5.439 reveals that the male and female leaders do not differ in significant way in term of their family sizes.

The family sizes of the sampled PR leaders are also examined in the light of their castes and relevant date is tabulated in Table 2.21. The data illustrates that the percentage of leaders belonging average sized families (5-6 members) is highest (51.7 per cent) in case of backward castes (A) and they are followed by backward castes (B) (40.5 per cent). The proportion of other castes is (39.2 per cent); scheduled castes (A) for scheduled castes (B) (39.1 per cent); for (35.4 per cent) farming castes; and for (32.5 per cent) upper castes.

It also indicates that the percentages of leaders belonging families up to six members are 57.6 per cent (farming castes); 60

TABLE 2.21

Classification of PR leaders based on their family sizes and castes

Family sizes	Castes						Total
	Farming castes	*Upper castes*	*Backward castes (A)*	*Backward castes (B)*	*Scheduled castes (A)*	*Scheduled castes (B)*	
(1)	(2)	(3)	(4)	(5)	(6)	(7)	(8)
Up to 2 members	0 .0%	0 .0%	0 .0%	0 .0%	1 2.0%	0 .0%	1 .3%
3-4 members	22 22.2%	11 27.5%	3 10.3%	6 16.2%	4 7.8%	9 14.1%	55 17.2%
5-6 members	35 35.4%	13 32.5%	15 51.7%	15 40.5%	20 39.2%	25 39.1%	123 38.4%
9-10 members	26 26.3%	12 30.0%	8 27.6%	13 35.1%	20 39.2%	26 40.6%	105 32.8%
Above 10 members	16 16.2%	4 10.0%	3 10.3%	3 8.1%	6 11.8%	4 6.3%	36 11.3%
Total	99 100.0%	40 100.0%	29 100.0%	37 100.0%	51 100.0%	64 100.0%	320 100.0%

Pearson chi-square 22.455.

per cent (upper castes); 62 per cent (backward castes (A); 56.7 per cent (backward castes (B)); 49 per cent (scheduled castes-A) and 53.2 per cent (scheduled castes-B).

Further, the proportion of leaders belonging large families are in the groups of SC-B (40.6 per cent) and SC-A (39.2 per cent). These castes groups are followed by BC-B (35.1 per cent) upper castes (30.0 per cent), farming castes (26.3 per cent), and BC-A (27.6 per cent). The trend of smaller families is highest among upper castes (27.2 per cent) followed by farming castes (22.2 per cent). Thus, the upper castes and farming castes leaders are more modern in their attitude in terms of the size of their families.

Thus, apparently there are some variations of family sizes among various castes' groups. However, the chi-square value, i.e. 22.410 indicates that the castes of leaders do not decide their family sizes. In other words, more or less every caste have similar pattern of family sizes. It is attributed to the two children norms and social awareness of people living in villages. Therefore, the panchayats and leadership are more instrumental and effective institutions, for promoting population awareness in the villages.

The family sizes of the sampled leaders are also examined with their educational levels and information is tabulated in Table 2.22. The data indicates that the families comprising 3-4 members and 5-6 members are having an edge in terms of educational achievement but as chi-square value is 20.572, therefore, it is concluded that family sizes do not differ with the educational levels of the sampled leaders.

Lastly, the data pertaining to family sizes of the PR leaders are analyzed with their annual income repeated by the sampled leaders. The data is tabulated in Table 2.23 and clearly indicates that the family sizes are not different in significant way if classified on estimated annual income basis. The chi-square value 17.371 confirms it.

The cross-examination of family sizes with gender, castes, educational achievements, and incomes reveals that most active family size is average family size, i.e. 5-6 members (38.4 per cent) followed by the bigger size, i.e. 9-10 members (32.8 per cent).

TABLE 2.22

Classification of PR leaders based on their family sizes and education levels

Family sizes	Education Levels								Total
	Illiterate	*Literate*	*Primary*	*Middle*	*Matri-culation*	*Senior secondary*	*Graduate*	*Other*	
(1)	(2)	(3)	(4)	(5)	(6)	(7)	(8)	(9)	(10)
Up to 2 members	1 1.1%	0 .0%	0 .0%	0 .0%	0 .0%	0 .0%	0 .0%	0 .0%	1 .3%
3-4 members	12 12.9%	5 20.0%	9 24.3%	7 13.0%	11 17.7%	4 26.7%	6 25.0%	1 10.0%	55 17.2%
5-6 members	38 40.9%	11 44.0%	10 27.0%	20 37.0%	27 43.5%	4 26.7%	7 29.2%	6 60.0%	123 38.4%
9-10 members	29 31.2%	6 24.0%	15 40.5%	24 44.4%	16 25.8%	5 33.3%	7 29.2%	3 30.0%	105 32.8%
Above 10 members	13 14.0%	3 12.0%	3 8.1%	3 5.6%	8 12.9%	2 13.3%	4 16.7%	0 .0%	36 11.3%
Total	93 100.0%	25 100.0%	37 100.0%	54 100.0%	62 100.0%	15 100.0%	24 100.0%	10 100.0%	320 100.0%

Pearson chi-square 20.572.

TABLE 2.23

Classification of PR leaders based on their family sizes and incomes

Family Sizes	*Incomes*							*Total*
	Upto 12,500	*12,501-25,000*	*25,001-50,000*	*50,001-1,00,000*	*1,00,001-2,00,000*	*2,00,001-4,00,000*	*Above 4,00,000*	
(1)	(2)	(3)	(4)	(5)	(6)	(7)	(8)	(9)
Up to 2 members	0 .0%	1 1.7%	0 .0%	0 .0%	0 .0%	0 .0%	0 .0%	1 .3%
3-4 members	9 21.4%	11 18.6%	10 13.9%	5 11.9%	8 16.3%	6 18.8%	6 25.0%	55 17.2%
5-6 members	15 35.7%	18 30.5%	28 38.9%	20 47.6%	24 49.0%	11 34.4%	7 29.2%	123 38.4%
9-10 members	15 35.7%	24 40.7%	24 33.3%	11 26.2%	14 28.6%	10 31.3%	7 29.2%	105 32.8%
Above 10 members	3 7.1%	5 8.5%	10 13.9%	6 14.3%	3 6.1%	5 15.6%	4 16.7%	36 11.3%
Total	42 100.0%	59 100.0%	72 100.0%	42 100.0%	49 100.0%	32 100.0%	24 100.0%	320 100.0%

Pearson chi-square 17.371.

ECONOMIC BACKGROUND

The present study has identified four indicators to denote the economic background of the leaders, viz. occupations, land holdings, agricultural machinery and estimated annual incomes. Lastly, an attempt is also made to indicate their life standard. These indicators are the predicates of economic background of the PR leaders in the present study.

The social status and economic standing determines the individual's prospects to be elected in panchayat raj institutions. Therefore, the data was collected from the sampled leaders during field survey. The data is presented in Table 2.24.

TABLE 2.24
Occupations of the sampled PR leaders

		Frequency	*Percent*	*Cumulative Percent*
1.	Housewife/None	107	33.4	33.4
2.	Self-employed	15	4.7	38.1
3	Agriculture	113	35.3	73.4
4.	Artia	9	2.8	76.3
5.	Business	10	3.1	79.4
6.	Private jobs	4	1.3	80.6
7.	Shopkeeper/Traders	9	2.8	83.4
8.	Sweeper/Shoemaker, etc.	4	1.3	84.7
9.	Agri. labourer	49	15.3	100.0
	Total	320	100.0	

The data in Table 2.24 indicates that 33.4 per cent of the leaders stated that they are not engaged in any profession. Naturally, housewives and elders are in this group and they are dependent on their families for economic support. The data reveals that maximum proportion of them (35.3 per cent) is agriculturists. Others are self-employed (4.7 per cent), doing business (3.1 per cent), artias (2.8 per cent), shopkeepers/traders (2.8 per cent) and other private jobs (1.3 per cent). A sizeable section (15.3 per cent) of them is comprises of agricultural labourers. Thus, the sampled leaders are professing the occupations related to agriculture only.

The size of the land holding is fairly a reliable indicator for assessing the economic background of the rural leaders. Therefore, information pertaining to the land holdings possessed by them was obtained. It is presented in Table 2.25.

TABLE 2.25

Sizes of land holdings possessed by the sampled PR leaders

	Size of land holdings	*Frequency*	*Percent*	*Cumulative Percent*
1.	Nil	133	41.6	41.6
2.	Up to 1.25 acres	14	4.4	45.9
3.	1.25 - 2.5 acres	21	6.6	52.5
4.	2.5 - 5.0 acre	45	14.1	66.6
5.	5.0 - 12.5 acres	61	19.1	85.6
6.	12.5 - 25 acres	30	9.4	95.0
7.	Above 25 acres	16	5.0	100.0
	Total	320	100.0	

The data in Table 2.25 reveals that 41.6 of the sampled leaders are from the families who do not possess any kind of land holdings. However, about 60 per cent of the leaders reported that their families or they themselves possess land holdings of varied sizes. The biggest proportion (19.1 per cent) of farmers has land holdings of the sizes between 5.0-12.5 acres. It is followed by 14.1 per cent having lands measuring 2.5 to 5.0 acres. Further, about 15 per cent have more than 12.5 acres of land. It means that 33.5 per cent, i.e., more than half of land owning leaders are either average sized or big farmers. Thus, it is inferred that the big farmers and erstwhile big farmers are still active in village politics and constitute a sizeable section of village level leadership.

The second variable used as predicate of economic background is the agricultural machinery possessed by the farming class of leaders. The information in this regard is tabulated in Table 2.26.

TABLE 2.26

Agriculture machinery possessed by sampled PR leaders

Agricultural Machinery	*Frequency*	*Percent*	*Cumulative Percent*
1. Not applicable	194	60.6	60.6
2. Tractor	7	2.2	62.8
3. Electricity pump set	11	3.4	66.3
4. Diesel pump set	9	2.8	69.1
5. Solar pump set	1	.3	69.4
6. Tractor without agri. land	2	.6	70.0
7. Tractor + Harvester	20	6.3	76.3
8. Tractor + electric pump set	17	5.3	81.3
9. Tractor + diesel pump set	15	4.7	85.9
10. All including harvester	38	11.9	98.1
11. All kinds of machinery	6	1.9	100.0
Total	320	100.0	

The data in Table 2.26 reveals that 194 of the local leaders (which also include 133 non-land owning leaders) do not possess any kind of agricultural machinery. It means the farmers who are marginal/small or others may not have the ownership of such machinery as they are unable to afford it. However, 21 (6.5 per cent) of them have installed electricity pump set/diesel pump set or solar pump set for irrigating their land. About one-third of the sampled leaders are having tractor/tractor and harvester, etc. indicating the fact that leaders possessing sizeable land holdings are also possessing agricultural machinery for their own purposes or to earn rental income from small and other farmers who are not possessing those.

Thus, the information leads to conclude that the leaders possessing sizeable land holdings have also owned agriculture machinery, although the kind and number of agriculture machinery they possess largely depend upon size of land holdings and economic prosperity.

The information relating to the annual income of the sampled leaders during the last year was also probed. The information obtained is tabulated in Table 2.27.

TABLE 2.27
Estimated annual income levels of sampled PR leaders

	Incomes levels	*Frequency*	*Percent*	*Cumulative Percent*
1.	Up to 12500	42	13.1	13.1
2.	12,501-25,000	59	18.4	31.6
3.	25,001-50,000	72	22.5	54.1
4.	50,001- 1,00,000	42	13.1	67.2
5.	1,00,001- 2,00,000	49	15.3	82.5
6.	2,00,001- 4,00,000	32	10.0	92.5
7.	Above 4,00,000	24	7.5	100.0
	Total	320	100.0	

The data in Table 2.27 indictes that 31.6 percent of the leaders are having annual incomes below Rs. 25,000 which means they are very poor and live below poverty level. Further, most of these people are from scheduled castes (both groups) and backward classes (A) group (Table 2.28).

A sizeable percentage (35.6 per cent) of the leadership has the incomes in between Rs. 25,000 to Rs. 1,00,000 per annum. These leaders are not poor like the earlier section of leadership. However, they are not enough resourceful for mainstream politics. In real sense, they are in local politics due to their individual capacity, leadership traits and caste's support.

The group of remaining 32.8 per cent is of richer persons of the concerned villages. These leaders possess fairly bigger sizes of land holdings (more than 5 acres). Moreover, they are from upper castes, farming castes and 'B' group of backward classes. Further, these leaders are uniformly found in each caste (Table 2.28).

The information presented in the Tables 2.27 and 2.24 also illustrates that the income levels of the leaders correspond to the size of land holdings possessed by them. Thus, it is clear from

TABLE 2.28

Classification of sampled PR leaders based on their incomes and castes

Incomes	*Castes*						*Total*
	Farming castes	*Upper castes*	*Backward castes (A)*	*Backward castes (B)*	*Scheduled castes (A)*	*Scheduled castes (B)*	
(1)	*(2)*	*(3)*	*(4)*	*(5)*	*(6)*	*(7)*	*(8)*
Up to 12,500	2 2.0%	1 2.5%	6 20.7%	0 .0%	12 23.5%	21 32.8%	42 13.1%
12,501-25,000	6 6.1%	4 10.0%	9 31.0%	1 2.7%	18 35.3%	21 32.8%	59 18.4%
25,001-50,000	21 21.2%	9 22.5%	7 24.1%	15 40.5%	9 17.6%	11 17.2%	72 22.5%
50,001-1,00,000	15 15.2%	4 10.0%	2 6.9%	4 10.8%	9 17.6%	8 12.5%	42 13.1%
1,00,001-2,00,000	20 20.2%	10 25.0%	2 6.9%	12 32.4%	2 3.9%	3 4.7%	49 15.3%
2,00,001-4,00,000	21 21.2%	4 10.0%	2 6.9%	4 10.8%	1 2.0%	0 .0%	32 10.0%
Above 4,00,000	14 14.1%	8 20.0%	1 3.4%	1 2.7%	0 .0%	0 .0%	24 7.5%
Total	99 100.0%	40 100.0%	29 100.0%	37 100.0%	51 100.0%	64 100.0%	320 100.0%

the data that the leaders belonging farming and business occupations and residing in villages are not only holding offices in local institutions but also capable to influence the village politics. The poor are also represented and participating but all because of their castes' support and legal and constitutional provisions.

Last, the data in Table 2.29 indicates that the leadership lives a moderate or good life even in villages except 42.5 per cent as is evident from the data in Table 2.29.

TABLE 2.29

Life standard's indicators of the sampled PR leaders

	Indicators of Life Standard	*Frequency*	*Percent*	*Cumulative Percent*
1.	Radio + TV	136	42.5	42.5
2.	Radio + TV + Freeze	23	7.2	49.7
3.	TV + Washing machine + Furniture	3	.9	50.6
4.	TV + Home appliances + Furniture + two-wheeler	134	41.9	92.5
5	TV + Home appliances + Furniture + jeep/car	24	7.5	100.0
	Total	320	100.0	

The data in Table 2.29 reveals that the leaders possess all kinds of household amenities with them.

CONCLUSION

Thus, all kinds of rural people with varied social and economic backgrounds could get representation in the panchayati raj institutions of the state. Naturally, the present leadership is different from the earlier one in terms of their age, gender, caste, educational qualifications, incomes and living standards, etc. However, the domination of a particular class of people still persist but in different form.

NOTES AND REFERENCES

1. Scholars are like: Prodipto Roy (1951); Dube (1951); Oscar Lewis (1954); R. Bachenheimer (1956); A.P. Barnabas (1958); Yogendra Singh (1958); Orenstein (1959); Mackenzie Brown (1959); Morris E. Opler (1959); S.K Srivastava (1965); L.N. Sudhansu (1967); Hira Singh (1969); Iltija Khan (1969); N. Jha (1972); S.S. Sharma (1979); M. Shiviah (1980); Sivalinga Prasad (1981); Lakshminarayana (1985); Hargian Singh (1985) and many others
2. Jain, S.P. (1976). Panchayat Raj in Assam. Hyderabad: National Institute of Community Development, p. 110.
3. Bhargava, B.S. (1979). Panchayati Raj System and Political Parties. New Delhi: Ashish Publishing House.
4. Quoted in Singh, Surat and Rahim, C. A. (1989). Evolving Panchayat Raj Leadership. *Journal of Rural Development*, 8 (4), p. 420.
5. Shiviah, M. (1980). Quoted in *Ibid.*, p. 422.
6. M. Shiviah (1986). Quoted in *Ibid.*, p. 423.
7. Surat Singh and C.A. Rahim: (1989), *op. cit.*
8. See Chandrasekhar, B.K. and Ibanathan, Anand (1991). Profile and Participation of Women Zilla Parishad and Mandal Panchayat Members: The Case of Karnataka. *Journal of Rural Development*, 10 (5), pp. 578-79
9. Roy, M. Sam (1995). Emerging Panchayat Leadership and Polarisation of Political Power at Grass-root level. *Journal of Rural Development*, 14 (4), p. 346.
10. Miglani, D.C. (1993). Politics and Rural Power Structure: Emerging Trends, New Delhi: Deep & Deep Publications.
11. Chander, Subhash (1994). Rural Power Structure in Haryana: A Study of Three Panchayat Samities of Thanesar Sub-Division (Distt. Kurukshetra), Ph.D. Thesis (Unpublished) Department of Public Administration, Kurukshetra University, Kurukshetra.
12. The explanation of declining percentage of elder people in rural local institution is that their active period of life ends and they could not win against the more active and relatively younger leaders in the competition for power. However, others believe that the younger generation in Sirsikar, V.M. (1970). The Rural Elite in a Developing Society, New Delhi: Orient Longman, p. 40.
13. See Barnabas, A.P. (1958). Characteristics of 'Lay Leaders' in Extension work, *Journal of the M.S. University*, Baroda.
14. Orenstein (1959). Leadership and Caste in a Bombay Village in Park, R.L. and Tinker, I. (eds.), Leadership and Political Institutions in India, Madras.
15. Singh, Yogender (1958). Changing Power Structure of Village Community: A Case Study of Six Villages in Eastern U.P. in Desai, A.R. (ed.). *Rural Sociology in India*. Bombay: Popular Prakashan.
16. Srivastava, S.K. (1965). Directed Social Change and Rural Leadership and Rural leadership in India in Dube, S.C. (ed.). *Emerging Pattern of Rural Leadership in South Asia*.
17. See Jha, Nagesh (1972). Leadership and Local Politics. Bombay.

18. See Reddy, G. Ram (1967). Pattern of Panchayati Raj in India, Delhi: Macmillan.
19. Lewis, Oscar (1954). Group Dynamics in a North Indian Village. Delhi: Dhillon, H.S. (1955) Leadership and Groups in South Indian villages. New Delhi: Planning Commission; Hutton, J.H. (1969). Castes in India. Oxford University Press: Majumdar, R.C. (1918). Corporate Life in Ancient India and Mookerji, Radhakumud (1920). Local Government in Ancient India, Oxford, Clarendon Press.
20. Sen, Lalit K. (1976). Awareness of Community Devlopment in India. Hyderabad: National Institute of Rural Development, p. 56.
21. S.S. Sharma (1979). Rural Elites in India, New Delhi: Sterling Publishers.
22. Choudhry, D.S. (1984). Emerging Rural Leadership in an Indian State: A Case Study of Rajasthan, Rohtak: Manthan Publications, p. 52.
23. *Ibid.*
24. Chandrasekhar, B.K. and Ibanathan, Anand (1991). *op. cit.*, p. 576.
25. Prasad, V. Sivalinga (1981). Panchayats and Development, New Delhi: *Light and Life* quoted in Singh, Surat and Rahim, C.A. (1989). *op. cit.*, p. 423.
26. Singh, Hargian (1985). Panchayati Raj Administration in Haryana. Gurgaon: Indira Publications.
27. Shiviah, M. *et. al.*: (1986). Panchayati Raj Elections in Andhra Pradesh: 1981, A Study in Institution Building for Rural Development, Hyderabad: NIRD.
28. Roy, M. Sam (1995). Emerging Panchayat Leadership and Polarisation of Political Power at Grass-root level. *Journal of Rural Development*, 14 (4), p. 346.
29. The Haryana Panchayat Raj Act, 1994, Legislative Deparment, Government of Haryana, Chandigarh.
30. See Gahlan, Virender Kumar (2004). The Administrative Culture in Panchayat Raj Institutions : A Comparative Study of Two Districts in the State of Haryana. (Unpublished Thesis), Department of Public Administration, Kurukshetra University, *Kurukshetra*, pp. 51-53.
31. Shiviah, M. (1991). *op. cit.*
32. Chandrasekhar, B.K. and Inbanathan, Anand (1991). *op. cit.*
33. Roy, M. Sam (1995), *op. cit.*
34. Dhillon, H.S. (1955). Leadership and Groups in South Indian villages, New Delhi: Planning Commission.
35. Chaudhary, D.S. (1981). Emerging Rural Leadership in an Indian State: A Case Study of Rajasthan, Rohtak: Manthan Publications.
36. Sirsikar, V.M. (1970). The Rural Elite in a Developing Society—A Study in Political Sociology, New Delhi: Orient Longman.

3

Political Life

The idea that leaders are born and are not made has almost disappeared. It is true in case of panchayati raj as reservation provisions made therein the 73rd constitutional amendment and the states' legislations enacted for establishing panchayati raj, have helped in erasing this traditional belief. But it is also established that rural leadership is influenced by the social, economic and culture characteristics of village life and these characteristics shape the attitude, behaviour and value system of the rural local leadership. The wide scope of activities[1] of Panchayati Raj have given an opportunity to the so far neglected people of society to rise to position of leadership.[2] The political experience of this leadership not only empower it but also make it more effective and politically capable one. Moreover, as there have been many studies on socio-economic background of PR leaders but a comprehensive analysis of their political life is missing. Hence an effort is made here in this chapter to probe this aspect of political life of rural local leadership of the state.

In this effort, first of all, sampled Gram Panchayat (GP) and Panchayat Samities (PS) leaders were asked to state how many elections they have contested so far. The information is tabulated here in Table 3.1 given below:

TABLE 3.1

Number of elections contested by the sampled PR leaders

Number of elections contested	*Frequency*	*Percent*	*Cumulative Percent*
First time	269	84.1	84.1
Two times	36	11.3	95.3
Three times	14	4.4	99.7
More than four times	1	.3	100.0
Total	320	100.0	

The data in Table 3.1 reveals that a large majority (84.1 per cent) of them are first timer. These are the persons who are representatives rather than leaders as they are not contesting elections regularly but only when they are asked to do so by the people of their wards. It means that the basic principle of democracy, i.e., active and conscious involvement and participation of people actually takes place at this level. The people of the ward and panch elected by them are real representatives of the people and constitute the real foundation of democracy.

About one-tenth (11.3 per cent) contested second time. There are only 4.4 per cent leaders who contested the local body's election for third time. Thus, there are only about one-sixth of the sampled PR leaders who are active in regular sense in rural politics.

The regular and active involvement of these leaders is analysed on gender basis and the data in Table 3.2 presents an account of that information. The data that 82.8 per cent of male and 86.7 per cent of female joined local politics for the first time. There are 11.6 per cent male and 10.5 per cent female who have contested the election for the second time. The percentage of women is again lower (2.9 per cent) in relation to male (5.1 per cent) who have contested elections of PR office for third term.

TABLE 3.2

Classification of sampled PR leaders based on their gender and the number of elections contested by them

	Gender		*Total*
Number of elections contested	*Male*	*Female*	
First time	178 82.8%	91 86.7%	269 84.1%
Two times	25 11.6%	11 10.5%	36 11.3%
Three times	11 5.1%	3 2.9%	14 4.4%
More than four times	1 .5%	0 .0%	1 .3%
Total	215 100.0%	105 100.0%	320 100.0%

Pearson chi-square 1.521.

Thus, most of the leaders and particularly women have joined these institutions for the first time. It indicates that new panchayati raj has made these local institutions widely participated and more democratized in terms of participation of male and female leaders at the time of PR elections. But, the chi square value (1.521) does not indicate significant difference between male and female leaders in terms of frequency of contesting PR election by them. The reason most of the leaders, both male and female, are not contesting PR election on regular basis.

The information pertaining to the frequency of contesting election on caste basis is presented in Table 3.3.

The data in table shows that the percentage of upper castes leaders who stated that they are first timer is relatively lower (77.5 per cent) in relation to (84.1 per cent) the total sample. However, this percentage for backward castes (B) is 91.9 per cent and farming castes are 87.9 per cent for the first timers. The proportion of those who contested elections three times is the highest among upper castes candidates (7.5 percent) followed by backward castes (B) (5.4 per cent). Further, the leaders

Table 3.3
Classification of PR leaders based on their castes and number of elections contested by them

Number of elections contested	*Castes*						*Total*
	Farming castes	*Upper castes*	*Backward castes (A)*	*Backward castes (B)*	*Scheduled castes (A)*	*Scheduled castes (B)*	
(1)	*(2)*	*(3)*	*(4)*	*(5)*	*(6)*	*(7)*	*(8)*
First time	87 87.9%	31 77.5%	22 75.9%	34 91.9%	42 82.4%	53 82.8%	269 84.1%
Two times	9 9.1%	6 15.0%	6 20.7%	0 .0%	7 13.7%	8 12.5%	36 11.3%
Three times	3 3.0%	3 7.5%	1 3.4%	2 5.4%	2 3.9%	3 4.7%	14 4.4%
More than four times	0 .0%	0 .0%	0 .0%	1 2.7%	0 .0%	0 .0%	1 .3%
Total	99 100.0%	40 100.0%	29 100.0%	37 100.0%	51 100.0%	64 100.0%	320 100.0%

Pearson chi-square 17.780.

belonging backward castes (B) also contested more than four times (2.7 per cent).

Thus, the leaders from the upper castes followed by farming castes and backward castes (B) are relatively more regular and permanent leaders in comparison to other castes' leaders. It also reveals a trend that the new enactment has its impact in arousing interest among rural people of different castes to come forward for contesting elections of GP and PS elections. However, the chi square value (17.780) does not differentiate significantly, among the different caste groups of leaders based on caste in terms of their behaviour of contesting local election on regular basis.

The frequency of contesting election on regular basis is also studied with reference to their terms for which they were elected in PRIs. The data in Table 3.4 indicates that the frequency to contest election of PS and GP has increased from pre-73rd period to 2nd election after 73rd Amendment. But it has declined during the third election. The reason, although is not probed but may be because of the fact that the fascination or the illusion that these institutions will be endowed with real powers is almost over by the time third elections were held in the state. The chi-square value 43.041 confirms the significant distinction among the leaders who got elected to these institutions in different time period.

The regularity of election contested by the sampled leaders is also examined with the education level and information is tabulated in Table 3.5. It is clear from the data that the regularity of contesting elections does not differ in significant way with the educational levels of the sampled leaders. The chi-square value 18.784 indicates so.

Lastly, the income levels of the sampled leaders are interacted with the frequency of elections contested. The data in this regard to tabulated in Table 3.6 and it reveals that the leaders of each and every income class including poor have contested these elections more than once. However, this tendency is higher in upper income ranges, i.e. from Rs. 25,000 onwards. The chi-square value 26.400 indicates that the habit of contesting election again and again is not significantly attributed to the income levels of the sampled leaders.

TABLE 3.4

Classification of PR leaders based on their position and number of elections contested by them

Number of elections contested	*Positions*								*Total*
	PS leaders before 73rd amendment	*PS leaders after 73rd amendment (1st election)*	*PS leaders after 73rd amendment 2nd election)*	*PS leaders after 73rd amendment (3rd election)*	*GP leaders before 73rd amendment*	*GP leaders after 73rd amendment (1st election)*	*GP leaders after 73rd amendment (2nd election)*	*GP leaders after 73rd amendment (3rd election)*	
(1)	*(2)*	*(3)*	*(4)*	*(5)*	*(6)*	*(7)*	*(8)*	*(9)*	*(10)*
First time	2 50.0%	23 76.7%	52 82.5%	22 73.3%	20 74.1%	44 89.8%	62 87.3%	44 95.7%	269 84.1%
Two times	1 25.0%	6 20.0%	7 11.1%	3 10.0%	7 25.9%	3 6.1%	7 9.9%	2 4.3%	36 11.3%
Three times	1 25.0%	0 .0%	4 6.3%	5 16.7%	0 .0%	2 4.1%	2 2.8%	0 .0%	14 4.4%
More than four times	0 .0%	1 3.3%	0 .0%	0 .0%	0 .0%	0 .0%	0 .0%	0 .0%	1 .3%
Total	4 100.0%	30 100.0%	63 100.0%	30 100.0%	27 100.0%	49 100.0%	71 100.0%	46 100.0%	320 100.0%

Pearson chi-square 43.041.

TABLE 3.5

Classification of PR leaders based on their educational levels and number of elections contested by them

Number of elections contested	*Education Levels*								*Total*
	Illiterate	*Literate*	*Primary*	*Middle*	*Matri-culation*	*Senior secondary*	*Graduate*	*Other*	
(1)	(2)	(3)	(4)	(5)	(6)	(7)	(8)	(9)	(10)
First time	79 84.9%	21 84.0%	29 78.4%	47 87.0%	53 85.5%	14 93.3%	18 75.0%	8 80.0%	269 84.1%
Two times	9 9.7%	3 12.0%	7 18.9%	3 5.6%	7 11.3%	1 6.7%	5 20.8%	1 10.0%	36 11.3%
Three times	5 5.4%	1 4.0%	0 .0%	4 7.4%	2 3.2%	0 .0%	1 4.2%	1 10.0%	14 4.4%
More than four times	0 .0%	0 .0%	1 2.7%	0 .0%	0 .0%	0 .0%	0 .0%	0 .0%	1 .3%
Total	93 100.0%	25 100.0%	37 100.0%	54 100.0%	62 100.0%	15 100.0%	24 100.0%	10 100.0%	320 100.0%

Pearson chi-square 18.784.

TABLE 3.6
Classification of PR leaders based on their estimated annual and number of elections contested by them

Number of elections contested	*Incomes*							*Total*
	Up to 12,500	*12,501-25,000*	*25,001-50,000*	*50,001-1,00,000*	*1,00,001-2,00,000*	*2,00,001-4,00,000*	*Above 4,00,000*	
(1)	(2)	(3)	(4)	(5)	(6)	(7)	(8)	(9)
First time	37 88.1%	52 88.1%	60 83.3%	33 78.6%	44 89.8%	25 78.1%	18 75.0%	269 84.1%
Two times	5 11.9%	6 10.2%	6 8.3%	7 16.7%	3 6.1%	4 12.5%	5 20.8%	36 11.3%
Three times	0 .0%	1 1.7%	6 8.3%	2 4.8%	2 4.1%	3 9.4%	0 .0%	14 4.4%
More than four times	0 .0%	0 .0%	0 .0%	0 .0%	0 .0%	0 .0%	1 4.2%	1 .3%
Total	42 100.0%	59 100.0%	72 100.0%	42 100.0%	49 100.0%	32 100.0%	24 100.0%	320 100.0%

Pearson chi-square 26.400.

The discussion concludes that there are only a few panchayati raj leaders who are contesting PR elections almost on regular basis.

Further, it is also observed that these regular leaders are contesting election for Sarpanch's office. The data in Table 3.7 illustrates it in an empirical way.

TABLE 3.7
Classification of PR leaders based on sarpanch's elections contested by them

Number of elections contested	*Frequency*	*Percent*	*Cumulative Percent*
Nil	278	86.9	86.9
Contested once and win	34	10.6	97.5
Contested once and lose	3	.9	98.4
Contested thrice and win	2	.6	99.1
Contested twice, once win	3	.9	100.0
Total	320	100.0	

The data in Table 3.7 indicates that 86.9 per cent of the PR leaders did not contest the election for the office of the Sarpanch of a GP. In other words, only 13.1 per cent contested the election for this position and out of this, 10.6 per cent contested once and they win that election. A few of them (0.9 per cent) contested once and they lose it, whereas another 0.9 per cent contested twice once win it and 0.6 per cent contested thrice and remained successful each time.

The data indicates that on an average basis, there have been one or less than one person in each village (total villages surveyed are 8), who have keen interest in village politics and they are regularly contesting the election of Sarpanch. No doubt, the reservation provision has an adverse influence on such kind of dominance of individuals in village politics as that has disrupted the continuity to contest the election. Nevertheless, in such situation also they motivated a candidate from reserved caste or made their wife to contest the election.

Thus, the reservation has widened the scope for those candidates who in the absence of which had not thought of contesting sarpanch's election even as a proxy candidate. Therefore, it is concluded that there has been much democratization at local levels in general and office of sarpanch in particular after 73rd constitutional amendment act.

The data in Table 3.8 given below classifies the sampled leaders on gender basis and who contested election for the position of sarpanch.

TABLE 3.8

Classification of PR Leaders based on their Gender and Contested the Election for the Office of Sarpanch

	Gender		*Total*
Number of elections contested	*Male*	*Female*	
Nil	185 86.0%	93 88.6%	278 86.9%
Contested once and win	23 10.7%	11 10.5%	34 10.6%
Contested once and lose	2 .9%	1 1.0%	3 .9%
Contested thrice and win	2 .9%	0 .0%	2 .6%
Contested twice, once win	3 1.4%	0 .0%	3 .9%
Total	215 100.0%	105 100.0%	320 100.0%

Pearson chi-square 2.497.

The data in Table 3.8 reveals that 42 candidates contested the election of the position of sarpanch (30 male and 12 female). There is only one woman who contested this election twice but to loose and now (at the time of field survey) she is member panchayat. Thus, the women do not contest sarpanch's election unless they have to be the proxy of their husband or family. However, the chi square value 2.497 indicates that the regularity to contest election does not vary with the gender of leader.

The caste wise classification of the sampled leaders contested sarpanch's election is tabulated in Table 3.9. The data in the table reveals a very interesting pattern. It indicates that the percentage of leaders who contested the election of sarpanch more than once is relatively higher among farming castes. The scheduled castes (both A and B groups) followed them. The percentage of backward castes leaders who contested their elections thrice and win in real sense is not quite significant. However, the chi square value 20.736 does not support the above stated difference of frequency among the leaders of various castes groups in significant way.

The sampled leaders who contested sarpanch's office election are also studied with reference to their position that is office and term of their election in PRIs. The data in Table 3.10 illustrates that there are 12 Panchayat Samities' members who have previously contested the election for the office of sarpanch of gram panchayat but almost all of them contested it once. In case of the GP leaders, the number of such leaders is not much. The chi-square value 32.766 is not significant and thus the regularity of contesting election *viz.-a-viz.* position does not differ with each other.

The leaders who contested sarpanch's election are examined with their educational level and relevant information is presented in Table 3.11. The data in and chi square value 29.626 indicates that the change in educational levels does not bring significant change in regularity to contest election among leaders.

Similarly, the information in Table 3.12 and chi-square value 24.013 indicate that income is not significant to decide the regularity of contesting sarpanch's office election.

The information similar to the office of Sarpanch was also collected for the office of panch at Gram Panchayat level and tabulated in Table 3.13. The data in the data reveals that majority (54.1 per cent) of the elected panches in sampled gram panchayats have contested their first election to become a panch in the village panchayat and successful. Further the percentage of such leaders who contested elections for the office of panch more than once in a village panchayat is only 4.6 per cent.

The sampled PR leaders who contested the election of panch in the sample are 188. Frequency of election of Panch

TABLE 3.9

Classification of PR leaders based on their castes and elections contested for the position of sarpanch by them

Number of elections contested	*Castes*						*Total*
	Farming castes	*Upper castes*	*Backward castes (A)*	*Backward castes (B)*	*Scheduled castes (A)*	*Scheduled castes (B)*	
(1)	*(2)*	*(3)*	*(4)*	*(5)*	*(6)*	*(7)*	*(8)*
Nil	88 88.9%	35 87.5%	28 96.6%	32 86.5%	44 86.3%	51 79.7%	278 86.9%
Contested once and win	6 6.1%	5 12.5%	1 3.4%	4 10.8%	6 11.8%	12 18.8%	34 10.6%
Contested once and lose	1 1.0%	0 .0%	0 .0%	0 .0%	1 2.0%	1 1.6%	3 .9%
Contested thrice and win	1 1.0%	0 .0%	0 .0%	1 2.7%	0 .0%	0 .0%	2 .6%
Contested twice, once win	3 3.0%	0 .0%	0 .0%	0 .0%	0 .0%	0 .0%	3 .9%
Total	99 100.0%	40 100.0%	29 100.0%	37 100.0%	51 100.0%	64 100.0%	320 100.0%

Pearson chi-square 20.736.

TABLE 3.10

Classification of PR leaders based on their position and elections contested for the position of sarpanch by them

	Positions								*Total*
Number of elections contested	*PS leaders before 73rd amendment*	*PS leaders after 73rd amendment (1st election)*	*PS leaders after 73rd amendment 2nd election)*	*PS leaders after 73rd amendment (3rd election)*	*GP leaders before 73rd amendment*	*GP leaders after 73rd amendment (1st election)*	*GP leaders after 73rd amendment (2nd election)*	*GP leaders after 73rd amendment (3rd election)*	
(1)	*(2)*	*(3)*	*(4)*	*(5)*	*(6)*	*(7)*	*(8)*	*(9)*	*(10)*
Nil	4 100.0%	27 90.0%	59 93.7%	25 83.3%	20 74.1%	41 83.7%	60 84.5%	42 91.3%	278 86.9%
Contested once and win	0 .0%	2 6.7%	3 4.8%	3 10.0%	6 22.2%	6 12.2%	10 14.1%	4 8.7%	34 10.6%
Contested once and lose	0 .0%	0 .0%	1 1.6%	2 6.7%	0 .0%	0 .0%	0 .0%	0 .0%	3 .9%
Contested thrice and win	0 .0%	1 3.3%	0 .0%	0 .0%	0 .0%	1 2.0%	0 .0%	0 .0%	2 .6%
Contested twice, once win	0 .0%	0 .0%	0 .0%	0 .0%	1 3.7%	1 2.0%	1 1.4%	0 .0%	3 .9%
Total	4 100.0%	30 100.0%	63 100.0%	30 100.0%	27 100.0%	49 100.0%	71 100.0%	46 100.0%	320 100.0%

Pearson chi-square 32.766.

TABLE 3.11

Classification of PR leaders on the basis of their educational levels and elections contested for the position of sarpanch by them

Number of elections contested	*Education Levels*								*Total*
	Illiterate	*Literate*	*Primary*	*Middle*	*Matri-culation*	*Senior secondary*	*Graduate*	*Other*	
(1)	(2)	(3)	(4)	(5)	(6)	(7)	(8)	(9)	(10)
Nil	84 90.3%	21 84.0%	29 78.4%	49 90.7%	53 85.5%	15 100.0%	20 83.3%	7 70.0%	278 86.9%
Contested once and win	6 6.5%	4 16.0%	7 18.9%	3 5.6%	8 12.9%	0 .0%	3 12.5%	3 30.0%	34 10.6%
Contested once and lose	1 1.1%	0 .0%	0 .0%	2 3.7%	0 .0%	0 .0%	0 .0%	0 .0%	3 .9%
Contested thrice and win	0 .0%	0 .0%	1 2.7%	0 .0%	1 1.6%	0 .0%	0 .0%	0 .0%	2 .6%
Contested twice, once win	2 2.2%	0 .0%	0 .0%	0 .0%	0 .0%	0 .0%	1 4.2%	0 .0%	3 .9%
Total	93 100.0%	25 100.0%	37 100.0%	54 100.0%	62 100.0%	15 100.0%	24 100.0%	10 100.0%	320 100.0%

Pearson chi-square 29.626.

TABLE 3.12

Classification of PR leaders based on their estimated annual and elections contested for the position of sarpanch by them

Number of elections contested	Incomes							Total
	Up to 12,500	1,2,501-25,000	25,001-50,000	50,001-1,00,000	1,00,001-2,00,000	2,00,001-4,00,000	Above 4,00,000	
(1)	(2)	(3)	(4)	(5)	(6)	(7)	(8)	(9)
Nil	38 90.5%	53 89.8%	65 90.3%	33 78.6%	43 87.8%	24 75.0%	22 91.7%	278 86.9%
Contested once and win	4 9.5%	5 8.5%	5 6.9%	8 19.0%	5 10.2%	6 18.8%	1 4.2%	34 10.6%
Contested once and lose	0 .0%	1 1.7%	1 1.4%	0 .0%	0 .0%	1 3.1%	0 .0%	3 .9%
Contested thrice and win	0 .0%	0 .0%	0 .0%	0 .0%	1 2.0%	0 .0%	1 4.2%	2 .6%
Contested twice, once win	0 .0%	0 .0%	1 1.4%	1 2.4%	0 .0%	1 3.1%	0 .0%	3 .9%
Total	42 100.0%	59 100.0%	72 100.0%	42 100.0%	49 100.0%	32 100.0%	24 100.0%	320 100.0%

Pearson chi-square 24.013.

TABLE 3.13

Classification of PR leaders based on panch's election contested by them

Number of elections contested	*Frequency*	*Percent*	*Cumulative Percent*
Not contested	132	41.3	41.3
Contested once and win	173	54.1	95.3
Contested once and lose	2	.6	95.9
Contested twice and win	11	3.4	99.4
Contested thrice and win	2	.6	100.0
Total	320	100.0	

contested by the PR leaders is analysed with reference to their gender, castes, educational levels, etc.

TABLE 3.14

Classification of PR leaders based on their gender and panch's election contested by them

	Gender		*Total*
Number of elections contested	*Male*	*Female*	
Not contested	84 39.1%	48 45.7%	132 41.3%
Contested once and win	119 55.3%	54 51.4%	173 54.1%
Contested once and lose	1 .5%	1 1.0%	2 .6%
Contested twice and win	9 4.2%	2 1.9%	11 3.4%
Contested thrice and win	2 .9%	0 .0%	2 .6%
Total	215 100.0%	105 100.0%	320 100.0%

Pearson chi-square 3.268.

The data in Table 3.14 shows that out of total leaders who contested election for the office of panch, 131 are men and 57 are women. There are only two female panches who contested this election twice and remained successful. The percentage of male panches who contested more than once is again higher than the women panch. But chi-square value (3.268) failed to differentiate the male and female leaders in their habit to be regular in contesting the said election.

The caste based classification of leaders' frequencies to contest election for the position of panches is tabulated in Table 3.15.

The data in Table 3.15 indicates that the continuity of contesting election for the position of panches in gram panchayats is higher among scheduled castes (A), followed by upper castes, scheduled castes (B), backward castes (A) and farming castes. It means that upper castes and scheduled castes (A) are having stable leadership in the form of panches as their representatives. It is supported by significant chi square value (43.170) whish is higher than 31.410.

The panches tendency to contest election on regular basis is also examined in the light of their educational achievements. The data in Table 3.16 reveals that relatively better educated leaders do not prefer to be panch. The chi-square value (49.075) which is higher than the significant value 41.337) affirms that the frequency to contest election for the position of panch is influenced by the educational levels in significant way.

Like earlier, the leaders' frequency to contest panch's election is also examined with income levels as is given in Table 3.17. The data in the table indicates that the range of income level of the leaders who contested panches' election more than once is much broader, i.e. from Rs. 12,501 per annum to 2,00,000 per annum. Thus it is also evident that relatively lesser income level people have also contested this election more than once. The chi-square value (39.036 higher than the significant value of 36.415), however, testifies that the income levels differentiate between the frequencies of contesting panch's election. Normally higher income group leaders do not contest this election.

The election of panch and sarpanch in the GP is a village affair. It is considered to be a very graceful to win and even to lose election for the position of sarpanch. It is also true for the panch but in relatively lesser sense.

TABLE 3.15

Distribution of PR leaders on the basis of their castes and panch's elections contested by them

Number of elections contested	Castes						Total
	Farming castes	Upper castes	Backward castes (A)	Backward castes (B)	Scheduled castes (A)	Scheduled castes (B)	
(1)	(2)	(3)	(4)	(5)	(6)	(7)	(8)
Not contested	51 51.5%	14 35.0%	6 20.7%	21 56.8%	16 31.4%	24 37.5%	132 41.3%
Contested once and win	47 47.5%	22 55.0%	18 62.1%	16 43.2%	32 62.7%	38 59.4%	173 54.1%
Contested once and lose	0 .0%	0 .0%	0 .0%	0 .0%	1 2.0%	1 1.6%	2 .6%
Contested twice and win	1 1.0%	3 7.5%	5 17.2%	0 .0%	1 2.0%	1 1.6%	11 3.4%
Contested thrice and win	0 .0%	1 2.5%	0 .0%	0 .0%	1 2.0%	0 .0%	2 .6%
Total	99 100.0%	40 100.0%	29 100.0%	37 100.0%	51 100.0%	64 100.0%	320 100.0%

Pearson chi-square 43.170.

TABLE 3.16

Classification of PR leaders based on their educational levels and panch's elections contested by them

Number of elections contested	*Education Levels*								*Total*
	Illiterate	*Literate*	*Primary*	*Middle*	*Matri-culation*	*Senior secondary*	*Graduate*	*Other*	
(1)	*(2)*	*(3)*	*(4)*	*(5)*	*(6)*	*(7)*	*(8)*	*(9)*	*(10)*
Not contested	25 26.9%	7 28.0%	16 43.2%	20 37.0%	27 43.5%	11 73.3%	17 70.8%	9 90.0%	132 41.3%
Contested once and win	63 67.7%	16 64.0%	19 51.4%	32 59.3%	33 53.2%	4 26.7%	5 20.8%	1 10.0%	173 54.1%
Contested once and lose	1 1.1%	0 .0%	0 .0%	1 1.9%	0 .0%	0 .0%	0 .0%	0 .0%	2 .6%
Contested twice and win	4 4.3%	1 4.0%	2 5.4%	1 1.9%	1 1.6%	0 .0%	2 8.3%	0 .0%	11 3.4%
Contested thrice and win	0 .0%	1 4.0%	0 .0%	0 .0%	1 1.6%	0 .0%	0 .0%	0 .0%	2 .6%
Total	93 100.0%	25 100.0%	37 100.0%	54 100.0%	62 100.0%	15 100.0%	24 100.0%	10 100.0%	320 100.0%

Pearson chi-square 49.075.

TABLE 3.17
Classification of PR leaders based on their estimated annual income and panch's elections contested by them

Number of election contested	*Incomes*							*Total*
	Up to 12,500	*12,501-25,000*	*25,001-50,000*	*50,001-1,00,000*	*1,00,001-2,00,000*	*2,00,001-4,00,000*	*Above 4,00,000*	
(1)	(2)	(3)	(4)	(5)	(6)	(7)	(8)	(9)
Not contested	6 14.3%	20 33.9%	27 37.5%	23 54.8%	23 46.9%	20 62.5%	13 54.2%	132 41.3%
Contested once and win	34 81.0%	36 61.0%	40 55.6%	16 38.1%	25 51.0%	11 34.4%	11 45.8%	173 54.1%
Contested once and lose	0 .0%	1 1.7%	0 .0%	1 2.4%	0 .0%	0 .0%	0 .0%	2 .6%
Contested twice and win	2 4.8%	2 3.4%	3 4.2%	2 4.8%	1 2.0%	1 3.1%	0 .0%	11 3.4%
Contested thrice and win	0 .0%	0 .0%	2 2.8%	0 .0%	0 .0%	0 .0%	0 .0%	2 .6%
Total	42 100.0%	59 100.0%	72 100.0%	42 100.0%	49 100.0%	32 100.0%	24 100.0%	320 100.0%

Pearson chi-square 39.036*.

After discussing the GP the next level of PRIs is panchayat samiti. Therefore, like GP, the frequency to contest PS election is also probed here in the study. The information about the classification of leaders who contested PS election is given in Table 3.18.

TABLE 3.18

Classification of PR leaders based on PS elections contested by them

Number of elections contested	*Frequency*	*Percent*	*Cumulative Percent*
Not Contested	191	59.7	59.7
Contested once and win	122	38.1	97.8
Contested once and lose	1	.3	98.1
Contested twice and win	3	.9	99.1
Contested twice and win only once	2	.6	99.7
Contested thrice and win only once	1	.3	100.0
Total	320	100.0	

The data in Table 3.18 shows that 129 (about 40 percent) of the sampled leaders contested the PS election. Most of them contested the PS election for once. There are only 7 leaders who contested this election more than once.

Out of these, 82 are men and 47 are women as is evident from the data tabulated in Table 3.19.

The data in indicates that three women contested PS election more than once. The .number of respondents who reported that they contested PS elections is 129 instead of 90 PS leaders in the sample. This means that the leaders at GP level also contested PS elections. The chi-square value 3.908 is not significant and hence the frequency/regularity to contest PS elections can not be distinguished on the basis of gender of the sampled leaders.

The distribution of different castes' leaders in relation to the election contested by them for the panchayat samiti is also

TABLE 3.19

Classification of PR leaders based on their gender and PS election contested by them

Number of elections contested	Gender		Total
	Male	Female	
Not Contested	133 61.9%	58 55.2%	191 59.7%
Contested once and win	78 36.3%	44 41.9%	122 38.1%
Contested once and lose	1 .5%	0 .0%	1 .3%
Contested twice and win	2 .9%	1 1.0%	3 .9%
Contested twice and win only once	1 .5%	1 1.0%	2 .6%
Contested thrice and win only once	0 .0%	1 1.0%	1 .3%
Total	215 100.0%	105 100.0%	320 100.0%

Pearson chi-square 3.908.

studied. The data pertaining to this is presented in the Table 3.20 and apparently does not indicate any pattern on the regularity of leaders to contest PS election. However, it reveals that there have been some reserved classes of leaders who have contested this election more than once. However the chi-square value 49.343 is higher than the significant value 37.652 and that confirms the fact that the different castes leaders have different level of frequency or regularity in contesting PS elections. In simple words, some of the reserved class PS leaders (a very limited number) have adopted the political life on regular basis and contesting local elections every time they get the opportunity.

The behaviour pattern of PS leaders in contesting local body's election is studied in the context of their educational levels and the information is presented in Table 3.21. The data in does not predicate any kind of pattern but the chi square value 92.437 is significant which means differentiating the

TABLE 3.20

Classification of PR leaders based on their castes and PS elections contested by them

Number of elections contested	*Castes*						*Total*
	Farming castes	*Upper castes*	*Backward castes (A)*	*Backward castes (B)*	*Scheduled castes (A)*	*Scheduled castes (B)*	
(1)	(2)	(3)	(4)	(5)	(6)	(7)	(8)
Not Contested	51 51.5%	24 60.0%	21 72.4%	17 45.9%	36 70.6%	42 65.6%	191 59.7%
Contested once and win	48 48.5%	16 40.0%	8 27.6%	19 51.4%	12 23.5%	19 29.7%	122 38.1%
Contested once and lose	0 .0%	0 .0%	0 .0%	0 .0%	0 .0%	1 1.6%	1 .3%
Contested twice and win	0 .0%	0 .0%	0 .0%	0 .0%	3 5.9%	0 .0%	3 .9%
Contested twice and win only once	0 .0%	0 .0%	0 .0%	0 .0%	0 .0%	2 3.1%	2, .6%
Contested thrice and win only once	0 .0%	0 .0%	0 .0%	1 2.7%	0 .0%	0 .0%	1 .3%
Total	99 100.0%	40 100.0%	29 100.0%	37 100.0%	51 100.0%	64 100.0%	320 100.0%

Pearson chi-square 49.343.

classes of those who contested PS election only once and repeatedly by a few leaders only. The data reveals relatively the leaders placed in upper level of education and illiterate have higher tendency to contest PS election irrespective of frequency to be successful or not.

The behaviour pattern of contesting election on regular basis is also studied with reference to the income levels of the PS leaders. The information pertaining to this is tabulated in Table 3.22. The data in the table reveals that most of the leaders either did not contest the PS election or contested only once. The regularity of contesting election is not showing any trend in context with their annual income except a few poor persons who belong reserved classes and become full time political worker at village level or in the area. They may or may not have any affiliation with political parties but remain engaged to help their people in one way or the other. This becomes their profession. The chi-square value (57.987) although significant but might be because of the classes of those who did not contest elections and who contested it once only.

Thus the regularity to contest PS election is not very attractive and a few of the poor reserved classes of leaders who are not much educated have contested this election more than once.

The conclusions relating to the regularity in contesting local elections suffer from the following limitations:

(i) only elected candidates could be contacted for obtaining information;
(ii) the survey was conducted only to cover those panches/ sarpanches who are available in the village at the time of survey;
(iii) the percentage of such leaders is calculated from total population of PR leaders i.e. sarpanches, panches and PS members; and
(iv) the candidates who contested the local elections but failed to win could not be represented in the sample.

Even then, it is true that only a small part of local leadership consider it wise to adopt local politics as their permanent and regular career. The leaders, who reported

TABLE 3.21

Classification of PR leaders based on their educational levels and PS elections contested by them

Number of elections contested	*Education Levels*								*Total*
	Illiterate	*Literate*	*Primary*	*Middle*	*Matri-culation*	*Senior secondary*	*Graduate*	*Other*	
(1)	(2)	(3)	(4)	(5)	(6)	(7)	(8)	(9)	(10)
Not Contested	68 73.1%	20 80.0%	21 56.8%	31 57.4%	39 62.9%	3 20.0%	7 29.2%	2 20.0%	191 59.7%
Contested once and win	22 23.7%	5 20.0%	16 43.2%	22 40.7%	23 37.1%	12 80.0%	16 66.7%	6 60.0%	122 38.1%
Contested once and lose	0 .0%	0 .0%	0 .0%	0 .0%	0 .0%	0 .0%	0 .0%	1 10.0%	1 .3%
Contested twice and win	2 2.2%	0 .0%	0 .0%	0 .0%	0 .0%	0 .0%	1 4.2%	0 .0%	3 .9%
Contested twice and win only once	0 .0%	0 .0%	0 .0%	1 1.9%	0 .0%	0 .0%	0 .0%	1 10.0%	2 .6%
Contested thrice and win only once	1 1.1%	0 .0%	0 .0%	0 .0%	0 .0%	0 .0%	0 .0%	0 .0%	1 .3%
Total	93 100.0%	25 100.0%	37 100.0%	54 100.0%	62 100.0%	15 100.0%	24 100.0%	10 100.0%	320 100.0%

Pearson chi-square 92.437.

TABLE 3.22
Classification of PR leaders based on their estimated annual income and PS elections contested by them

Number of elections contested	*Incomes*							*Total*
	Up to 12,500	*12,501-25,000*	*25,001-50,000*	*50,001-1,00,000*	*1,00,001-2,00,000*	*2,00,001-4,00,000*	*Above 4,00,000*	
(1)	(2)	(3)	(4)	(5)	(6)	(7)	(8)	(9)
Not Contested	37 88.1%	42 71.2%	42 58.3%	21 50.0%	29 59.2%	14 43.8%	6 25.0%	191 59.7%
Contested once and win	5 11.9%	14 23.7%	29 40.3%	19 45.2%	20 40.8%	17 53.1%	18 75.0%	122 38.1%
Contested once and lose	0 .0%	0 .0%	0 .0%	1 2.4%	0 .0%	0 .0%	0 .0%	1 .3%
Contested twice and win	0 .0%	2 3.4%	0 .0%	0 .0%	0 .0%	1 3.1%	0 .0%	3 .9%
Contested twice and win only once	0 .0%	1 1.7%	0 .0%	1 2.4%	0 .0%	0 .0%	0 .0%	2 .6%
Contested thrice and win only once	0 .0%	0 .0%	1 1.4%	0 .0%	0 .0%	0 .0%	0 .0%	1 .3%
Total	42 100.0%	59 100.0%	72 100.0%	42 100.0%	49 100.0%	32 100.0%	24 100.0%	320 100.0%

Pearson chi-square 57.987.

regularity is in real sense, have adopted it in inheritance or these who have assimilated themselves in party politics of the state.

The low percentage of these leaders is because young leaders have just begun their career of joining this and contested for the first time or so. On the other hand, elders are not fascinated as they find that their career in the local politics is not fairly longer. Second, the reservation of seats and rotation of reserving a constituency and offices both on caste and gender basis (but not the wards of village panchayats) has also affected it (regularity of contesting elections) very much. The case study of some village panchayats may explain this phenomenon in more meaningful manner.

The field survey also testified the fact that the sampled leaders have not contested Zila Parishad or any other election other like cooperative institution, etc. Thus, the people in local politics are not recruited through cooperative institutions as it was in past. The reason attributed to this that the cooperative bodies have not remained so popular and vibrant now-a-days in the state in general or in the sampled villages in particular It means, the local leaders assume the role of leadership of a particular level (i.e. GP and PS) directly and definitely as per their capacity and strength in true sense of the term in political perspective. Thus, it is concluded that the reservation has provided a wider opportunity to develop much democratic and participative local leadership at GP and PS level.

The sampled leaders although not regularly contesting elections and the illusion of real devolution and decentralization of powers and functions to these institutions are over. One of the important reasons for this is inability of local politics and leadership to integrate with mainstream state level politics. It is verified from the local leaders themselves by asking the question, do they consider themselves as political worker of a political party'? The data is tabulated in Table 3.23.

The data in Table 3.23 indicates that only 14.1 per cent admitted that they have acquired the role of political leader after becoming local representative in PRIs. Another 10 percent feel that their position has made them to behave somewhat like political leader. Others have denied or they had not asked to express their opinions in response to this question or uncertain to say anything. Thus as most of these leaders joined local

TABLE 3.23

Perceptions of PR leaders regarding rural leaders are acquiring the role of political worker

Perceptions	*Frequency*	*Percent*	*Cumulative Percent*
Yes	45	14.1	14.1
No	165	51.6	65.6
Somewhat	32	10.0	75.6
Uncertain	2	.6	76.3
Not asked	76	23.8	100.0
Total	320	100.0	

institutions first time therefore they consider that they have not acquired the role of political worker.

The perceptions of sampled leaders on this proposition are distributed on gender basis in Table 3.24 and the data indicates

TABLE 3.24

Classification of perceptions of PR leaders based on their gender regarding rural leaders are acquiring the role of political worker

	Gender		*Total*
Perception to be a political worker	*Male*	*Female*	
Yes	38 17.7%	7 6.7%	45 14.1%
No	100 46.5%	65 61.9%	165 51.6%
Somewhat	28 13.0%	4 3.8%	32 10.0%
Uncertain	1 .5%	1 1.0%	2 .6%
Not asked	48 22.3%	28 26.7%	76 23.8%
Total	215 100.0%	105 100.0%	320 100.0%

Pearson chi-square 16.137.

that the percentage of women (61.9 per cent) who do not consider themselves as political worker is higher in comparison to male (46.5 per cent). The chi-square value (16.137) is significant indicating the difference in perceptions on gender basis.

The caste-wise classification of leaders' perceptions on this issue is tabulated in Table 3.25 and the data reveals that the leaders, who perceive themselves in political workers' role is higher among farming castes followed by scheduled castes (B), upper castes and backward castes (A) and scheduled castes (A). In addition, the backward castes are relatively less developed in political sense in comparison to backward castes (B). It is also concluded from the data that farming castes, backward castes (B) and upper castes are politically active castes and backward castes (A) and scheduled castes as a whole, find themselves lesser active castes in the sampled villages. The chi-square value (34.966) is also significant which means that leaders belonging different castes have different perceptions and thus the backward castes could not integrate themselves in main stream politics like the forward castes.

The perceptions of sampled leaders are also classified on the basis of their educational levels. The data in Table 3.26 indicate a relationship between the education levels of the leaders and their perceptions to be political workers. The data indicates that the percentage of leaders who consider that they have acquired the role of political worker more or less increases with the rise in educational levels of the sampled leaders. This trend is also getting repeated in case of those leaders who feel that they have acquired the role of political worker up to some extent only. Thus, the education may be considered as responsible factor facilitating the assimilation of PR leader in localized mainstream politics of the state. The chi-square value (45.363) is significant and confirms the difference of perception on the basis of educational levels of the sampled leaders.

The sampled PR leaders' feeling that they become political worker is also associated with their income level as is evident from the data in Table 3.27. The data in the chi-square value (39.587) confirms the similar trend as is there in the case of educational levels of the leaders. In other words, the political

TABLE 3.25

Classification of perceptions of PR leaders based on their castes regarding rural leaders are acquiring the role of political worker

Number of elections contested	Castes						Total
	Farming castes	Upper castes	Backward castes (A)	Backward castes (B)	Scheduled castes (A)	Scheduled castes (B)	
(1)	(2)	(3)	(4)	(5)	(6)	(7)	(8)
Yes	22 22.2%	5 12.5%	2 6.9%	5 13.5%	5 9.8%	6 9.4%	45 14.1%
No	42 42.4%	23 57.5%	21 72.4%	11 29.7%	29 56.9%	39 60.9%	165 51.6%
Somewhat	12 12.1%	4 10.0%	1 3.4%	8 21.6%	5 9.8%	2 3.1%	32 10.0%
Uncertain	0 .0%	1 2.5%	0 .0%	0 .0%	1 2.0%	0 .0%	2 .6%
Not asked	23 23.2%	7 17.5%	5 17.2%	13 35.1%	11 21.6%	17 26.6%	76 23.8%
Total	99 100.0%	40 100.0%	29 100.0%	37 100.0%	51 100.0%	64 100.0%	320 100.0%

Pearson chi-square 34.966.

TABLE 3.26
Classification of perceptions of PR leaders based on their educational levels regarding rural leaders are acquiring the role of political worker

Perception to be a political worker	*Education Levels*								*Total*
	Illiterate	*Literate*	*Primary*	*Middle*	*Matri-culation*	*Senior secondary*	*Graduate*	*Other*	
(1)	(2)	(3)	(4)	(5)	(6)	(7)	(8)	(9)	(10)
Yes	9 9.7%	2 8.0%	3 8.1%	8 14.8%	11 17.7%	4 26.7%	7 29.2%	1 10.0%	45 14.1%
No	62 66.7%	17 68.0%	23 62.2%	22 40.7%	27 43.5%	3 20.0%	9 37.5%	2 20.0%	165 51.6%
Somewhat	3 3.2%	2 8.0%	4 10.8%	7 13.0%	7 11.3%	3 20.0%	5 20.8%	1 10.0%	32 10.0%
Uncertain	1 1.1%	0 .0%	0 .0%	0 .0%	1 1.6%	0 .0%	0 .0%	0 .0%	2 .6%
Not asked	18 19.4%	4 16.0%	7 18.9%	17 31.5%	16 25.8%	5 33.3%	3 12.5%	6 60.0%	76 23.8%
Total	93 100.0%	25 100.0%	37 100.0%	54 100.0%	62 100.0%	15 100.0%	24 100.0%	10 100.0%	320 100.0%

Pearson chi-square 45.363.

TABLE 3.27

Classification of perceptions of PR leaders based on their estimated annual incomes regarding rural leaders are acquiring the role of political worker

Perception to be a political worker	*Incomes*							*Total*
	Up to 12,500	*12,501-25,000*	*25,001-50,000*	*50,001-1,00,000*	*1,00,001-2,00,000*	*2,00,001-4,00,000*	*Above 4,00,000*	
(1)	*(2)*	*(3)*	*(4)*	*(5)*	*(6)*	*(7)*	*(8)*	*(9)*
Yes	2 4.8%	7 11.9%	9 12.5%	6 14.3%	9 18.4%	9 28.1%	3 12.5%	45 14.1%
No	34 81.0%	35 59.3%	31 43.1%	18 42.9%	21 42.9%	13 40.6%	13 54.2%	165 51.6%
Somewhat	1 2.4%	2 3.4%	6 8.3%	7 16.7%	7 14.3%	5 15.6%	4 16.7%	32 10.0%
Uncertain	0 .0%	1 1.7%	1 1.4%	0 .0%	0 .0%	0 .0%	0 .0%	2 .6%
Not asked	5 11.9%	14 23.7%	25 34.7%	11 26.2%	12 24.5%	5 15.6%	4 16.7%	76 23.8%
Total	42 100.0%	59 100.0%	72 100.0%	42 100.0%	49 100.0%	32 100.0%	24 100.0%	320 100.0%

Pearson chi-square 39.587.

socialization more or less moves up with the income levels of the sampled PR leaders.

Last, the external and internal conditions motivate a person to do or no to do an action. Politics needs time, money and energy. The discussion above also support that caste, education, income etc. have been the resources of the successful PR leadership in the state. Even after utilizing resources, it is not necessary one may be successful in it or not? Hence, only certain strong conditions can motivate the people to join politics. Ch. Balaramulu and Raghavender Rao in their study[3] based on the opinions expressed by the presidents of mandal praja parishads found that most of them joined the panchayati raj institutions with a view to serving the people and improving the economic conditions of the weaker sections of the society. However, considerable numbers of them (40 per cent) have joined these institutions with the motive of capturing political power. It means the main motive is to be in localized mainstream politics. Therefore the question what motivate the rural leaders to join local politics is also probed with the help of opinions expressed by the leaders themselves.

The data in Table 3.28 indicates that many leaders got this leadership in inheritance (9.7 per cent). In addition to this, some of them are also big farmers (0.9 per cent) or they are unanimously elected (3.8 per cent). Others narrated that they did not get it in inheritance but being the big farmers of the village (.9 per cent) they are in politics. In other words, 15.3 per cent of the sampled leaders are in local politics because of being elite in rural society.

About 12 percent of leaders accepted that fascination of political power allures them to join politics. A few of them are political workers of a political party (.9 per cent) or their relatives are in politics (1.3 per cent), they themselves have interest in politics (10.0 per cent). Thus, politics allure them to join local politics. The discussion leads to conclude that they are or consider themselves somewhat as political worker or in the midst of political life of the society in general and village in particular.

The reservation provision introduced by amendment has also pushed many village people into local politics. A sizeable percentage (19.1 per cent) confirmed this belief. Not only this

TABLE 3.28
Reasons to be in local politics

Sl. No. Reasons	*Frequency*	*Percent*	*Cumulative Percent*
1. Family tradition	31	9.7	9.7
2. Family tradition+big farmer	3	.9	10.6
3. Unanimous choice/family tradition/big farmer	12	3.8	14.4
4. Big farmers of the village	3	.9	15.3
5. Active worker of a political party	3	.9	16.3
6. Relatives are in politics	4	1.3	17.5
7. Interest in politics	32	10.0	27.5
8. Reservation pushed to join local politics	61	19.1	46.6
9. Fellow villagers motivated to do so	44	13.8	60.3
10. Neighborhood asked to contest	14	4.4	64.7
11. Popularity allures to do so	1	.3	65.0
12. Concerned for village development	47	14.7	79.7
13. To oppose certain contestant	1	.3	80.0
14. Social service	21	6.6	86.6
15. Other multiple reasons	43	13.4	100.0
Total	320	100.0	

fellow villagers (13.8 per cent) and neighborhood (4.4 per cent) and gaining popularity (.3 per cent) are other factors which made a sizeable portion of leaders to take local politics in a casual manner. This group of persons (reserved classes etc.) is the local representatives who not only provide opposition to dominant leadership but also prevent misuse of power by the dominant leadership especially at grown panchayat level. They are instrumental in preventing the misuse of power by the panchayat. However, usually they do not find their integration into the political process of the areas as a whole.

About 21 per cent of leaders find themselves concerned for development of the village or social service. Another 13.4 per cent have many reasons to tell why they are in local politics.

Thus the discussion based on data leads to conclude that big farmers and many of those who get the local politics in inheritance, reservation introduced by new panchayat raj, interest to promote political interests and concern for development/welfare activities are the motivating factors for sampled rural leaders to take local politics as political career.

The rural life is quite latent one. It is quiet and calm unless disturbed. The people possess limited wants and aspire within their means and available opportunities advancement for them. They lead a settled life and have restricted mobility. Therefore, it is presumed that life in village might be an inactive life. This is asked from the sampled PR leaders during survey as it is related to the inactivity of leaders also.

TABLE 3.29

Perceptions of PR leaders on the incidence of inactive life in rural areas

	Frequency	*Percent*	*Cumulative Percent*
Yes	177	55.3	55.3
No	28	8.8	64.1
Uncertain	86	26.9	90.9
No response	29	9.1	100.0
Total	320	100.0	

The data in Table 3.29 reveals that a majority of them (55.3 per cent) agreed to accept village life is an inactive one. There were only 8.8 per cent who rejected the incidence of this characteristic in village society. Others are either uncertain or did not respond to when asked this. Thus, the village leadership in general believes that the life is slow one but a few of the leaders possess progressive thinking.

The perceptions of sampled leaders regarding inactive life in villages are classified on gender basis and data is presented in Table 3.30.

The data in Table 3.30 clearly states that a majority (61.9 per cent) of sampled male leaders accepted the incidence of inactive life in rural areas of the state. About 20 per cent were

TABLE 3.30
Classification of perceptions of PR leaders based on their gender regarding the incidence of inactive life in rural areas

Perceptions	Gender		Total
	Male	Female	
Yes	133 61.9%	44 41.9%	177 55.3%
No	20 9.3%	8 7.6%	28 8.8%
Uncertain	43 20.0%	43 41.0%	86 26.9%
No response	19 8.8%	10 9.5%	29 9.1%
Total	215 100.0%	105 100.0%	320 100.0%

Pearson chi-square 16.868.

uncertain to say something when this is asked from them. However, in case of female sampled leaders the proportion who admitted inactiveness in rural life and uncertainty to answer the question was found almost equal, i.e. 41.9 per cent and 41 per cent respectively. Surprisingly, the percentage of leaders who denied the incidence of inactive life is quite minimum both among male and female leaders (9.3 and 7.6%). The chi-square value (16.868) also makes it clear that there is a difference of perceptions among male and female leaders. Nevertheless, there is inactiveness in rural life and it is realized by a majority of the leadership. In other words, the emerging political leadership at local level is well aware of progressive needs of the society.

The reality of inactive life is also well understood by the leaders belonging different castes (Table 3.31).

The data in Table 3.31 indicates that majority of leaders of different castes (except backward castes (B) and scheduled castes (B)) affirmed the inactiveness of life in villages and only a small percentage of them denied it. Many of the leaders remained uncertain to this issue. The chi-square value 15.913 indicates the difference of perceptions about inactive life in

TABLE 3.31
Classification of perceptions of PR leaders based on their castes regarding the incidence of inactive life in rural areas

Perceptions	*Castes*						*Total*
	Farming castes	*Upper castes*	*Backward castes (A)*	*Backward castes (B)*	*Scheduled castes (A)*	*Scheduled castes (B)*	
(1)	*(2)*	*(3)*	*(4)*	*(5)*	*(6)*	*(7)*	*(8)*
Yes	58 58.6%	25 62.5%	18 62.1%	17 45.9%	28 54.9%	31 48.4%	177 55.3%
No	13 13.1%	3 7.5%	2 6.9%	3 8.1%	2 3.9%	5 7.8%	28 8.8%
Uncertain	23 23.2%	11 27.5%	7 24.1%	10 27.0%	15 29.4%	20 31.3%	86 26.9%
No response	5 5.1%	1 2.5%	2 6.9%	7 18.9%	6 11.8%	8 12.5%	29 9.1%
Total	99 100.0%	40 100.0%	29 100.0%	37 100.0%	51 100.0%	64 100.0%	320 100.0%

Pearson chi-square 15.913.

village is not perceived differently by the leaders of the different castes groups.

The data about the perceptions of the leaders on the proposition regarding the incidence of inactive life in rural areas is also classified on the basis of their position or the terms during which they were/have been elected in panchayati raj. The data in this regard is tabulated in Table 3.32 and it indicates that the proportion of PS leaders who find village life as an inactive one is higher in comparison to GP leaders. The proportion of such leaders is again higher among those who were elected during first and second PR elections after amendment. Further, the data also reveals that the percentages of GP leaders who denied the inactive life in villages is also lesser than the PS leaders holding such perception. The data also shows that a large number of them are confused and uncertain to respond to this proposition. The chi-square value 133.740 however, indicates a significant difference of perception among various groups of PR leaders.

The data about the perceptions of the leaders on the said proposition is also examined in context with their educational levels and it is clear from the information in Table 3.33 that the leaders of different educational levels have interpreted the proposition of inactive life in villages in different ways. Naturally it is as per their understanding developed and depends on their educational levels. The chi-square value 72.824 supports the difference of perceptions in significant manner.

The data reveals that the proportion of relatively much educated leaders considers that there is inactiveness in village life. They are also not confused and therefore their proportion is less in comparison to lesser educated leaders.

The perceptions of sampled leaders on the proposition about the inactiveness in village life are also analyzed in context with their annual incomes. The data so obtained is tabulated in Table 3.34 and it reveals that the percentage of leaders having perception that village life is inactive one decreases with the increase in income levels. However, the chi-square value 25.132 do not indicate significant difference of perceptions among the leaders of various income levels.

TABLE 3.32

Classification of perceptions of PR leaders based on their position regarding the incidence of inactive life in rural areas

Perceptions	*Positions*								*Total*
	PS leaders before 73rd amendment	*PS leaders after 73rd amendment (1st election)*	*PS leaders after 73rd amendment 2nd election)*	*PS leaders after 73rd amendment (3rd election)*	*GP leaders before 73rd amendment*	*GP leaders after 73rd amendment (1st election)*	*GP leaders after 73rd amendment (2nd election)*	*GP leaders after 73rd amendment (3rd election)*	
(1)	(2)	(3)	(4)	(5)	(6)	(7)	(8)	(9)	(10)
Yes	2 50.0%	20 66.7%	43 68.3%	16 53.3%	15 55.6%	30 61.2%	36 50.7%	15 32.6%	177 55.3%
No	1 25.0%	2 6.7%	11 17.5%	4 13.3%	1 3.7%	3 6.1%	1 1.4%	5 10.9%	28 8.8%
Uncertain	1 25.0%	8 26.7%	9 14.3%	4 13.3%	11 40.7%	15 30.6%	33 46.5%	5 10.9%	86 26.9%
No response	0 .0%	0 .0%	0 .0%	6 20.0%	0 .0%	1 2.0%	1 1.4%	21 45.7%	29 9.1%
Total	4 100.0%	30 100.0%	63 100.0%	30 100.0%	27 100.0%	49 100.0%	71 100.0%	46 100.0%	320 100.0%

Pearson chi-square 133.740.

TABLE 3.33

Classification of perceptions of PR leaders based on their educational levels regarding the incidence of inactive life in rural areas

Perceptions	*Education Levels*								*Total*
	Illiterate	*Literate*	*Primary*	*Middle*	*Matri-culation*	*Senior secondary*	*Graduate*	*Other*	
(1)	*(2)*	*(3)*	*(4)*	*(5)*	*(6)*	*(7)*	*(8)*	*(9)*	*(10)*
Yes	49 52.7%	8 32.0%	17 45.9%	34 63.0%	37 59.7%	13 86.7%	16 66.7%	3 30.0%	177 55.3%
No	3 3.2%	2 8.0%	3 8.1%	6 11.1%	3 4.8%	0 .0%	7 29.2%	4 40.0%	28 8.8%
Uncertain	31 33.3%	14 56.0%	16 43.2%	9 16.7%	14 22.6%	1 6.7%	1 4.2%	0 .0%	86 26.9%
No response	10 10.8%	1 4.0%	1 2.7%	5 9.3%	8 12.9%	1 6.7%	0 .0%	3 30.0%	29 9.1%
Total	93 100.0%	25 100.0%	37 100.0%	54 100.0%	62 100.0%	15 100.0%	24 100.0%	10 100.0%	320 100.0%

Pearson chi-square 72.824

TABLE 3.34

Classification of perceptions of PR leaders based on their incomes levels regarding the incidence of inactive life in rural areas

Perceptions	*Incomes*							*Total*
	Up to 12,500	*12,501-25,000*	*25,001-50,000*	*50,001-1,00,000*	*1,00,001-2,00,000*	*2,00,001-4,00,000*	*Above 4,00,000*	
(1)	*(2)*	*(3)*	*(4)*	*(5)*	*(6)*	*(7)*	*(8)*	*(9)*
Yes	27 64.3%	35 59.3%	45 62.5%	19 45.2%	25 51.0%	15 46.9%	11 45.8%	177 55.3%
No	0 .0%	1 1.7%	6 8.3%	7 16.7%	4 8.2%	6 18.8%	4 16.7%	28 8.8%
Uncertain	11 26.2%	17 28.8%	15 20.8%	10 23.8%	16 32.7%	8 25.0%	9 37.5%	86 26.9%
No response	4 9.5%	6 10.2%	6 8.3%	6 14.3%	4 8.2%	3 9.4%	0 .0%	29 9.1%
Total	42 100.0%	59 100.0%	72 100.0%	42 100.0%	49 100.0%	32 100.0%	24 100.0%	320 100.0%

Pearson chi-square 25.132.

Political development is pre-requisite to economic progress of a society. Feelings of the sample leaders obtained is tabulated in Table 3.35 which indicates that the sampled leaders have not realized the significance of political development and only 6.6 per cent admitted that political development is pre-requisite of economic progress in a society. The important thing is that a majority of sampled leaders (60 per cent) denied it. This leads to conclude that the process of developing a political understanding in rural society has just begun. However, the PR leadership has not been successful in acquiring the understanding how to get it integrated with the mainstream of politics of the state. They are not visionary of development. The routine political activities are considered as development by them.

TABLE 3.35

Perceptions of PR leaders regarding political development are pre-requisite of economic progress

	Frequency	*Percent*	*Cumulative Percent*
Yes	21	6.6	6.6
No	192	60.0	66.6
Uncertain	33	10.3	76.9
No response	4	1.3	78.1
Not asked	70	21.9	100.0
Total	320	100.0	

As the percentage of those who affirmed that political development is pre requisite of economic development is quite low therefore its analysis with the gender, caste, position, educational qualification and income, etc. is not presented. However, an examination of the chi-square values which are Gender (10.836*); Castes (15.864); Position (338.756); Educational level (34.298); and Income (29.667) indicate that the male and the PS leaders elected particularly post-amendment period in higher proposition than their counterparts respectively.

The absence of political development is also get confirmed from the data in Table 3.36 which indicate that only 9.4 per cent of the sampled leaders admitted holding GP elections on political party basis. But, a large majority (74.7 per cent) disfavoured it.

TABLE 3.36

Perceptions of PR leaders regarding holding of GP elections on political party basis

	Frequency	*Percent*	*Cumulative Percent*
Yes	30	9.4	9.4
No	239	74.7	84.1
Uncertain	49	15.3	99.4
No response	2	.6	100.0
Total	320	100.0	

Like earlier, the information relating to the analysis of these perceptions of the leadership with Gender (58.044)[4]; Castes (18.593); Educational levels (51.837*); and Incomes (15.198). It is evident from the data that the proportion of leaders who disfavoured holding GP election on political party basis are significantly higher among males and the leaders possessing educational level higher than matriculation level.

The sampled leaders were also asked to state whether the elections in panchayati raj are actually contested on political party basis or not? It is probed in general for local elections i.e. elections other than state legislature and Lok Sabha. The responses of the leaders are tabulated in Table 3.37.

The data in Table 3.37 reveals that 22.5 percent of the sampled leadership affirmed that local elections are contested on political party basis. A majority (61.9 per cent) denied it. It simply means some of the local elections may acquire this characteristic due to the fact that if a candidate contesting the said election is a political worker of a particular political party in such situation it may be fought on party basis. Besides this, sometime (in Zila Parishad) the political party field and support its candidates particularly to win chairman office elected indirectly.

TABLE 3.37
Perceptions regarding local elections contested on political party basis

	Frequency	*Percent*	*Cumulative Percent*
Yes	72	22.5	22.5
No	198	61.9	84.4
Sometimes	32	10.0	94.4
practiced only in a few villages	10	3.1	97.5
No response	8	2.5	100.0
Total	320	100.0	

In last, the leaders were also asked to narrate the reason why the election of PRIs should not be on non-partisan basis. The information obtained from them is tabulated in Table 3.38

The data in Table 3.38 indicates that 29.7 per cent of the leaders simply answered that non-partisan election helps in

TABLE 3.38
Reasons why elections should be on non-partisans basis

	Frequency	*Percent*	*Cumulative Percent*
Ensuring harmony	41	12.8	12.8
Maintaining peace	6	1.9	14.7
For overall development/ participation	11	3.4	18.1
To avoid enmity	66	20.6	38.8
To avoid groupism	95	29.7	68.4
Avoiding groupism + ensuring harmony	3	.9	69.4
Avoiding groupism + enmity	21	6.6	75.9
Avoiding groupism + overall development	5	1.6	77.5
Avoiding enmity + ensuring harmony	2	.6	78.1
Unaware	36	11.3	89.4
Uncertain	19	5.9	95.3
No response	15	4.7	100.0
Total	320	100.0	

avoiding the process of grouping of people in village politics. The grouping of people in village is bad for ensuring harmony and another 12.5 percent leaders expressed so. Further, avoiding grouping and maintaining harmony means removing enmity usually found in traditional communities. It is again endorsed by a sizeable percentage (20.6 per cent) of leaders. Thus, in total 62.8 percent of leaders in different words said the same that village harmony requires non-partisan kind of local elections. Remaining leaders either expressed the combination of above stated reason or were uncertain to say something. In other words, maintaining harmony and avoiding conflict is still a motto the village people like to cherish in their society. The political parties by not indulging in local elections are also trying to respect those sentiments.

CONCLUSION

Thus, it is concluded that panchayat leadership at gram panchayat and panchayat samiti levels in is not politically progressive one. The ethical premises and spirit of the rural local political system is guided by the value system prevalent and practiced in the rural areas of state but within the existing democratic and modern value system laid down in constitution and legislations in this regard. But, at sometime, tendency to integrate local politics with mainstream politics is a very positive indication of political development taking place at grassroot level in the state.

NOTES AND REFERENCES

1. The post-amendment panchayati raj has enlarged this opportunity to a greater extent in the country. If it is realized in true spirit, it is definite that then the third stratum of federal set-up will emerge in the country.
2. Darshankar, Arjunrao Y. (1979). Leadership in Panchayati Raj, Jaipur; Panchsheel Prakashan, p. 102.
3. Balaramulu, Ch. and Rao, Raghavender (Jan.-June 1995). Political Leadership in Panchayati Raj: A Study of Mandal Praja Parishad Leadership in Andhra Pradesh. Administrative Change, 22(2), p. 173.
4. The figures in brackets are the chi-square values of the said variable with another variable taken in the table.

Political Practices

The studies of rural local political system make one to conclude that there are few castes in the villages, which are politically active. These castes are dominant in terms of their numerical strength or possessing land holdings or owning relatively large sized land holdings and/or socially or economically superior or possessing any combination of the above stated traits. Therefore, an effort is made to understand the emerging political practices in the light of social and economic conditions prevailing in the villages of the state.

The politically active castes in villages possess the requisite resources required to be successful in local politics. It is also believed that the resourceful people dominate in PRIs and numerical strength is instrumental in deciding the nature of leadership at village level. Many times, it is argued that the Sarpanch belonging upper castes can only be successful. It means that the caste plays an important role in decision-making process of PRIs. It is also true that the reservation system introduced particularly after 73rd constitutional amendment act (1992) has facilitated the representation of SC/women and naturally that has elevated their status in politics in particular and society in general. Nevertheless, the unanimous elections are preferred in this traditional or transitional society. The above stated propositions pertaining to local political practices are probed and tested with the help of empirical data collected from the sampled leadership.

In pursuance of the above stated objective, first of all, the information relating to the politically active castes of the sampled villages is presented in Table 4.1.

TABLE 4.1
Political active castes based on the responses of the sampled respondents

	Frequency	*Valid Percent*	*Cumulative Percent*
Farming castes	3	.9	.9
Upper castes	1	.3	1.3
Scheduled castes + Upper castes	29	9.1	10.3
Scheduled castes	2	.6	10.9
Farming castes + Upper castes + others	5	1.6	12.5
Farming + Backward castes (B)	5	1.6	14.1
Backward castes (A) + Backward castes (B)	2	.6	14.7
Farming castes + Scheduled castes	39	12.2	26.9
Backward castes + Scheduled castes	7	2.2	29.1
SC(A) + SC (B)	2	.6	29.7
Farming castes + Upper castes + Scheduled castes	15	4.7	34.4
Not willing to tell	7	2.2	36.6
All castes have their role in local politics	203	63.4	100.0
Total	320	100.0	

The data in Table 4.1 illustrates that the village leaders are fairly mature in political sense as a large majority (63.4 per cent) of them stated that all castes have their independent role in electing GP leaders. How every caste plays an independent role in electing GP leaders? The credit to involve every caste is attributed to the ward system introduced after 73rd constitutional amendment. The wards for GP elections were carved out in such a manner that each caste may get its significance as per their numerical strength in electing their representatives. It may be intentional or unintentional on the part of those who have remained involved in framing rules and regulations and executing those rules and regulations for demarcating the wards in the villages of the state. Another factor responsible for this state of affairs is that almost all villages of the state have unique characteristics in the form that the houses of numerically weak castes are concentrated at one place or live together in a single street or in separate vicinity. Whatever the reason, one thing is quite clear that all castes have their significance in sending their representatives to GP in particular.

A sizeable (12.2 per cent) proportion of the respondents, however, stated that the farming castes and scheduled castes are the active castes. Further, 4.7 per cent opined that upper castes along with farming and scheduled castes are active. About 9 per cent holds the view that farming plus upper and other (i.e., depending upon the village) castes are active in village politics. Thus, the information indicates although all castes have independent role in GP elections but the group of three castes, i.e. farming, upper and scheduled castes are active in general. The backward castes are not so active if those are not numerically and economically dominating one in a village.

The responses of the sampled leaders on political active castes are examined in context with their gender, castes, educational levels, estimated annual incomes, etc.

The examination lead to conclude[1] (See Tables 4.42-4.46 after notes and references of the chapter) that the percentage of male leaders (60.5 per cent) who hold that all castes play independent role in electing their local representatives, is apparently lesser than the female sampled leaders (69.5 per cent) (Table 4.42). Similarly, the GP leaders (average more than 63.0 percent) in comparison to PS leaders (average less than 63 per cent) have higher in (significant manner) proportion that hold this view point (Tale 4.43).

However, the leaders of various castes' groups have responded differently and the percentage of those who consider that the all castes have independent in electing their representatives is lowest (35.3 per cent) among scheduled castes (A) representatives indicating their inability to compete with all other castes of their respective villages. Surprisingly, the leaders belonging scheduled castes (B) are active in most vigrous way (78.1 per cent). It means these leaders are asserting to reject the domination of traditional castes in PRIs. (Table 4.44).

The data with reference to educational levels reveals that the senior secondary passed leaders are at the lowest (53.3 per cent) and graduate leaders are at the highest level (75 per cent) on the continuum (with the average of 63.4 percent and the leaders of other educational levels supported this view more or less in uniform proportion around 60 per cent) of respondents who stated that all castes have independent role in local elections. Other leaders having percentage more than the average are either literate or studied up to middle level (Table 4.45). Besides, the role of all castes is not much perceived by the leaders of higher income groups (Table 4.46). The chi-square values (except in the cases of gender and incomes) calculated for the above stated variables are significant and therefore support the differentiation of perceptions across castes groups and educational levels.

The empowerment, i.e. power to the people decides the efficacy of local leader in relation to his/her role performance. Therefore, it becomes essential to find out the social, economic and political resources, which they utilize to promote themselves as leaders. Therefore, information pertaining to this aspect was obtained during field survey.

The data in Table 4.2 indicates that sizeable percentage (30.3 per cent) of leaders are either big landlords or political active or influential persons of the village/area or persons having relationships in state bureaucracy. It means about one third of them are socially, economically and politically resourceful leaders. They are enough empowered, mature and in the mainstream of rural society who find themselves fit and successful in running PRIs.

A group of 8.4 per cent of the sampled leaders stated that they are in mainstream of the society and having relationships with political leaders or bureaucrats or local influential persons.

TABLE 4.2

Political resources of the sampled local leaders

		Frequency	*Valid Percent*	*Cumulative Percent*
1	Big landlords + Rich + Active in politics+ Influential	97	30.3	30.3
1	Big landlords + Politically active + Influential + Relations with bureaucrats	51	15.9	57.2
2	Closeness with pol. leaders/ bureaucracy + Influential	27	8.4	38.7
3	Rich Persons	54	16.9	55.6
3	Influential Persons			
3	+ Related with bureaucracy			
3	Party worker + Close to pol. Leader + influential			
3	Active in politics			
4	Party worker	5	1.6	57.2
5	Other	22	6.9	64.1
6	No response	115	35.9	100.0
	Total	320	100.0	

Similarly another 16.9 percent are either rich persons or influential or party workers or close to a political leader or active in politics.

Some of the leaders (1.6 percent) stated that to be political worker is also an important resource of the local rural leadership. However, a large percentage of them (i.e. 35.9 percent) did not respond because they do not consider themselves as resourceful leaders.

The data in Table 4.3 tells the relationship between the gender of the leaders and the resources they possess and a close perusal of the data in reveals that the male leaders are more resourceful than the female in significant way (the chi-square value 37.759 is very much higher than the significant value 18.307).

The most important resource to reserve a berth in rural local political system is the caste and its social hierarchical level

TABLE 4.3
Classification of resources of the sampled leaders based on their gender

	Gender		*Total*
	Male	*Female*	
Party worker	4 1.9%	1 1.0%	5 1.6%
Big landlords + Rich + Active in politics + Influential	35 16.3%	11 10.5%	46 14.4%
Rich Persons	2 .9%	0 .0%	2 .6%
Influential Persons	9 4.2%	5 4.8%	14 4.4%
Influential + Related with bureaucracy	7 3.3%	1 1.0%	8 2.5%
Party worker + Close to political leader + influential	12 5.6%	2 1.9%	14 4.4%
Rich + Active in politics + Influential	14 6.5%	2 1.9%	16 5.0%
Closeness with political leaders/ bureaucracy + Influential	25 11.6%	2 1.9%	27 8.4%
Big landlords + Politically active + Influential + Relations with bureaucracy	36 16.7%	15 14.3%	51 15.9%
Other	16 7.4%	6 5.7%	22 6.9%
No response	55 25.6%	60 57.1%	115 35.9%
Total	215 100.0%	105 100.0%	320 100.0%

Pearson chi-square 37.759*.

and numerical strength in the village concerned. The upper castes and land owning castes leaders are more resourceful in social, economic and political sense. Therefore the data is tabulated in Table 4.4 which is revealing about the interactions between the variable of possession of resources and the castes of the leadership.

TABLE 4.4

Classification of resources of the sampled leaders based on their castes

Resources	*Castes*						*Total*
	Farming castes	*Upper castes*	*Backward castes (A)*	*Backward castes (B)*	*Scheduled castes (A)*	*Scheduled castes (B)*	
(1)	*(2)*	*(3)*	*(4)*	*(5)*	*(6)*	*(7)*	*(8)*
Party worker	2 2.0%	0 .0%	0 .0%	1 2.7%	0 .0%	2 3.1%	5 1.6%
Big landlords + Rich + Active in politics + Influential	16 16.2%	10 25.0%	2 6.9%	4 10.8%	5 9.8%	9 14.1%	46 14.4%
Rich Persons	0 .0%	2 5.0%	0 .0%	0 .0%	0 .0%	0 .0%	2 .6%
Influential Persons	5 5.1%	2 5.0%	1 3.4%	0 .0%	4 7.8%	2 3.1%	14 4.4%
Influential + Related with bureaucracy	4 4.0%	3 7.5%	1 3.4%	0 .0%	0 .0%	0 .0%	8 2.5%
Party worker + Close to political leader + influential	5 5.1%	1 2.5%	0 .0%	3 8.1%	4 7.8%	1 1.6%	14 4.4%
Rich + Active in politics + Influential	9 9.1%	2 5.0%	0 .0%	1 2.7%	3 5.9%	1 1.6%	16 5.0%
Closeness with political	4	4	4	1	10	4	27

leaders/bureaucracy + Influential	4.0%	10.0%	13.8%	2.7%	19.6%	6.3%	8.4%
Big landlords + Politically active + Influential + Relations with bureaucracy	17 17.2%	6 15.0%	6 20.7%	10 27.0%	3 5.9%	9 14.1%	51 15.9%
Other	8 8.1%	3 7.5%	1 3.4%	4 10.8%	1 2.0%	5 7.8%	22 6.9%
No response	29 29.3%	7 17.5%	14 48.3%	13 35.1%	21 41.2%	31 48.4%	115 35.9%
Total	99 100.0%	40 100.0%	29 100.0%	37 100.0%	51 100.0%	64 100.0%	320 100.0%

Pearson chi-square 79.662*.

The data in Table 4.4 reveals that upper castes, farming castes and land possessing backward castes i.e., BC (B) leaders expressed their affirmation of possessing the resources required in local politics. However, the scheduled castes and BC (A) leaders preferred to be silent on the issue. The reason, these leaders are not much resourceful in social, economic and political sense.

Further, whosoever has responded they find that the leaders are rich, influential, and active in politics or have closeness with mainstream political leadership/bureaucracy. The chi-square value 79.662 affirms the fact that leaders of different castes differ in term of possessing resources by them. The resources of the leaders are examined in the light of their term for which they are elected and pertinent information is tabulated in Table 4.5, which reveals that the PS leaders before 73rd amendment were used to be rich, influential, party workers and having closeness with the mainstream political leadership of the state. But, the PS leaders elected after amendment are from the different classes of people, no doubt, maximum of them are rich, influential and active in politics instead of closely related with mainstream political leadership of the state.

Similarly, in case of Gram Panchayat leaders, most of them used to be rich and big landlords, active in politics, influential and closely related to mainstream political leaders and bureaucrats But they are now coming from all classes of rural people. It means pre-dominance of earlier dominant class has diluted to the extent that the base of recruiting leaders in local politics has widened to include more common and poor people. The chi-square value, which is 142.928, affirms the distinction between the various positions of the leaders having different kinds of political resources.

The variable of resources is also treated with the educational level. The data obtained is tabulated in Table 4.6 and it makes it clear that a large percentage of leaders who are illiterate, primary and middle passed did not respond to this question. They are not very resourceful. The chi-square value (121.415) affirms that the resources of the leaders of different education levels are different from each other.

TABLE 4.5

Classification of resources of the sampled leaders based on their positions

Number of elections contested	Positions								Total
	PS leaders before 73rd amendment	PS leaders after 73rd amendment (1st election)	PS leaders after 73rd amendment 2nd election)	PS leaders after 73rd amendment (3rd election)	GP leaders before 73rd amendment	GP leaders after 73rd amendment (1st election)	GP leaders after 73rd amendment (2nd election)	GP leaders after 73rd amendment (3rd election)	
(1)	(2)	(3)	(4)	(5)	(6)	(7)	(8)	(9)	(10)
Party worker	0 .0%	1 3.3%	0 .0%	0 .0%	1 3.7%	1 2.0%	0 .0%	2 4.3%	5 1.6%
Big landlords + Rich + Active in politics + Influential	0 .0%	5 16.7%	11 17.5%	3 10.0%	4 14.8%	7 14.3%	12 16.9%	4 8.7%	46 14.4%
Rich Persons	0 .0%	0 .0%	0 .0%	0 .0%	2 7.4%	0 .0%	0 .0%	0 .0%	2 .6%
Influential Persons	0 .0%	0 .0%	2 3.2%	1 3.3%	1 3.7%	3 6.1%	3 4.2%	4 8.7%	14 4.4%
Influential + Related with bureaucracy	0 .0%	2 6.7%	4 6.3%	0 .0%	0 .0%	0 .0%	1 1.4%	1 2.2%	8 2.5%
Party worker + Close to political leader + influential	1 25.0%	0 .0%	1 1.6%	7 23.3%	0 .0%	1 2.0%	1 1.4%	3 6.5%	14 4.4%

(*Contd.*)

TABLE 4.5 (Contd.)

(1)	(2)	(3)	(4)	(5)	(6)	(7)	(8)	(9)	(10)
Rich + Active in politics + Influential	2 50.0%	1 3.3%	2 3.2%	2 6.7%	2 7.4%	3 6.1%	2 2.8%	2 4.3%	16 5.0%
Closeness with political leaders/bureaucracy + Influential	0 0%	1 3.3%	5 7.9%	3 10.0%	4 14.8%	5 10.2%	8 11.3%	1 2.2%	27 8.4%
Big landlords + Politically active + Influential + Relations with bureaucracy	0 .0%	8 26.7%	7 11.1%	1 3.3%	7 25.9%	10 20.4%	16 22.5%	2 4.3%	51 15.9%
Other	1 25.0%	2 6.7%	10 15.9%	4 13.3%	1 3.7%	0 .0%	2 2.8%	2 4.3%	22 6.9%
No response	0 .0%	10 33.3%	21 33.3%	9 30.0%	5 18.5%	19 38.8%	26 36.6%	25 54.3%	115 35.9%
Total	4 100.0%	30 100.0%	63 100.0%	30 100.0%	27 100.0%	49 100.0%	71 100.0%	46 100.0%	320 100.0%

Pearson Chi-square 142.928.

TABLE 4.6

Classification of resources of the sampled leaders based on their educational levels

	Education Levels								Total
	Illiterate	*Literate*	*Primary*	*Middle*	*Matri-culation*	*Senior secondary*	*Graduate*	*Other*	
(1)	(2)	(3)	(4)	(5)	(6)	(7)	(8)	(9)	(10)
Party worker	0 .0%	0 .0%	0 .0%	3 5.6%	1 1.6%	1 6.7%	0 .0%	0 .0%	5 1.6%
Big landlords + Rich + Active in politics + Influential	7 7.5%	4 16.0%	6 16.2%	4 7.4%	8 12.9%	3 20.0%	9 37.5%	5 50.0%	46 14.4%
Rich Persons	0 .0%	0 .0%	0 .0%	0 .0%	2 3.2%	0 .0%	0 .0%	0 .0%	2 .6%
Influential Persons	5 5.4%	0 .0%	1 2.7%	4 7.4%	4 6.5%	0 .0%	0 .0%	0 .0%	14 4.4%
Influential + Related with bureaucracy	0 .0%	0 .0%	1 2.7%	1 1.9%	4 6.5%	0 .0%	2 8.3%	0 .0%	8 2.5%
Party worker + Close to political leader + influential	3 3.2%	0 .0%	1 2.7%	2 3.7%	5 8.1%	2 13.3%	0 .0%	1 10.0%	14 4.4%
Rich + Active in politics + Influential	6 6.5%	3 12.0%	2 5.4%	0 .0%	2 3.2%	1 6.7%	2 8.3%	0 .0%	16 5.0%

(Contd.)

TABLE 4.6 (*Contd.*)

(1)	(2)	(3)	(4)	(5)	(6)	(7)	(8)	(9)	(10)
Closeness with political leaders/bureaucracy + Influential	7 7.5%	5 20.0%	1 2.7%	6 11.1%	5 8.1%	1 6.7%	2 8.3%	0 .0%	27 8.4%
Big landlords + Politically active + Influential + Relations with bureaucracy	15 16.1%	9 36.0%	4 10.8%	12 22.2%	9 14.5%	0 .0%	2 8.3%	0 .0%	51 15.9%
Other	4 4.3%	1 4.0%	3 8.1%	3 5.6%	4 6.5%	3 20.0%	1 4.2%	3 30.0%	22 6.9%
No response	46 49.5%	3 12.0%	18 48.6%	19 35.2%	18 29.0%	4 26.7%	6 25.0%	1 10.0%	115 35.9%
Total	93 100.0%	25 100.0%	37 100.0%	54 100.0%	62 100.0%	15 100.0%	24 100.0%	10 100.0%	320 100.0%

Pearson chi-square 121.415*.

Lastly, the resources of the leaders are studied with reference to the estimated annual income of the sampled leaders. The data in Table 4.7 affirms relationship between income levels and resources of the local leaders. It is evident from the data that poorer the leader lesser the incidence of response on the issue which means they are resourceless. Further, the richer people responded that the resources are important to be successful in local politics.

It is believed that the resourceful persons (in terms of wealth, education, influence and morally sound) not only get elected in PRIs but they can also participate in a local democratic politics of the village in an effective manner. Therefore the sampled leaders were asked respond to the proposition 'the resourceful and influential persons alone influence the election and working of panchayats. The data is tabulated in Table 4.8.

The data in Table 4.8 indicates that 32.8 per cent agreed and 31.9 per cent disagreed to the proposition that resourceful and influential persons alone influence the election and working of panchayats. About one-fourth of them (26.3 per cent) were undecided. Therefore, valid conclusion cannot be laid down based on the data.

The perceptions on this aspect are classified on the basis of their gender and the data in Table 4.9 and chi-square value (2.542 which is not significant) do not indicate the difference of perceptions between male and female leaders on the said proposition.

Further the above stated perceptions are classified on the basis of the castes of the leaders and information relating to it is tabulated in Table 4.10. The data in the table does not present a clear picture and the chi-square value 17.005, which is not significant, also indicates that the perceptions of the leaders belonging different castes do not differ in significant way.

The perceptions relating to the influence of resourceful leaders are also studied with reference to their educational level and tabulated in the Table 4.11. It is clear from the information that apparently there is a difference of opinion among the leaders of different educational levels (Chi-square 30.258 less than the significant value 32.671) but it is not significant and uniformity of any pattern is missing.

TABLE 4.7

Classification of resources of the sampled leaders based on their annual incomes

	Incomes							*Total*
	Up to 12,500	*12,501-25,000*	*25,001-50,000*	*50,001-1,00,000*	*1,00,001-2,00,000*	*2,00,001-4,00,000*	*Above 4,00,000*	
(1)	*(2)*	*(3)*	*(4)*	*(5)*	*(6)*	*(7)*	*(8)*	*(9)*
Party worker	1 2.4%	1 1.7%	2 2.8%	0 .0%	1 2.0%	0 .0%	0 .0%	5 1.6%
Big landlords + Rich + Active in politics + Influential	3 7.1%	3 5.1%	8 11.1%	9 21.4%	8 16.3%	6 18.8%	9 37.5%	46 14.4%
Rich Persons	0 .0%	0 .0%	1 1.4%	0 .0%	1 2.0%	0 .0%	0 .0%	2 .6%
Influential Persons	1 2.4%	4 6.8%	7 9.7%	2 4.8%	0 .0%	0 .0%	0 .0%	14 4.4%
Influential + Related with bureaucracy	0 .0%	1 1.7%	3 4.2%	2 4.8%	1 2.0%	1 3.1%	0 .0%	8 2.5%
Party worker + Close to political leader + influential	0 .0%	3 5.1%	2 2.8%	4 9.5%	3 6.1%	1 3.1%	1 4.2%	14 4.4%
Rich + Active in politics + Influential	1 2.4%	1 1.7%	2 2.8%	4 9.5%	3 6.1%	4 12.5%	1 4.2%	16 5.0%

Closeness with political leaders/bureaucracy + Influential	5 11.9%	5 8.5%	5 6.9%	2 4.8%	5 10.2%	4 12.5%	1 4.2%	27 8.4%
Big landlords + Politically active + Influential + Relations with bureaucracy	9 21.4%	3 5.1%	5 6.9%	5 11.9%	9 18.4%	11 34.4%	9 37.5%	51 15.9%
Other	1 2.4%	1 1.7%	4 5.6%	4 9.5%	8 16.3%	2 6.3%	2 8.3%	22 6.9%
No response	21 50.0%	37 62.7%	33 45.8%	10 23.8%	10 20.4%	3 9.4%	1 4.2%	115 35.9%
Total	42 100.0%	59 100.0%	72 100.0%	42 100.0%	49 100.0%	32 100.0%	24 100.0%	320 100.0%

Pearson chi-square 120.622.

TABLE 4.8

Perceptions of sampled leaders on the proposition that resourceful and influential persons alone influence the election and working of panchayats

	Frequency	*Valid Percent*	*Cumulative Percent*
Yes	105	32.8	32.8
No	102	31.9	64.7
Undecided	84	26.3	90.9
No response	29	9.1	100.0
Total	320	100.0	

TABLE 4.9

Classification of the perceptions of sampled leaders based on gender on the proposition that resourceful and influential persons influence the election and working of panchayats

	Gender		*Total*
	Male	*Female*	
Yes	73 34.0%	32 30.5%	105 32.8%
No	71 33.0%	31 29.5%	102 31.9%
Undecided	55 25.6%	29 27.6%	84 26.3%
No response	16 7.4%	13 12.4%	29 9.1%
Total	215 100.0%	105 100.0%	320 100.0%

Pearson chi-square 2.542.

Thus in total it is concluding that there is not any difference of opinion on the basis of gender, castes and educational level regarding the dominance of resourceful and morally sound persons in local democratic system except in an apparent manner.

TABLE 4.10

Classification of the perceptions of sampled leaders based on castes on the proposition that resourceful and influential persons influence the election and working of panchayats

Resources	*Castes*						*Total*
	Farming castes	*Upper castes*	*Backward castes (A)*	*Backward castes (B)*	*Scheduled castes (A)*	*Scheduled castes (B)*	
(1)	*(2)*	*(3)*	*(4)*	*(5)*	*(6)*	*(7)*	*(8)*
Yes	41 41.4%	16 40.0%	10 34.5%	11 29.7%	11 21.6%	16 25.0%	105 32.8%
No	29 29.3%	12 30.0%	12 41.4%	9 24.3%	15 29.4%	25 39.1%	102 31.9%
Undecided	22 22.2%	9 22.5%	6 20.7%	11 29.7%	18 35.3%	18 28.1%	84 26.3%
No response	7 7.1%	3 7.5%	1 3.4%	6 16.2%	7 13.7%	5 7.8%	29 9.1%
Total	99 100.0%	40 100.0%	29 100.0%	37 100.0%	51 100.0%	64 100.0%	320 100.0%

Pearson chi-square 17.005.

TABLE 4.11

Classification of the perceptions of sampled leaders based on educational levels on the proposition that resourceful and influential persons influence the election and working of panchayats

	Education Levels								*Total*
	Illiterate	*Literate*	*Primary*	*Middle*	*Matri-culation*	*Senior secondary*	*Graduate*	*Other*	
(1)	*(2)*	*(3)*	*(4)*	*(5)*	*(6)*	*(7)*	*(8)*	*(9)*	*(10)*
Yes	29 31.2%	14 56.0%	9 24.3%	18 33.3%	18 29.0%	3 20.0%	9 37.5%	5 50.0%	105 32.8%
No	25 26.9%	3 12.0%	14 37.8%	19 35.2%	23 37.1%	4 26.7%	11 45.8%	3 30.0%	102 31.9%
Undecided	32 34.4%	7 28.0%	11 29.7%	12 22.2%	14 22.6%	4 26.7%	4 16.7%	0 .0%	84 26.3%
No response	7 7.5%	1 4.0%	3 8.1%	5 9.3%	7 11.3%	4 26.7%	0 .0%	2 20.0%	29 9.1%
Total	93 100.0%	25 100.0%	37 100.0%	54 100.0%	62 100.0%	15 100.0%	24 100.0%	10 100.0%	320 100.0%

Pearson chi-square 30.258.

The numerical strength of a caste determines its prospects to be represented in village panchayat or other PRIs.

TABLE 4.12

Distribution of perceptions of the sampled leaders regarding the role of numerical strength of a specific caste in deciding the nature of local leadership in a village

	Frequency	*Valid Percent*	*Cumulative Percent*
Yes	107	33.4	33.4
No	128	40.0	73.4
Undecided	54	16.9	90.3
No response	31	9.7	100.0
Total	320	100.0	

The data in Table 4.12 reveals that one-third of the sampled leaders (33.4 per cent) favoured this viewpoint and 40 per cent disagreed to it. A sizeable proportion (16.9 per cent) of them could not decide and another 9.7 did not respond to this proposition when put to them.

The role of numerical strength in influencing the nature of local leadership is studied with reference to the gender, castes and education levels of the sampled leaders and related information is presented in Tables 4.13, 4.14 and 4.15 as under.

An analysis of the information presented in Table 4.13 reveals that there is a difference between men and women leaders on accepting the proposition that the numerical dominance of a caste decides the nature of village leadership. It is apparently somewhat higher among males in comparison to females. However, the chi-square value (2.639) is not significant and hence there is no significant difference between male and female leaders' perceptions on the role of numerical strength in composing the local leadership particularly at village level.

Similarly, the data in Table 4.14 indicates that a majority (51 per cent) of the accepted scheduled castes (A) leaders admitted the effectiveness of caste in sending the representative to PRIs. But the chi-square value (18.060) is less than the significant

TABLE 4.13

Distribution of perceptions of the sampled leaders based on their gender regarding the role of numerical strength of a specific caste in deciding the nature of local leadership in a village

	Gender		*Total*
	Male	*Female*	
Yes	77 35.8%	30 28.6%	107 33.4%
No	83 38.6%	45 42.9%	128 40.0%
Undecided	37 17.2%	17 16.2%	54 16.9%
No response	18 8.4%	13 12.4%	31 9.7%
Total	215 100.0%	105 100.0%	320 100.0%

Pearson chi-square 2.639.

value therefore the perceptions of leaders of different castes do not differ from each other in significant manner. In other words, only a sizeable portion of leaders, almost uniformly belonging to various castes of the sample, hold that the numerical strength of a caste plays an important role in deciding the nature of leadership.

The data in Table 4.15 indicates that the leaders who are literate and graduate are holding the opinion of accepting the instrumentality role of caste in electing PR representatives. This is confirmed by the significant chi-square value 33.517 which clearly specify that the perceptions differ with the educational levels but any specific pattern in this regard is missing.

Thus, analysis of the data indicates that only about one third of the sampled leaders endorsed the proposition that numerical strength of a specific caste is an active and contributory condition, which decides the composition and nature of village leadership. In real sense, the instrumentality of numerical strength in deciding the composition of village leadership is undermined by the reservation provision and

TABLE 4.14

Distribution of perceptions of the sampled leaders based on their castes regarding the role of numerical strength of a specific caste in deciding the nature of local leadership in a village

Resources	*Castes*						*Total*
	Farming castes	*Upper castes*	*Backward castes (A)*	*Backward castes (B)*	*Scheduled castes (A)*	*Scheduled castes (B)*	
(1)	(2)	(3)	(4)	(5)	(6)	(7)	(8)
Yes	35 35.4%	14 35.0%	9 31.0%	9 24.3%	26 51.0%	14 21.9%	107 33.4%
No	39 39.4%	19 47.5%	12 41.4%	16 43.2%	13 25.5%	29 45.3%	128 40.0%
Undecided	18 18.2%	5 12.5%	5 17.2%	6 16.2%	6 11.8%	14 21.9%	54 16.9%
No response	7 7.1%	2 5.0%	3 10.3%	6 16.2%	6 11.8%	7 10.9%	31 9.7%
Total	99 100.0%	40 100.0%	29 100.0%	37 100.0%	51 100.0%	64 100.0%	320 100.0%

Pearson chi-square 18.060.

TABLE 4.15

Distribution of perceptions of the sampled leaders based on their educational levels regarding the role of numerical strength of a specific caste in deciding the nature of local leadership in a village

	Education Levels								*Total*
	Illiterate	*Literate*	*Primary*	*Middle*	*Matri-culation*	*Senior secondary*	*Graduate*	*Other*	
(1)	*(2)*	*(3)*	*(4)*	*(5)*	*(6)*	*(7)*	*(8)*	*(9)*	*(10)*
Yes	33 35.5%	14 56.0%	12 32.4%	13 24.1%	15 24.2%	6 40.0%	12 50.0%	2 20.0%	107 33.4%
No	32 34.4%	9 36.0%	13 35.1%	26 48.1%	28 45.2%	6 40.0%	10 41.7%	4 40.0%	128 40.0%
Undecided	19 20.4%	2 8.0%	9 24.3%	8 14.8%	12 19.4%	2 13.3%	2 8.3%	0 .0%	54 16.9%
No response	9 9.7%	0 .0%	3 8.1%	7 13.0%	7 11.3%	1 6.7%	0 .0%	4 40.0%	31 9.7%
Total	93 100.0%	25 100.0%	37 100.0%	54 100.0%	62 100.0%	15 100.0%	24 100.0%	10 100.0%	320 100.0%

Pearson chi-square 33.517.

ward system introduced after reforms. However, the sampled leaders who are either literate or graduate and who belong to the SC (A) group of castes are much (50 percent or more) in favour of this belief. Thus it is concluded that numerical strength is one of the factor which decide the composition of GP or the nature of the gram panchayat leadership.

It has been believed (before 73rd Amendment) that the person from scheduled castes or other reserved classes of people is not a good choice for the office of a Sarpanch of the village. Therefore, an effort has been made here to test the above stated belief on the basis of empirical information obtained from the sampled respondents of the study.

TABLE 4.16

Why a sarpanch should be from upper caste?

	Frequency	*Valid Percent*	*Cumulative Percent*
Not applicable	244	76.3	76.3
SC people are poor	8	2.5	78.8
Ineffective leaders/no one listen them	7	2.2	80.9
Infested with inferiority stigma	2	.6	81.6
People don't care about them	9	2.8	84.4
Uncertain	20	6.3	90.6
Prone to pressures	4	1.3	91.9
Upper caste people don't visit them	4	1.3	93.1
Upper castes are not prone to pressure	1	.3	93.4
Can't mix up	1	.3	93.8
Upper caste leaders are rich	7	2.2	95.9
Upper castes leaders can take decisions	6	1.9	97.8
Influence upper caste people is good	7	2.2	100.0
Total	320	100.0	

The data in Table 4.16 clearly reveals that a large majority of leaders (76.3 per cent) did not involve themselves in this kind of caste controversy. However, 11 per cent of the sampled leaders found one or the other weakness with SC person as sarpanch of the village. At the same time, 6.6 per cent of the leaders stated that they consider non-SC person as good as any other person to be a sarpanch.

It is observed that non-SC leaders avoided criticizing the scheduled castes as an ineffective in public mainly because of legal protection and their significance in popular democracy. Besides it, the reserved class of rural population's economic dependence has not only improved over the time rather a few of them have better economic position in comparison to upper castes' families of the village. Therefore, they reserved category of the sarpanch may be as successful as the one from non-reserved class.

Further analysis of this aspect (as is evident from the data in Table 4.17) reveals that almost all the scheduled castes (B), backward castes (A), scheduled castes (A) leaders preferred not to be involved in responding to this question. However, many of the farming castes, backward castes (A) and upper castes leaders responded to this but the higher proportion of these responding leaders rated upper castes/farming castes/land-owning castes leaders are effective instead of finding reserved classes of leaders as ineffective. In other words, a relatively low proportion of them criticized the reserved class of leaders as ineffective to deliver the responsibilities of the office for which they are elected. The leaders who responded to the proposition have found reserved category of Sarpanch as ineffective in one sense or the other. Thus, it is true that the social, economic background and lesser political resourcefulness are responsible for relatively less empowered one.

However, the chi-square value, i.e. 79.803 does not indicate significant relationship between the responses and the castes of the leaders. The constitutional and legal provisions along with political development which has been taking place at local level made these leaders not to respond such sensitive question.

The above stated aspects is also probed indirectly. The sampled leaders were asked to narrate their opinion on the assertion that 'caste plays an important role in decision-making process of a panchayat'. The data obtained is tabulated in Table 4.18.

TABLE 4.17

Distribution of perceptions based on caste regarding why sarpanch should be from upper caste?

Why sarpanch from upper caste?	*Castes*						*Total*
	Farming castes	*Upper castes*	*Backward castes (A)*	*Backward castes (B)*	*Scheduled castes (A)*	*Scheduled castes (B)*	
(1)	(2)	(3)	(4)	(5)	(6)	(7)	(8)
Not involved	60 60.6%	29 72.5%	27 93.1%	25 67.6%	42 82.4%	61 95.3%	244 76.3%
SC people are poor	3 3.0%	1 2.5%	0 .0%	2 5.4%	0 .0%	2 3.1%	8 2.5%
Ineffective leaders/no one listen them	5 5.1%	0 .0%	0 .0%	2 5.4%	0 .0%	0 .0%	7 2.2%
Infested with inferiority stigma	0 .0%	1 2.5%	0 .0%	0 .0%	1 2.0%	0 .0%	2 .6%
People don't care about them	3 3.0%	1 2.5%	1 3.4%	1 2.7%	3 5.9%	0 .0%	9 2.8%
can't mix up	0 .0%	1 2.5%	0 .0%	0 .0%	0 .0%	0 .0%	1 .3%
Prone to pressures	1 1.0%	2 5.0%	0 .0%	0 .0%	1 2.0%	0 .0%	4 1.3%

(*Contd.*)

Table 4.17 (*Contd.*)

(1)	(2)	(3)	(4)	(5)	(6)	(7)	(8)
Upper caste people don't visit them	4 4.0%	0 .0%	0 .0%	0 .0%	0 .0%	0 .0%	4 1.3%
Upper castes are not prone to pressure	1 1.0%	0 .0%	0 .0%	0 .0%	0 .0%	0 .0%	1 .3%
Upper caste leaders are rich	5 5.1%	0 .0%	0 .0%	1 2.7%	1 2.0%	0 .0%	7 2.2%
Upper castes leaders can take decisions	4 4.0%	1 2.5%	0 .0%	1 2.7%	0 .0%	0 .0%	6 1.9%
Influence of upper caste people is good	5 5.1%	0 .0%	0 .0%	1 2.7%	0 .0%	1 1.6%	7 2.2%
Uncertain	8 8.1%	4 10.0%	1 3.4%	4 10.8%	3 5.9%	0 .0%	20 6.3%
Total	99 100.0%	40 100.0%	29 100.0%	37 100.0%	51 100.0%	64 100.0%	320 100.0%

Pearson chi-square 79.803.

TABLE 4.18

Caste plays an important role in decision-making process of a panchayat

Perceptions	*Frequency*	*Valid Percent*	*Cumulative Percent*
Yes	76	23.8	23.8
No	176	55.0	78.8
Undecided	44	13.8	92.5
No response	13	4.1	96.6
Not asked	11	3.4	100.0
Total	320	100.0	

It is quite clear from the data in Table 4.18 that a simple majority (55 per cent) denied that caste plays an important role in decision making process of a panchayat. There is only less than a quarter (23.8 per cent) who affirmed this. A sizeable percentage (13.8 per cent) could not decide on it. Thus, the caste is not the only and very significant factor in decision-making process of the panchayats.

The responses tabulated in Table 4.18 are studied in gender and caste perspective and tabulated in Tables 4.19 and 4.20.

TABLE 4.19

Gender based perceptions regarding the role of caste in decision-making process of a panchayat

	Gender		*Total*
Perceptions	*Male*	*Female*	
Yes	50 23.3%	26 24.8%	76 23.8%
No	127 59.1%	49 46.7%	176 55.0%
Undecided	26 12.1%	18 17.1%	44 13.8%
No response	4 1.9%	9 8.6%	13 4.1%
Not asked	8 3.7%	3 2.9%	11 3.4%
Total	215 100.0%	105 100.0%	320 100.0%

Pearson chi-square 11.323.

TABLE 4.20

Caste based perceptions regarding the role of caste in decision-making process of a panchayat

Perceptions	*Castes*						*Total*
	Farming castes	*Upper castes*	*Backward castes (A)*	*Backward castes (B)*	*Scheduled castes (A)*	*Scheduled castes (B)*	
(1)	*(2)*	*(3)*	*(4)*	*(5)*	*(6)*	*(7)*	*(8)*
Yes	32 32.3%	6 15.0%	6 20.7%	8 21.6%	16 31.4%	8 12.5%	76 23.8%
No	47 47.5%	27 67.5%	17 58.6%	23 62.2%	22 43.1%	40 62.5%	176 55.0%
Undecided	16 16.2%	3 7.5%	4 13.8%	5 13.5%	4 7.8%	12 18.8%	44 13.8%
No response	3 3.0%	2 5.0%	0 .0%	1 2.7%	4 7.8%	3 4.7%	13 4.1%
Not asked	1 1.0%	2 5.0%	2 6.9%	0 .0%	5 9.8%	1 1.6%	11 3.4%
Total	99 100.0%	40 100.0%	29 100.0%	37 100.0%	51 100.0%	64 100.0%	320 100.0%

Pearson chi-square 32.219*

The data in Table 4.19 although does not differentiate in terms of accepting the significance of caste but it does so in rejecting the significance of caste. More the percentage of leaders remained undecided are slightly higher among women in comparison to men. The chi-square value (11.323) lends support to the difference of men and women leaders in rejecting the significance of caste in decision-making process.

The responses of the leaders on the significance of caste in decision-making process are analyzed in context with the castes of the leaders.

The data in Table 4.20 indicates that the farming castes and scheduled castes (A) leaders recognize the role of caste much more in comparison to others. Interestingly, the backward castes and in particular their B group who are landowning castes and scheduled castes (B) do not find the caste so important in local political decision-making. Thus, it is concluded that backward castes and scheduled castes (B) have realized their political potential and asserting to negate the dominance of traditional castes in panchayati raj. At the same time, the scheduled castes (A) could not get them empowered as much as the other could do in this regard. The chi-square value 32.219 supports the conclusion that the leaders differ in their opinion regarding the role played by the caste of the leaders in decision-making process of a panchayat.

Lastly, the responses of the leaders interacted with their educational levels and tabulated in Table 4.21 indicates that higher the level of education of the leader, lesser the recognition of the role of caste in local political system leaving some exceptions. The chi-square value 49.646 also confirms the distinction of leaders' opinions about the role of caste in decision making process of the panchayat.

Thus the data in Tables 4.18 to 4.21 make it clear that only about a quarter of the sampled leaders believe that caste play an important role in decision-making process of a panchayat but the leaders of different gender, castes and educational levels differ in their perceptions on this issue.

The sampled leaders were further asked to give their perceptions on another similar proposition, i.e., 'the caste of a

TABLE 4.21

Education levels of the leaders and their perceptions about the role of caste in decision-making process of a panchayat

Perceptions	*Education Levels*								*Total*
	Illiterate	*Literate*	*Primary*	*Middle*	*Matri-culation*	*Senior secondary*	*Graduate*	*Other*	
(1)	(2)	(3)	(4)	(5)	(6)	(7)	(8)	(9)	(10)
Yes	31 33.3%	6 24.0%	6 16.2%	11 20.4%	9 14.5%	6 40.0%	5 20.8%	2 20.0%	76 23.8%
No	37 39.8%	14 56.0%	20 54.1%	35 64.8%	41 66.1%	6 40.0%	18 75.0%	5 50.0%	176 55.0%
Undecided	15 16.1%	5 20.0%	8 21.6%	7 13.0%	6 9.7%	0 .0%	1 4.2%	2 20.0%	44 13.8%
No response	4 4.3%	0 .0%	3 8.1%	1 1.9%	2 3.2%	3 20.0%	0 .0%	0 .0%	13 4.1%
Not asked	6 6.5%	0 .0%	0 .0%	0 .0%	4 6.5%	0 .0%	0 .0%	1 10.0%	11 3.4%
Total	93 100.0%	25 100.0%	37 100.0%	54 100.0%	62 100.0%	15 100.0%	24 100.0%	10 100.0%	320 100.0%

Pearson chi-square 49.646*.

leader determines how much he/she contributes to a decision of the panchayat'. The responses are presented in Table 4.22.

TABLE 4.22

The caste of a leader decides how much he/she contributes towards the decision of a panchayat

Perceptions	*Frequency*	*Valid Percent*	*Cumulative Percent*
Yes	64	20.0	20.0
No	170	53.1	73.1
Undecided	59	18.4	91.6
No response	27	8.4	100.0
Total	320	100.0	

The data in Table 4.22 reveals that 20 per cent agreed and 53.1 per cent disagreed respectively in response to this assertion. (These percentages are 23.8 per cent and 55 per cent for those who stated that role of caste is instrumental in decision making

TABLE 4.23

Classification of perceptions based on their gender regarding contribution of a leader in a decision taken by a panchayat

	Gender		*Total*
Perceptions	*Male*	*Female*	
Yes	42 19.5%	22 21.0%	64 20.0%
No	118 54.9%	52 49.5%	170 53.1%
Undecided	39 18.1%	20 19.0%	59 18.4%
No response	16 7.4%	11 10.5%	27 8.4%
Total	215 100.0%	105 100.0%	320 100.0%

Pearson chi-square 1.254.

process of panchayat. The only difference is that the percentage of leaders who were undecided has increased from 13.8 per cent to 18.4 per cent (4.18).

However, the classification of these perceptions on gender Table 4.23 indicates that men and women do not differ in their responses on the contributions of caste of a leader in deciding a matter in panchayat. In other words, both of them equally endorse that caste is not instrumental to contribute to a decision of a village panchayat. The conditions other than caste may contribute to that. The chi-square value 1.254 which is less than the significant value 7.815 confirms the non-existence of difference between men and women.

Further when these responses of leaders were classified as per their castes the trend is again almost similar. The data in Table 4.24 indicates the difference of opinion of the sampled leaders belonging different castes. The chi-square value 28.244 is also significant one. Thus, it is clear that more SC (A) and farming castes' leaders support the proposition that contribution to the decision of a panchayat depend on the caste of the leader in relation to SC (B) and backward castes leaders.

Lastly, the responses on the proposition are also examined with the educational levels of the leaders. The data in Table 4.25 indicates that the affirmation of the role of caste decreases and denial increases as one move from illiterate to higher educational level. But, there is discontinuity to this generalized statement in case of primary and secondary passed leaders. Above all, the chi-square value, 32.384 is nearly significant and confirms the above stated trend.

Thus, the caste of a leader is significant in terms of the contribution of the leader towards the panchayat decision but only about one fifth leadership accept it significance. The education and political empowerment of leaders is playing an important in diminishing the role of castes in decision-making process of a panchayat.

The provision for reserving seats in PRIs has been made for lesser-empowered classes of people like scheduled castes, backward castes and women. Reservation is very much useful for bringing about socio-economic transformation for Dalit community through the panchayat[2]. Therefore, it is probed here with the help of the responses collected from the sampled

TABLE 4.24

Classification of perceptions based on caste regarding contribution of a leader in a decision taken by a panchayat

Perceptions	*Castes*						*Total*
	Farming castes	*Upper castes*	*Backward castes (A)*	*Backward castes (B)*	*Scheduled castes (A)*	*Scheduled castes (B)*	
(1)	*(2)*	*(3)*	*(4)*	*(5)*	*(6)*	*(7)*	*(8)*
Yes	29 29.3%	6 15.0%	4 13.8%	6 16.2%	16 31.4%	3 4.7%	64 20.0%
No	46 46.5%	25 62.5%	17 58.6%	17 45.9%	24 47.1%	41 64.1%	170 53.1%
Undecided	19 19.2%	7 17.5%	5 17.2%	7 18.9%	7 13.7%	14 21.9%	59 18.4%
No response	5 5.1%	2 5.0%	3 10.3%	7 18.9%	4 7.8%	6 9.4%	27 8.4%
Total	99 100.0%	40 100.0%	29 100.0%	37 100.0%	51 100.0%	64 100.0%	320 100.0%

Pearson chi-square 28.244.

TABLE 4.25

Classification of perceptions based on their education levels regarding contribution of a leader in a decision taken by a panchayat

Perceptions	*Education Levels*								*Total*
	Illiterate	*Literate*	*Primary*	*Middle*	*Matri-culation*	*Senior secondary*	*Graduate*	*Other*	
(1)	(2)	(3)	(4)	(5)	(6)	(7)	(8)	(9)	(10)
Yes	29 31.2%	7 28.0%	4 10.8%	10 18.5%	8 12.9%	3 20.0%	3 12.5%	0 .0%	64 20.0%
No	38 40.9%	12 48.0%	21 56.8%	30 55.6%	38 61.3%	7 46.7%	18 75.0%	6 60.0%	170 53.1%
Undecided	19 20.4%	6 24.0%	10 27.0%	7 13.0%	10 16.1%	2 13.3%	3 12.5%	2 20.0%	59 18.4%
No response	7 7.5%	0 .0%	2 5.4%	7 13.0%	6 9.7%	3 20.0%	0 .0%	2 20.0%	27 8.4%
Total	93 100.0%	25 100.0%	37 100.0%	54 100.0%	62 100.0%	15 100.0%	24 100.0%	10 100.0%	320 100.0%

Pearson chi-square 32.384.

leadership on the proposition that "the election of SC people and women in PRIs is possible only because of reservation, otherwise not." The responses of the leaders are presented in Table 4.26 given as under.

TABLE 4.26

Reservation facilitates in the election of scheduled castes and women representatives

Perceptions	*Frequency*	*Valid Percent*	*Cumulative Percent*
Yes	121	37.8	37.8
No	119	37.2	75.0
Undecided	74	23.1	98.1
No response	6	1.9	100.0
Total	320	100.0	

The data in Table 4.26 reveals that 37.8 per cent of the sampled leaders admitted that the reservation has helped the SC and women to get elected in panchayats and practically equal percentage (37.2 per cent) denied it. About one-quarter of the total sampled leaders (23.1 per cent) were found undecided when this proposition was put to them. Thus there is a lack of unanimity of responses on the proposition.

Therefore, like earlier, the responses were studied with reference to the caste, gender and educational levels of the leaders.

The data in Table 4.27 reveals that the men and women leaders do not differ in their responses on the efficacy of reservation provision to elect scheduled castes and women candidates to PRIs. The chi-square value 1.885, which is not significant, supports the conclusion.

The responses classified on the basis of castes (Table 4.28) indicates that the castes like backward castes, farming castes and scheduled castes (A) leaders agreed to the proposition much more in comparison to the leaders from the upper castes and scheduled castes (B).

Surprisingly, scheduled castes (B) denied that the reservation is helpful in electing SC in particular from their

TABLE 4.27

Classification of responses based on their gender on the proposition that reservation facilitates the election of scheduled castes and women representatives in PRIs

	Gender		*Total*
	Male	*Female*	
Yes	81 37.7%	40 38.1%	121 37.8%
No	84 39.1%	35 33.3%	119 37.2%
Undecided	47 21.9%	27 25.7%	74 23.1%
No response	3 1.4%	3 2.9%	6 1.9%
Total	215 100.0%	105 100.0%	320 100.0%

Pearson chi-square 1.885.

castes to PRIs. The reason is attributed to the fact, where scheduled castes (A) candidates could be successful in getting their representation because of their caste's numerical strength in village or ward. However, the scheduled castes (B) people could not do so. In other words, the SC (A) is more resourceful in social, economic and political context and has much more numerical dominance in comparison to scheduled castes (B). Similarly, it is true for the backward castes (A) also (as 44.8 per cent of them) denied the said proposition. In case of upper castes, a larger percentage (37.5 per cent) remained undecided. But, the chi-square value is not significant (20.110), therefore the difference of perception is not significant and only about one-third agreed to the efficacy of reservation in electing a representative to PRIs. The reason to this state of affairs is attributed to numerical strength of the caste, demarcation of wards and political awareness among reserved classes of population.

The data in Table 4.29 gives an account of information of the responses of the leaders classified on the basis of their educational levels on the proposition that reservation facilitates

TABLE 4.28

Classification of responses based on their castes on the proposition that reservation facilitates the election of scheduled castes and women representatives in PRIs

Resources	*Castes*						*Total*
	Farming castes	*Upper castes*	*Backward castes (A)*	*Backward castes (B)*	*Scheduled castes (A)*	*Scheduled castes (B)*	
(1)	*(2)*	*(3)*	*(4)*	*(5)*	*(6)*	*(7)*	*(8)*
Yes	43 43.4%	10 25.0%	13 44.8%	16 43.2%	20 39.2%	19 29.7%	121 37.8%
No	32 32.3%	14 35.0%	13 44.8%	12 32.4%	15 29.4%	33 51.6%	119 37.2%
Undecided	22 22.2%	15 37.5%	2 6.9%	9 24.3%	15 29.4%	11 17.2%	74 23.1%
No response	2 2.0%	1 2.5%	1 3.4%	0 .0%	1 2.0%	1 1.6%	6 1.9%
Total	99 100.0%	40 100.0%	29 100.0%	37 100.0%	51 100.0%	64 100.0%	320 100.0%

Pearson chi-square 20.110.

TABLE 4.29

Classification of responses based on the education levels of the leaders on the proposition that reservation facilitates the election of scheduled castes and women representatives in PRIs

	Education Levels								*Total*
	Illiterate	*Literate*	*Primary*	*Middle*	*Matri-culation*	*Senior secondary*	*Graduate*	*Other*	
(1)	(2)	(3)	(4)	(5)	(6)	(7)	(8)	(9)	(10)
Yes	40 43.0%	15 60.0%	11 29.7%	25 46.3%	21 33.9%	3 20.0%	2 8.3%	4 40.0%	121 37.8%
No	24 25.8%	6 24.0%	18 48.6%	16 29.6%	31 50.0%	7 46.7%	13 54.2%	4 40.0%	119 37.2%
Undecided	28 30.1%	4 16.0%	7 18.9%	13 24.1%	10 16.1%	3 20.0%	8 33.3%	1 10.0%	74 23.1%
No response	1 1.1%	0 .0%	1 2.7%	0 .0%	0 .0%	2 13.3%	1 4.2%	1 10.0%	6 1.9%
Total	93 100.0%	25 100.0%	37 100.0%	54 100.0%	62 100.0%	15 100.0%	24 100.0%	10 100.0%	320 100.0%

Pearson chi-square 47.963.

the election of scheduled castes and women representatives in PRIs.

The data in Table 4.29 indicates that the better educated leaders do not assign much significance to the provision of reservation in electing leaders. The chi-square value (47.963) confirms that the responses on the issue vary with the educational level in significant manner. Thus, the reservation of seats is an important issue but many of the leaders perceive other conditions like ward system, caste consciousness, political awakening and above all the different level of political development of different castes in the rural areas of the state are also responsible for giving wider representation to the people in local institutions.

Many studies have pointed out that the reservation has made it possible for women and SC leaders to be represented in these elected bodies of local governance. Not only this, the reservation provision has gone beyond it and it has not only attracted many competent persons of all castes and classes but also empowered the reserved classes of leaders to contest election to establish themselves as leaders of local self-government.

Many of the leaders belonging reserved classes including women, who contested Panchayati Raj election after 73rd constitutional amendment, contested the election even when the office has not remained reserved for them. No doubt, such instances are not in abundance but there is a healthy beginning at least. How it happened? The studies pointed out, when a person elected to an office, then people start to respect him/her as their leader. Further most of the leaders who are in PRIs are not professional politicians or regular in politics. They are very casual and there is not much competition to contest the election from the ward from which the said leader has already got elected. It has motivated the leader to contest even when the office or seat is not reserved for the reserved class of person. This is probed and sampled leaders were requested to react to the proposition that 'the reservation of seats in PRIs for SC and women has enhanced their respect in society'.

The data in Table 4.30 supports the proposition stated above as a large majority (73.4 per cent) affirmed that, 'the reservation of seats in PRIs for SC and women has elevated their respect in society'.

TABLE 4.30

Reservation of seats in PRIs for SC and women has elevated their respect in society

	Frequency	*Valid Percent*	*Cumulative Percent*
Yes	235	73.4	73.4
No	58	18.1	91.6
Undecided	25	7.8	99.4
Uncertain	2	.6	100.0
Total	320	100.0	

The perceptions on reservation of the sampled leaders contained in Table 4.30 are classified based on the gender, caste and educational levels of the sampled leaders and tabulated in Tables 4.31, 4.32 and 4.33.

TABLE 4.31

Classification of perceptions based on gender on efficacy of reservation of seats in PRIs in elevating respect of SC and women in society

	Gender		*Total*
	Male	*Female*	
Yes	165 76.7%	70 66.7%	235 73.4%
No	36 16.7%	22 21.0%	58 18.1%
Undecided	12 5.6%	13 12.4%	25 7.8%
Uncertain	2 .9%	0 .0%	2 .6%
Total	215 100.0%	105 100.0%	320 100.0%

Pearson chi-square 6.817.

It is evident from the data in Table 4.31 that the percentage of women (66.7 percent) who found that the reservation has helped in elevating the respect of reserved classes of leaders including women in society is lesser than the males (76.6 per cent). However, the chi-square value (6.817) is not significant, therefore, the difference of perception in this regard is only an apparent one.

The data in Table 4.32 and chi-square value 16.006 confirms that the leaders from different castes do not differ in significant manner in this regard. Similarly, the classification of perceptions on this issue is independent of educational levels of the leader as is evident from the data in Table 4.33 and chi-square value (19.998) which is not significant.

Thus the data in Tables 4.30 to 4.33 makes it clear that irrespective of caste, gender and educational level a large majority of leaders perceive that the reservation of seats in PRIs has elevated the respect of SC and women in society.

The village society is a single unit and more or less homogenous in terms of social and cultural manner. The panchayat system in past was based on fraternity of the village people as a whole. Even today, many village people prefer to elect their representatives on consensus basis. Therefore, the sampled leaders were asked to express their feelings on the proposition that 'Unanimous elections are better than the contested one'. The responses obtained are tabulated in Table 4.34 and clearly reveals that almost every-one (93.1 per cent) likes it and only 19 per cent are not in favour of unanimous election. Further, there is not any difference in this liking among men and women and the leaders from different castes as is evident from the data in Tables 4.35 and 4.36).

The data in Table 4.35 and chi-square value 1.184 that both male and female leaders have similar kind of perception on the proposition under discussion. Similarly, the data in Table 4.36 and the chi-square value 12.323 make it quite clear that the unanimous elections of PRIs are almost equally welcomed by the leaders of various castes.

Similarly there is not any difference of opinion among sampled leaders on this proposition when the perceptions are classified on educational levels as is evident from the data in Table 4.37.

TABLE 4.32
Classification of perceptions based on castes on efficacy of reservation of seats in PRIs in elevating respect of SC and women in society

	Castes						*Total*
	Farming castes	*Upper castes*	*Backward castes (A)*	*Backward castes (B)*	*Scheduled castes (A)*	*Scheduled castes (B)*	
(1)	*(2)*	*(3)*	*(4)*	*(5)*	*(6)*	*(7)*	*(8)*
Yes	77 77.8%	27 67.5%	20 69.0%	26 70.3%	39 76.5%	46 71.9%	235 73.4%
No	14 14.1%	9 22.5%	8 27.6%	9 24.3%	10 19.6%	8 12.5%	58 18.1%
Undecided	7 7.1%	3 7.5%	1 3.4%	2 5.4%	2 3.9%	10 15.6%	25 7.8%
Uncertain	1 1.0%	1 2.5%	0 .0%	0 .0%	0 .0%	0 .0%	2 .6%
Total	99 100.0%	40 100.0%	29 100.0%	37 100.0%	51 100.0%	64 100.0%	320 100.0%

Pearson chi-square 16.006.

TABLE 4.33

Classification of responses based on educational levels on the efficacy of reservation of seats in PRIs in elevating respect of SC and women in society

	Education Levels								*Total*
	Illiterate	*Literate*	*Primary*	*Middle*	*Matri-culation*	*Senior secondary*	*Graduate*	*Other*	
(1)	(2)	(3)	(4)	(5)	(6)	(7)	(8)	(9)	(10)
Yes	63 67.7%	19 76.0%	29 78.4%	40 74.1%	47 75.8%	14 93.3%	16 66.7%	7 70.0%	235 73.4%
No	16 17.2%	5 20.0%	5 13.5%	9 16.7%	12 19.4%	1 6.7%	7 29.2%	3 30.0%	58 18.1%
Undecided	14 15.1%	1 4.0%	3 8.1%	4 7.4%	2 3.2%	0 .0%	1 4.2%	0 .0%	25 7.8%
Uncertain	0 .0%	0 .0%	0 .0%	1 1.9%	1 1.6%	0 .0%	0 .0%	0 .0%	2 .6%
Total	93 100.0%	25 100.0%	37 100.0%	54 100.0%	62 100.0%	15 100.0%	24 100.0%	10 100.0%	320 100.0%

Pearson chi-square 19.998.

TABLE 4.34

Unanimous election is much better than contested one

	Frequency	*Valid Percent*	*Cumulative Percent*
Yes	298	93.1	93.1
No	6	1.9	95.0
Undecided	12	3.8	98.8
No response	4	1.3	100.0
Total	320	100.0	

TABLE 4.35

Classification of perceptions based on gender of leaders on unanimous and contested elections

	Gender		*Total*
	Male	*Female*	
Yes	203 94.4%	95 90.5%	298 93.1%
No	3 1.4%	3 2.9%	6 1.9%
Undecided	7 3.3%	5 4.8%	12 3.8%
No response	2 .9%	2 1.9%	4 1.3%
Total	215 100.0%	105 100.0%	320 100.0%

Pearson chi-square 1.184.

The data in Table 4.37 and chi-square value 23.632 confirms that there is not any difference among the leaders of different education levels on the proposition that unanimous election is much better than contested one.

Further the sampled leaders were asked to respond to the statement 'unanimous election of Sarpanch or panch promotes higher participation opportunity to scheduled castes and women leaders'. The information obtained from the sampled leaders in this regard is presented in Table 4.38.

TABLE 4.36

Classification of perceptions based on castes of leaders on unanimous and contested elections

	Castes						*Total*
	Farming castes	*Upper castes*	*Backward castes (A)*	*Backward castes (B)*	*Scheduled castes (A)*	*Scheduled castes (B)*	
(1)	*(2)*	*(3)*	*(4)*	*(5)*	*(6)*	*(7)*	*(8)*
Yes	91 91.9%	39 97.5%	28 96.6%	36 97.3%	48 94.1%	56 87.5%	298 93.1%
No	4 4.0%	0 .0%	0 .0%	0 .0%	0 .0%	2 3.1%	6 1.9%
Undecided	2 2.0%	1 2.5%	1 3.4%	1 2.7%	2 3.9%	5 7.8%	12 3.8%
No response	2 2.0%	0 .0%	0 .0%	0 .0%	1 2.0%	1 1.6%	4 1.3%
Total	99 100.0%	40 100.0%	29 100.0%	37 100.0%	51 100.0%	64 100.0%	320 100.0%

Pearson chi-square 12.323.

TABLE 4.37

Classification of perceptions based on education levels of leaders on unanimous and contested elections

	Education Levels								*Total*
	Illiterate	*Literate*	*Primary*	*Middle*	*Matri-culation*	*Senior secondary*	*Graduate*	*Other*	
(1)	*(2)*	*(3)*	*(4)*	*(5)*	*(6)*	*(7)*	*(8)*	*(9)*	*(10)*
Yes	83 89.2%	25 100.0%	33 89.2%	51 94.4%	59 95.2%	15 100.0%	24 100.0%	8 80.0%	298 93.1%
No	2 2.2%	0 .0%	2 5.4%	1 1.9%	0 .0%	0 .0%	0 .0%	1 10.0%	6 1.9%
Undecided	6 6.5%	0 .0%	2 5.4%	1 1.9%	3 4.8%	0 .0%	0 .0%	0 .0%	12 3.8%
No response	2 2.2%	0 .0%	0 .0%	1 1.9%	0 .0%	0 .0%	0 .0%	1 10.0%	4 1.3%
Total	93 100.0%	25 100.0%	37 100.0%	54 100.0%	62 100.0%	15 100.0%	24 100.0%	10 100.0%	320 100.0%

Pearson chi-square 23.632.

TABLE 4.38

Unanimous election of sarpanch or panch promote higher participation opportunity to SC and women leaders

	Frequency	*Valid Percent*	*Cumulative Percent*
Yes	160	50.0	50.0
No	95	29.7	79.7
Uncertain	36	11.3	90.9
No response	29	9.1	100.0
Total	320	100.0	

The data in Table 4.38 indicates that 50 per cent of sampled leaders affirmed but 29.7 per cent are not optimistic of creating higher participation opportunity for Scheduled Castes and women leaders by unanimous elections of sarpanch or panch. However, about 20 per cent of the respondents either remained undecided or did not respond.

The responses of the leaders on this issue are classified on the gender basis and presented in Table 4.39.

TABLE 4.39

Classification of responses based on gender of leaders on the efficacy of unanimous election of sarpanch or panch in promoting higher participation opportunity for SC and women leaders

	Gender		*Total*
	Male	*Female*	
Yes	107 49.8%	53 50.5%	160 50.0%
No	67 31.2%	28 26.7%	95 29.7%
Uncertain	26 12.1%	10 9.5%	36 11.3%
No response	15 7.0%	14 13.3%	29 9.1%
Total	215 100.0%	105 100.0%	320 100.0%

Pearson chi-square 4.047.

The data in Table 4.39 clearly shows that male and female leaders do not differ in their perceptions on this issue. It is confirmed by the chi-square value which is 4.047 and not significant one.

Like earlier the responses are also classified on caste and educational level basis and presented in Tables 4.40 and 4.41.

The data in Table 4.40 reveals that the leaders of different castes apparently have variation in their responses on the efficacy of unanimous election in ensuring participation of Scheduled Castes and women in panchayat raj when classified on caste basis but the chi-square value 20.630 is not significant. It means the perception regarding unanimous election is more or less is found to be similar. Similarly, the data in Table 4.41 depicts the distinctions among the differently educated leaders. It is apparent from the information that the proportion of better educated persons having realization of the efficacy of unanimous election of panch or sarpanch is higher. The chi-square value, which is 30.213, however does not indicate significant difference between better educated and less educated leaders.

CONCLUSION

Thus, it is concluded that the number of politically active castes and leaders is very much limited one. The political active caste may or may not be resourceful but one has to be enough resourceful to be an active leader at least to be a successful sarpanch of the village. These leaders utilize their richness and other tangible and intangible resources along with their castes for maintaining their presence and dominance in village politics. However, the data in the chapter also suggests that the new panchayati raj, introduced after constitutional amendment, has diluted the influence of caste and other physical resources in the rural political system of the state and the reservation has alleviated the respect of women and the scheduled castes in the rural society.

TABLE 4.40

Classification of responses based on castes of leaders on the efficacy of unanimous election of sarpanch or banch in promoting higher participation opportunity for SC and women leaders

	Castes						*Total*
	Farming castes	*Upper castes*	*Backward castes (A)*	*Backward castes (B)*	*Scheduled castes (A)*	*Scheduled castes (B)*	
(1)	*(2)*	*(3)*	*(4)*	*(5)*	*(6)*	*(7)*	*(8)*
Yes	55 55.6%	24 60.0%	14 48.3%	10 27.0%	20 39.2%	37 57.8%	160 50.0%
No	29 29.3%	12 30.0%	9 31.0%	13 35.1%	19 37.3%	13 20.3%	95 29.7%
Uncertain	8 8.1%	2 5.0%	4 13.8%	7 18.9%	7 13.7%	8 12.5%	36 11.3%
No response	7 7.1%	2 5.0%	2 6.9%	7 18.9%	5 9.8%	6 9.4%	29 9.1%
Total	99 100.0%	40 100.0%	29 100.0%	37 100.0%	51 100.0%	64 100.0%	320 100.0%

Pearson chi-square 20.630.

TABLE 4.41

Classification of responses based on educational levels of leaders on the efficacy of unanimous election of sarpanch or panch in promoting higher participation opportunity for SC and women leaders

	Education Levels								*Total*
	Illiterate	*Literate*	*Primary*	*Middle*	*Matri-culation*	*Senior secondary*	*Graduate*	*Other*	
(1)	*(2)*	*(3)*	*(4)*	*(5)*	*(6)*	*(7)*	*(8)*	*(9)*	*(10)*
Yes	40 43.0%	8 32.0%	21 56.8%	27 50.0%	31 50.0%	8 53.3%	18 75.0%	7 70.0%	160 50.0%
No	29 31.2%	13 52.0%	10 27.0%	15 27.8%	19 30.6%	4 26.7%	5 20.8%	0 .0%	95 29.7%
Uncertain	14 15.1%	4 16.0%	4 10.8%	5 9.3%	6 9.7%	2 13.3%	1 4.2%	0 .0%	36 11.3%
No response	10 10.8%	0 .0%	2 5.4%	7 13.0%	6 9.7%	1 6.7%	0 .0%	3 30.0%	29 9.1%
Total	93 100.0%	25 100.0%	37 100.0%	54 100.0%	62 100.0%	15 100.0%.	24 100.0%	10 100.0%	320 100.0%

Pearson chi-square 30.213.

TABLE 4.42
Perceptions of the sampled leaders based on their gender regarding political active castes of their respective villages

Political active castes	*Gender*		*Total*
	Male	*Female*	
Farming castes	3 1.4%	0 .0%	3 .9%
Upper castes	1 .5%	0 .0%	1 .3%
Scheduled castes + Upper castes	20 9.3%	9 8.6%	29 9.1%
Scheduled castes	2 .9%	0 .0%	2 .6%
Farming castes + Upper castes + others	5 2.3%	0 .0%	5 1.6%
Farming + Backward castes (B)	4 1.9%	1 1.0%	5 1.6%
Backward castes (A) + Backward castes (B)	2 .9%	0 .0%	2 .6%
Farming castes + Scheduled castes	29 13.5%	10 9.5%	39 12.2%
Backward castes + Scheduled castes	5 2.3%	2 1.9%	7 2.2%
SC (A) + SC (B)	2 .9%	0 .0%	2 .6%
Farming castes + Upper castes + Scheduled castes	11 5.1%	4 3.8%	1 4.7%
Not willing to tell	1 .5%	6 5.7%	7 2.2%
All castes have their role in local politics	130 60.5%	73 69.5%	203 63.4%
Total	215 100.0%	105 100.0%	320 100.0%

Pearson chi-square 18.762.

TABLE 4.43
Perceptions of the sampled leaders based on their positions regarding political active castes of their respective villages

Number of elections contested	*Positions*								*Total*
	PS leaders before 73rd amendment	*PS leaders after 73rd amendment (1st election)*	*PS leaders after 73rd amendment 2nd election)*	*PS leaders after 73rd amendment (3rd election)*	*GP leaders before 73rd amendment*	*GP leaders after 73rd amendment (1st election)*	*GP leaders after 73rd amendment (2nd election)*	*GP leaders after 73rd amendment (3rd election)*	
(1)	*(2)*	*(3)*	*(4)*	*(5)*	*(6)*	*(7)*	*(8)*	*(9)*	*(10)*
Farming castes	0 .0%	0 .0%	2 3.2%	1 3.3%	0 .0%	0 .0%	0 .0%	0 .0%	3 .9%
Upper castes	0 .0%	0 .0%	0 .0%	1 3.3%	0 .0%	0 .0%	0 .0%	0 .0%	1 .3%
Scheduled castes + Upper castes	0 .0%	3 10.0%	0 .0%	1 3.3%	4 14.8%	4 8.2%	9 12.7%	8 17.4%	29 9.1%
Scheduled castes	0 .0%	0 .0%	1 1.6%	0 .0%	0 .0%	0 .0%	1 1.4%	0 .0%	2 .6%
Farming castes + Upper castes + others	1 25.0%	3 10.0%	0 .0%	0 .0%	0 .0%	0 .0%	1 1.4%	0 .0%	5 1.6%
Farming + Backward castes (B)	0 .0%	0 .0%	1 1.6%	3 10.0%	0 .0%	0 .0%	0 .0%	1 2.2%	5 1.6%

Backward castes (A) + Backward castes (B)	0 .0%	1 3.3%	0 .0%	0 .0%	0 .0%	1 2.0%	0 .0%	0 .0%	2 .6%
Farming castes + Scheduled castes	1 25.0%	3 10.0%	9 14.3%	5 16.7%	4 14.8%	4 8.2%	4 5.6%	9 19.6%	39 12.2%
Backward castes + Scheduled castes	0 .0%	1 3.3%	3 4.8%	2 6.7%	0 .0%	1 2.0%	0 .0%	0 .0%	7 2.2%
SC (A) + SC (B)	0 .0%	0 .0%	2 3.2%	0 .0%	0 .0%	0 .0%	0 .0%	0 .0%	2 .6%
Farming castes + Upper castes + Scheduled castes	0 .0%	0 .0%	2 3.2%	1 3.3%	2 7.4%	5 10.2%	3 4.2%	2 4.3%	15 4.7%
Not willing to tell	0 .0%	0 .0%	4 6.3%	1 3.3%	0 .0%	0 .0%	0 .0%	2 4.3%	7 2.2%
All castes have their role in local politics	2 50.0%	19 63.3%	39 61.9%	15 50.0%	17 63.0%	34 69.4%	53 74.6%	24 52.2%	203 63.4%
Total	4 100.0%	30 100.0%	63 100.0%	30 100.0%	27 100.0%	49 100.0%	71 100.0%	46 100.0%	320 100.0%

Pearson chi-square 129.207.

Table 4.44
Perceptions of the sampled leaders based on their castes regarding political active castes of their respective villages

Political active castes	*Castes*						*Total*
	Farming castes	*Upper castes*	*Backward castes (A)*	*Backward castes (B)*	*Scheduled castes (A)*	*Scheduled castes (B)*	
(1)	*(2)*	*(3)*	*(4)*	*(5)*	*(6)*	*(7)*	*(8)*
Farming castes	3 3.0%	0 .0%	0 .0%	0 .0%	0 .0%	0 .0%	3 .9%
Upper castes	0 .0%	0 .0%	0 .0%	0 .0%	0 .0%	1 1.6%	1 .3%
Scheduled castes + Upper castes	1 1.0%	6 15.0%	2 6.9%	0 .0%	19 37.3%	1 1.6%	29 9.1%
Scheduled castes	0 .0%	0 .0%	0 .0%	0 .0%	2 3.9%	0 .0%	2 .6%
Farming castes + Upper castes + others	2 2.0%	2 5.0%	0 .0%	0 .0%	0 .0%	1 1.6%	5 1.6%
Farming + Backward castes (B)	1 1.0%	2 5.0%	0 .0%	2 5.4%	0 .0%	0 .0%	5 1.6%
Backward castes (A) + Backward castes (B)	0 .0%	0 .0%	1 3.4%	1 2.7%	0 .0%	0 .0%	2 .6%

Farming castes + Scheduled castes	22 22.2%	1 2.5%	3 10.3%	0 .0%	6 11.8%	7 10.9%	39 12.2%
Backward castes + Scheduled castes	0 .0%	1 2.5%	0 .0%	6 16.2%	0 .0%	0 .0%	7 2.2%
SC (A) + SC (B)	0 .0%	0 .0%	0 .0%	0 .0%	2 3.9%	0 .0%	2 .6%
Farming castes + Upper castes + Scheduled castes	9 9.1%	2 5.0%	0 .0%	0 .0%	3 5.9%	1 1.6%	15 4.7%
Not willing to tell	0 .0%	1 2.5%	2 6.9%	0 .0%	1 2.0%	3 4.7%	7 2.2%
All castes have their role in local politics	61 61.6%	25 62.5%	21 72.4%	28 75.7%	18 35.3%	50 78.1%	203 63.4%
Total	99 100.0%	40 100.0%	29 100.0%	37 100.0%	51 100.0%	64 100.0%	320 100.0%

Pearson chi-square 195.295.

TABLE 4.45

Perceptions of the sampled leaders based on their educational level regarding political active castes of their respective villages

Political active castes	Education Levels								Total
	Illiterate	*Literate*	*Primary*	*Middle*	*Matri-culation*	*Senior secondary*	*Graduate*	*Other*	
(1)	(2)	(3)	(4)	(5)	(6)	(7)	(8)	(9)	(10)
Farming castes	0 .0%	0 .0%	0 .0%	0 .0%	2 3.2%	0 .0%	0 .0%	1 10.0%	3 .9%
Upper castes	0 .0%	0 .0%	0 .0%	0 .0%	0 .0%	0 .0%	0 .0%	1 10.0%	1 .3%
Scheduled castes + Upper castes	9 9.7%	4 16.0%	5 13.5%	4 7.4%	6 9.7%	0 .0%	0 .0%	1 10.0%	29 9.1%
Scheduled castes	1 1.1%	0 .0%	1 2.7%	0 .0%	0 .0%	0 .0%	0 .0%	0 .0%	2 .6%
Farming castes + Upper castes + others	1 1.1%	0 .0%	1 2.7%	0 .0%	0 .0%	0 .0%	3 12.5%	0 .0%	5 1.6%
Farming + Backward castes (B)	1 1.1%	0 .0%	0 .0%	1 1.9%	2 3.2%	1 6.7%	0 .0%	0 .0%	5 1.6%
Backward castes (A) + BC (B)	0 .0%	0 .0%	0 .0%	0 .0%	1 1.6%	1 6.7%	0 .0%	0 .0%	2 .6%

Farming castes + Scheduled castes	13 14.0%	2 8.0%	3 8.1%	9 16.7%	7 11.3%	2 13.3%	2 8.3%	1 10.0%	39 12.2%
Backward castes + Scheduled castes	1 1.1%	2 8.0%	1 2.7%	2 3.7%	0 .0%	1 6.7%	0 .0%	0 .0%	7 2.2%
SC (A) + SC (B)	0 .0%	0 .0%	0 .0%	0 .0%	0 .0%	1 6.7%	1 4.2%	0 .0%	2 .6%
Farming castes + Upper castes + SCs	6 6.5%	1 4.0%	0 .0%	1 1.9%	6 9.7%	1 6.7%	0 .0%	0 .0%	15 4.7%
Not willing to tell	3 3.2%	0 .0%	2 5.4%	2 3.7%	0 .0%	0 .0%	0 .0%	0 .0%	7 2.2%
All castes have their role in local politics	58 62.4%	16 64.0%	24 64.9%	35 64.8%	38 61.3%	8 53.3%	18 75.0%	6 60.0%	203 63.4%
Total	93 100.0%	25 100.0%	37 100.0%	54 100.0%	62 100.0%	15 100.0%	24 100.0%	10 100.0%	320 100.0%

Pearson chi-square 134.557.

TABLE 4.46

Perceptions of sampled leaders based on their income regarding political active castes of their respective villages

Political active castes	*Incomes*							*Total*
	Up to 12,500	*12,501-25,000*	*25,001-50,000*	*50,001-1,00,000*	*1,00,001-2,00,000*	*2,00,001-4,00,000*	*Above 4,00,000*	
(1)	(2)	(3)	(4)	(5)	(6)	(7)	(8)	(9)
Farming castes	0 .0%	0 .0%	0 .0%	0 .0%	2 4.1%	0 .0%	1 4.2%	3 .9%
Upper castes	0 .0%	0 .0%	0 .0%	1 2.4%	0 .0%	0 .0%	0 .0%	1 .3%
Scheduled castes + Upper castes	2 4.8%	8 13.6%	6 8.3%	6 14.3%	5 10.2%	0 .0%	2 8.3%	29 9.1%
Scheduled castes	1 2.4%	0 .0%	0 .0%	0 .0%	1 2.0%	0 .0%	0 .0%	2 .6%
Farming castes + Upper castes + others	0 .0%	0 .0%	2 2.8%	0 .0%	1 2.0%	2 6.3%	0 .0%	5 1.6%
Farming + Backward castes (B)	0 .0%	0 .0%	2 2.8%	1 2.4%	0 .0%	1 3.1%	1 4.2%	5 1.6%
Backward castes (A) + Backward castes (B)	0 .0%	0 .0%	1 1.4%	1 2.4%	0 .0%	0 .0%	0 .0%	2 .6%

Farmings castes + Scheduled castes	7 16.7%	5 8.5%	10 13.9%	2 4.8%	5 10.2%	5 15.6%	5 20.8%	39 12.2%
Backward castes + Scheduled castes	0 .0%	0 .0%	2 2.8%	0 .0%	4 8.2%	0 .0%	1 4.2%	7 2.2%
SC (A) + SC (B)	0 .0%	0 .0%	0 .0%	1 2.4%	0 .0%	1 3.1%	0 .0%	2 .6%
Farming castes + Upper castes + Scheduled castes	2 4.8%	1 1.7%	0 .0%	1 2.4%	7 14.3%	2 6.3%	2 8.3%	15 4.7%
Not willing to tell	1 2.4%	3 5.1%	1 1.4%	1 2.4%	0 .0%	1 3.1%	0 .0%	7 2.2%
All castes have their role in local politics	29 69.0%	42 71.2%	48 66.7%	28 66.7%	24 49.0%	20 62.5%	12 50.0%	203 63.4%
Total	42 100.0%	59 100.0%	72 100.0%	42 100.0%	49 100.0%	32 100.0%	24 100.0%	320 100.0%

Pearson chi-square 92.428.

Notes and References

1. Tables 4.42 to 4.46.
2. G. Palanithurai, (2005) Emerging Dimensions in Decentralisation. New Delhi; Concept Publishing Company, p. 382.

5

Attributes and Abilities

Decentralization of government authority is the heart of democratic politics and management. This is so because the essence of democracy rests on the right of the individual to decide and participate in defining and shaping the society he wants to live in.[1] But, how the individuals will decide and what is good for them and their community? These are some of the questions which are usually decided by the leadership either individually in anticipation of acceptance by the members of their community or in consultation with the members of their community. Therefore the leadership must possess certain capacities which can make it capable to discharge its responsibilities.

The society expects that the leadership must possess certain attributes and abilities required for managing and ensuring progress and change in the community. Therefore, the person who can take initiative and endowed with requisite independence along with a high standard of integrity can become a choice, as leader, of the people at village level. The leader must be skilled to solve the problems of the people or fellow villagers who come to him for this purpose. It is expected that he must be able to communicate well with all, with whom he interact. He must be a consensus builder but at the same time, enough assertive to make others to understand his viewpoint. He must possess the required knowledge and motivation to serve his men. The local leader in a community must be a person who considers himself committed to the welfare of community and required level of understanding or social vision. The leader is expected to have enough time to interact with the people who have faith in his leadership.

Other attributes possessed by the leaders are that the leader must be enthusiastic, empathetic, creative, altruistic and able to share a vision with others. He must be a person who is able to relate himself with people and can be an ambassador of the village community at various platforms including for the adjoining villages. Above all, he must be an organized person who can behave in fearless manner, can be a successful leader. Glen Paoletto listed nine qualities of a leader, which are: communication; network; offer new solutions; build consensus; action-oriented; opportunity seeking; marketing; goal-oriented and persistency.[2]

It does not mean that the leaders possessing above stated attributes will join or joining the PRIs in the state but the leadership not possessing the requisite competence or anticipatory learning capacities to get hold of the organizations entrusted to them for managing are liable to be ineffective. In other words, the community rejects them whenever their performance is reviewed, in a popular democracy through periodic election.

The emergence of leadership in panchayats might be conditioned by: (i) the preference of the electorates to vote for their own caste and status caste candidates; (ii) the caste-wise distribution of electoral population in which numerical dominance is maintained by almost all castes in a number of electoral constituencies at the ward level so does a few castes among the backward castes at Panchayat Samities' and Zila Parishad's level electoral constituencies; (iii) the increasing requirement of men and material to mobilize the votes particularly at higher levels of panchayats' bodies which many times permit economically sound person to contest for the office of the panchayat president; and (iv) the policy of reservation of seats for scheduled castes followed in different levels of panchayats' election.[3]

Keeping in view these aspects and the characteristics of leadership discussed in first chapter, it becomes imperative to find out the behavioural attributes and abilities of panchayati raj's elected leaders. An effort is also made in particular to differentiate the traits among the various categories of leaders (i.e. non-reserved and reserved including women) elected in PRIs after the constitutional amendment of 1992.

First of all, it is essential to state that many of the leaders are either illiterate or just literate (36.9 per cent as given in Table 2.14) Naturally, these leaders are deprived of opportunity to learn about society or to understand the society as they cannot read the news paper, an effective instrument to educate people and develop requisite understanding about socio-economic and political conditions of their surrounding in an analytical way. No doubt, the electronic media has reduced the limitations of illiterate in this regard but education has its role in understanding the society and its socio-cultural, economic and political dimensions. The reading habit contrіbutes to the leader's capacity in understanding, interacting, communicating and establishing a vision and setting goals for transforming the community in general. Therefore, the sampled leaders were asked to narrate about their newspaper reading habit.

TABLE 5.1

Newspaper reading habit of the sampled leaders

Responses	*Frequency*	*Valid Percent*	*Cumulative Percent*
Yes	128	40.0	40.0
No	145	45.3	85.3
Sometimes	40	12.5	97.8
Undecided	7	2.2	100.0
Total	320	100.0	

The data in Table 5.1 clearly reveals that that 40 per cent of the sampled leaders read newspapers regularly and another 12.5 per cent are casual readers. Thus majority of those who are literate enough to read newspaper have this habit. It simply means leaders are interested to get acquainted with about their surroundings. This attribute of leadership is classified on gender, caste and educational basis and information is tabulated in Tables 5.2 and 5.3.

TABLE 5.2

Classification of the perceptions based on their gender on newspaper reading habit of the leaders

Perceptions	*Gender*		*Total*
	Male	*Female*	
Yes	111 51.6%	17 16.2%	128 40.0%
No	69 32.1%	76 72.4%	145 45.3%
Sometimes	31 14.4%	9 8.6%	40 12.5%
Undecided	4 1.9%	3 2.9%	7 2.2%
Total	215 100.0%	105 100.0%	320 100.0%

Pearson chi-square 49.669.

The data in Table 5.2 clearly shows that there is significant difference between male (51.6 per cent) and female (16.2 per cent and those are also the leaders of panchayat samities) leaders on this attributes. The chi-square value 49.669 is highly significant and confirms that the habit of reading newspaper among male leaders is very much higher in comparison to female leaders. The reasons are: lesser level of education among female leaders; absence of social independence; and women are proxy of their families.

The data in Table 5.3 reveals that the upper castes, followed by backward castes and farming castes have relatively higher proportion of leaders having newspaper reading habit. The chi-square value 26.887 also confirms the distinction of this trait among the leaders of different castes of the sampled population.

TABLE 5.3

Classification of perceptions based on their castes on newspaper reading habit of the leaders

Perceptions	Castes						Total
	Farming castes	*Upper castes*	*Backward castes (A)*	*Backward castes (B)*	*Scheduled castes (A)*	*Scheduled castes (B)*	
(1)	(2)	(3)	(4)	(5)	(6)	(7)	(8)
Yes	42 42.4%	24 60.0%	8 27.6%	18 48.6%	16 31.4%	20 31.3%	128 40.0%
No	43 43.4%	10 25.0%	16 55.2%	10 27.0%	31 60.8%	35 54.7%	145 45.3%
Sometimes	12 12.1%	4 10.0%	4 13.8%	8 21.6%	3 5.9%	9 14.1%	40 12.5%
Undecided	2 2.0%	2 5.0%	1 3.4%	1 2.7%	1 2.0%	0 .0%	7 2.2%
Total	99 100.0%	40 100.0%	29 100.0%	37 100.0%	51 100.0%	64 100.0%	320 100.0%

Pearson chi-square 26.887.

The newspaper reading habit is also investigated to find out the newspaper which they are reading.

TABLE 5.4

Type of newspaper read by the sampled leaders

Types	*Frequency*	*Valid Percent*	*Cumulative Percent*
Hindi paper	111	34.7	34.7
English + Hindi	3	.9	35.6
Any one which is available	62	19.4	55.0
Illiterate	94	29.4	84.4
None	50	15.6	100.0
Total	320	100.0	

The data in Table 5.4 makes it clear that out of 40 per cent regular and 12.5 per cent casual leaders (Table 5.1), 34.7 per cent read Hindi newspaper and 19.4 per cent stated any paper whichever is available to them. There are only .9 per cent who responded that they read both English and Hindi newspaper.

The newspaper reading attribute needs some explanation. First, this habit must be considered in context with leaders' educational levels and their knowledge of English language. Second, the understanding and requirement of the village or local level leaders does not go beyond their area or state and in some cases (social and political system) up to national level. Therefore the Hindi dailies can satiate this urge of the said leaders.

It is also important to find out from leaders' point of view why they are reading newspapers? It may or may not be useful for them to look after the affairs of their panchayat or local body with which they are associated. The Table 5.5 contains opinions in this regard.

The data in the Table 5.5 indicates that only 17.5 per cent affirmed the utility of newspaper reading habit in understanding local governance. and another 14.1 per cent consider that this habit helps in developing wisdom to run the

TABLE 5.5
Utilization of newspaper reading habit in understanding local governance by them

Perceptions	*Frequency*	*Valid Percent*	*Cumulative Percent*
Yes	56	17.5	17.5
No	67	20.9	38.4
Develops some kind of wisdom	45	14.1	52.5
Uncertain	152	47.5	100.0
Total	320	100.0	

affairs of PRIs. But most of them (68.4 per cent) rejected the idea that this habit has helped them in their local political pursuit.

Although, it (utility of newspaper reading habit) is not acceptable to the majority of the leaders even then it is analyzed here in context with the leaders' gender, caste and positions and data is presented in Tables 5.6, 5.7 and 5.8.

TABLE 5.6
Classification of the leaders' perceptions based on their gender on the utilization of newspaper reading habit

	Gender		*Total*
Perceptions	*Male*	*Female*	
Yes	51 23.7%	5 4.8%	56 17.5%
No	54 25.1%	13 12.4%	67 20.9%
Develops some kind of wisdom	36 16.7%	9 8.6%	45 14.1%
Uncertain	74 34.4%	78 74.3%	152 47.5%
Total	215 100.0%	105 100.0%	320 100.0%

Pearson chi-square 46.911.

TABLE 5.7

Classification of the leaders' perceptions based on their castes on the utilization of newspaper reading habit

Perceptions	*Castes*						*Total*
	Farming castes	*Upper castes*	*Backward castes (A)*	*Backward castes (B)*	*Scheduled castes (A)*	*Scheduled castes (B)*	
(1)	*(2)*	*(3)*	*(4)*	*(5)*	*(6)*	*(7)*	*(8)*
Yes	22 22.2%	9 22.5%	3 10.3%	7 18.9%	6 11.8%	9 14.1%	56 17.5%
No	22 22.2%	7 17.5%	5 17.2%	12 32.4%	7 13.7%	14 21.9%	67 20.9%
Develops some kind of wisdom	11 11.1%	11 27.5%	4 13.8%	8 21.6%	5 9.8%	6 9.4%	45 14.1%
Uncertain	44 44.4%	13 32.5%	17 58.6%	10 27.0%	33 64.7%	35 54.7%	152 47.5%
Total	99 100.0%	40 100.0%	29 100.0%	37 100.0%	51 100.0%	64 100.0%	320 100.0%

Pearson chi-square 27.132.

The data in Table 5.6 reveals that male and female leaders consider the utility of newspaper reading habit is significantly different one. The chi-square 46.911 confirms it. It is obvious also as most of the women do not have news paper reading habit.

The information relating to the newspaper reading habit and the castes of the leaders presented in Table 5.7 reveals that the leaders of upper castes and farming castes find the efficacy of newspaper reading habit in much proportion in comparison to the leaders of other castes. The chi-square value 27.132 is significant and therefore confirms the difference among the leaders of various castes' groups.

The Table 5.8 consists of the information pertaining to the classification of leaders on their perceptions on the utilization of news paper reading habit as per their positions they held in the PRIs. The data in Table 5.8 supports that there is an efficacy of newspaper reading habit in terms of developing the necessary wisdom and accepting that this trait is helpful in discharging the panchayat affairs which people entrusted to them. The chi-square value 56.208 confirms the difference of perception among the leaders holding different positions in different period of time. It is evident from the table that the PS members particularly those who were elected before and after the amendment consider it more useful than the gram panchayat leaders.

Thus, the proposition that about half of leaders read newspapers, particularly Hindi dailies, and they consider that it is helpful in developing wisdom required to discharge their responsibilities as local leaders. Further, the level of this characteristic is higher among male, upper castes and farming castes' leaders and the PS leaders. The female, scheduled castes and GP leaders are relatively backward in this context

The village leadership performs certain responsibilities of local institution mainly under the influence of prevailing social, economic, political and cultural conditions. The education helps in proper understanding of these different kinds of conditions and forces based on these conditions taking place within the community. Education not only helps in acquiring knowledge required for understanding and developing skills of local

TABLE 5.8

Classification of the leaders' perceptions based on their positions on the utilization of newspaper reading habit

Perceptions	Positions								Total
	PS leaders before 73rd amendment	*PS leaders after 73rd amendment (1st election)*	*PS leaders after 73rd amendment 2nd election)*	*PS leaders after 73rd amendment (3rd election)*	*GP leaders before 73rd amendment*	*GP leaders after 73rd amendment (1st election)*	*GP leaders after 73rd amendment (2nd election)*	*GP leaders after 73rd amendment (3rd election)*	
(1)	(2)	(3)	(4)	(5)	(6)	(7)	(8)	(9)	(10)
Yes	1 25.0%	6 20.0%	19 30.2%	6 20.0%	6 22.2%	7 14.3%	8 11.3%	3 6.5%	56 17.5%
No	0 .0%	6 20.0%	14 22.2%	15 50.0%	4 14.8%	9 18.4%	4 5.6%	15 32.6%	67 20.9%
Develops some kind of wisdom	1 25.0%	8 26.7%	7 11.1%	2 6.7%	3 11.1%	7 14.3%	14 19.7%	3 6.5%	45 14.1%
Uncertain	2 50.0%	10 33.3%	23 36.5%	7 23.3%	14 51.9%	26 53.1%	45 63.4%	25 54.3%	152 47.5%
Total	4 100.0%	30 100.0%	63 100.0%	30 100.0%	27 100.0%	49 100.0%	71 100.0%	46 100.0%	320 100.0%

Pearson chi-square 56.208.

governance but also imparts communication skills to the leader in person. Therefore, the sampled leaders were asked to narrate their opinion to the question: 'Do you think that Sarpanch of the village must be an educated person'? It is an indirect question aimed to find out the role of education in building up a successful leader at the village level. The information obtained is tabulated in Table 5.9 given below.

TABLE 5.9
Perceptions on the need of educated person to be a sarpanch of a village

Perceptions	*Frequency*	*Valid Percent*	*Cumulative Percent*
Yes	285	89.1	89.1
No	18	5.6	94.7
Not necessary	15	4.7	99.4
No response	2	.6	100.0
Total	320	100.0	

It is evident from the data in Table 5.9 that 89.1 per cent consider that sarpanch must be an educated person. There are about 6 per cent of the leaders who reject it and in their opinion it is not necessary to be educated to become successful sarpanch of the village. Further a few of the leaders 4.7 per cent found that it is not necessary that educated person may always be a successful sarpanch of the village. Thus, it is concluded that almost everyone consider the necessity of educated sarpanch in the village panchayat but about 11 per cent of them find education is not a necessary condition to be a sarpanch rather it is contingent or contributory condition which enrich the personality of a sarpanch.

The above stated perceptions (efficacy of education) of the sampled leaders are examined *vis-a-vis* the gender, castes and education levels of the leaders.

It is evident from the data in Table 5.10 that the perceptions of male and female leaders do not differ much and chi-square value 2.783 confirms this fact. It means both male and female leaders understand the efficacy of education as they like an

TABLE 5.10

Classification of the perceptions based on their gender on the need of educated person to be a sarpanch of a village

Perceptions	Gender		Total
	Male	Female	
Yes	190 88.4%	95 90.5%	285 89.1%
No	15 7.0%	3 2.9%	18 5.6%
Not necessary	9 4.2%	6 5.7%	15 4.7%
No response	1 .5%	1 1.0%	2 .6%
Total	215 100.0%	105 100.0%	320 100.0%

Pearson chi -square 2.783.

educated person to be the sarpanch of the village panchayat.

Similarly, the perceptions classified on the basis of castes also indicate the above stated trend. The data in Table 5.11 reveals that although it appears that the proportion of leaders of farming castes and SC-B is relatively lower but the chi-square value 23.469 confirms the absence of any significant difference of perceptions on castes group basis on this issue.

The perceptions of leaders are also classified on educational levels and the data in Table 5.12 and chi-square value 40.766 clearly indicates the distinction of perceptions among the leaders possessing different levels of education. The illiterate leaders do not attach much importance to the education of the sarpanch but almost all leaders who are even fairly educated to the village standard affirmed the need of educated sarpanch in the village.

It is not necessary that the sarpanch of the village is always an educated person. There are some sarpanch who are not educated but more successful than the educated one. Therefore some of the leaders stated (Table 5.8) that it is not necessary always to have educated sarpanch. Keeping in view this aspect,

TABLE 5.11

Classification of the perceptions based on their castes on the need of educated person to be a sarpanch of a village

Perceptions	*Castes*						*Total*
	Farming castes	*Upper castes*	*Backward castes (A)*	*Backward castes (B)*	*Scheduled castes (A)*	*Scheduled castes (B)*	
(1)	*(2)*	*(3)*	*(4)*	*(5)*	*(6)*	*(7)*	*(8)*
Yes	81 81.8%	39 97.5%	27 93.1%	36 97.3%	49 96.1%	53 82.8%	285 89.1%
No	7 7.1%	1 2.5%	1 3.4%	1 2.7%	1 2.0%	7 10.9%	18 5.6%
Not necessary	10 10.1%	0 .0%	1 3.4%	0 .0%	0 .0%	4 6.3%	15 4.7%
No response	1 1.0%	0 .0%	0 .0%	0 .0%	1 2.0%	0 .0%	2 .6%
Total	99 100.0%	40 100.0%	29 100.0%	37 100.0%	51 100.0%	64 100.0%	320 100.0%

Pearson chi-square 23.469.

TABLE 5.12

Classification of the perceptions based on their educational levels about the need of educated person to be a sarpanch of a village

Perceptions	*Education Levels*								*Total*
	Illiterate	*Literate*	*Primary*	*Middle*	*Matri-culation*	*Senior secondary*	*Graduate*	*Other*	
(1)	*(2)*	*(3)*	*(4)*	*(5)*	*(6)*	*(7)*	*(8)*	*(9)*	*(10)*
Yes	69 74.2%	22 88.0%	32 86.5%	53 98.1%	61 98.4%	15 100.0%	23 95.8%	10 100.0%	285 89.1%
No	11 11.8%	2 8.0%	3 8.1%	1 1.9%	0 .0%	0 .0%	1 4.2%	0 .0%	18 5.6%
Not necessary	12 12.9%	1 4.0%	2 5.4%	0 .0%	0 .0%	0 .0%	0 .0%	0 .0%	15 4.7%
No response	1 1.1%	0 .0%	0 .0%	0 .0%	1 1.6%	0 .0%	0 .0%	0 .0%	2 .6%
Total	93 100.0%	25 100.0%	37 100.0%	54 100.0%	62 100.0%	15 100.0%	24 100.0%	10 100.0%	320 100.0%

Pearson chi-square value40.766.

the leaders were also asked to give their perceptions if the sarpanch is not an educated person then he/she must be having requisite understanding and wisdom to run the panchayats.

TABLE 5.13

Perceptions of sampled leaders regarding the ability of a sarpanch if not an èducated one

Perceptions	*Frequency*	*Valid Percent*	*Cumulative Percent*
Yes	316	98.8	98.8
No	4	1.3	100.0
Total	320	100.0	

The data in Table 5.13 on the basis of the perceptions of the sampled leaders confirms that the Sarpanch of the village if not educated must be a person possessing the requisite traits to understand his/her job, community and the surrounding in which he or she interacts while discharging his/her responsibilities. Thus, it is concluded that the people expect that persons having requisite level of education or understanding are the successful local leaders.

What should be the age of the sarpanch? It is understood that this indicates the required level of maturity and responsibility in the person eligible to be a sarpanch. The leaders were asked this question to find out an expected level of maturity in local leadership. The information collected is presented in Table 5.14.

TABLE 5.14

Perceptions of the sampled leaders regarding expected age of the sarpanch

Expected Age Groups	*Frequency*	*Valid Percent*	*Cumulative Percent*
Young (upto 35 years	81	25.3	25.3
Mature (36-50 years)	173	54.1	79.4
Elders (50-65 years)	66	20.6	100.0
Total	320	100.0	

It is evident from the data given in Table 5.14 that a majority of the leaders (54.1 per cent) expected that the sarpanch must be a mature in age, followed by another 20.6 per cent who stated that they expected that elder persons must be their sarpanch in the village. It is important to note that about 25 per cent of leaders are there of this age group in the sample. It means, even the sampled elders preferred for younger and mature person to be the sarpanch of the village. One fourth (25.3 per cent) of the sampled leadership preferred young person to be a sarpanch of the village. Thus, the elder persons are not finding much preference in this regard. It indicates that a new enthusiastic, motivated and competent leadership in the PRIs is replacing traditional leadership culture.

Classification of this expectation is examined on gender and caste basis and data is presented in Tables 5.15 and 5.16.

Table 5.15

Classification of perceptions of the leaders based on their gender and regarding expected age of the sarpanch

	Gender		*Total*
Perceptions	*Male*	*Female*	
Young	54 25.1%	27 25.7%	81 25.3%
Mature	114 53.0%	59 56.2%	173 54.1%
Elders	47 21.9%	19 18.1%	65 20.6%
Total	215 100.0%	105 100.0%	320 100.0%

Pearson chi-square 1.007.

The data in Table 5.15 clearly establishes that the perceptions of male and female leaders do not differ in significant manner on the issue of what should be the preferred age of the sarpanch of the village? It is interesting to state that majority of them wish to find that a mature person in the age group of 36-50 years should be the sarpanch of a village. The

TABLE 5.16

Classification of perceptions of the leaders based on their castes and regarding expected age of the sarpanch

Perceptions	*Castes*						*Total*
	Farming castes	*Upper castes*	*Backward castes (A)*	*Backward castes (B)*	*Scheduled castes (A)*	*Scheduled castes (B)*	
(1)	(2)	(3)	(4)	(5)	(6)	(7)	(8)
Young	20 20.2%	9 22.5%	3 10.3%	12 32.4%	17 33.3%	20 31.3%	81 25.3%
Mature	53 53.5%	23 57.5%	17 58.6%	20 54.1%	29 56.9%	31 48.4%	173 54.1%
Elders	26 26.3%	8 20.0%	9 31.0%	5 13.5%	5 9.8%	13 20.3%	65 20.6%
Total	99 100.0%	40 100.0%	29 100.0%	37 100.0%	51 100.0%	64 100.0%	320 100.0%

Pearson chi-square value 22.729.

ch-i square value 1.007 also confirms the absence of difference of opinion on the said issue.

The data in Table 5.16 reveals that the majority of leaders of backward castes-A and upper castes followed by scheduled castes-A and others rated mature leaders as their preference for the office of the sarpanch of the village. Further, the percentages of sampled leaders belonging to scheduled castes (33.3 and 31.3 percent) and backward castes-B (32.4 percent) are higher than other castes leaders (average is 25.3 percent) who prefer young leadership. The elders are preferred much by the backward castes and farming castes in comparison to other castes' leaders. However, the chi-square value (22.729) confirms that the caste based difference of perceptions is an apparent one and not enough significant to draw valid conclusion.

Nevertheless, the data make it apparent (but not in scientific sense) that: (i) the young leadership is expected; (ii) mature leaders are preferred almost by all castes and this proposition is in quite conformity to the conclusion made relating to age of the leaders while discussing their socio-economic background; (iii) the backward castes (A) leaders are still conservative in their attitude in terms of expectation of the age of sarpanch in the village; and (iv) the upper caste leaders represent the average expectation; (v) farming castes are little bit traditional and backward castes-B is quite progressive in its attitude towards younger age leadership.

Another attribute which is expected to be there in the sarpanch of a village is his ability to provide moral leadership to the whole of the panchayat and the village. Therefore, the proposition that the sarpanch should be a person who should be able to provide moral leadership was put to the sampled respondents for their comments. The data is compiled in Table 5.17.

The data in Table 5.17 indicates that a large majority (86.3 per cent) affirms this expectation from the sarpanch. But 2.5 per cent said that it is not possible to have this kind of attribute in the village sarpanch. Some (5.0 percent) negated and others (6.3 per cent) did not respond. Thus almost everyone likes that the sarpanch must be a person able to provide moral leadership and their proportion is so large that their classification on gender and castes basis may not lead to any deviation in the conclusion based on information contained in the table.

TABLE 5.17

Perceptions regarding the sarpanch should provide moral leadership to the GP

Perceptions	*Frequency*	*Valid Percent*	*Cumulative Percent*
Yes	276	86.3	86.3
No	16	5.0	91.3
Not possible	8	2.5	93.8
No response	20	6.3	100.0
Total	320	100.0	

The leader must behave in responsible manner. The elector of a leader in a democratic set up and particularly at the level where the voters are in face to face contact with their leadership this attribute is very much intense one. The information relating to this aspect is collected from the panches, sarpanches and Panchayat samiti members. Therefore, the sampled leaders were asked to answer 'Do you find that your representative (sarpanch or panch) or village leadership feel responsible towards the panchayats works? The responses are tabulated in Table 5.18.

TABLE 5.18

Perceptions of leaders regarding the possession of responsibility attribute by the sarpanch and panches

Perceptions	*Frequency*	*Valid Percent*	*Cumulative Percent*
Yes	164	51.3	51.3
No	28	8.8	60.0
Average	51	15.9	75.9
No response	1	.3	76.3
Not asked	76	23.8	100.0
Total	320	100.0	

The data in Table 5.18 indicates that a majority (51.3 per cent) of the leaders find that the sarpanch or panch who represent them is mature and responsible with regard to the responsibilities entrusted to him/her by their electors. There is another sizeable group of leaders (15.9 per cent) who consider that their feeling of responsibility is average one. However, a small section of 8.8 per cent of the total sampled leaders is pessimistic and considers that village leadership is not behaving in a responsible way.

These perceptions are also classified based on their gender and castes and tabulated in Table 5.19 and 5.20.

TABLE 5.19

Classification of perceptions based on the gender of the leaders regarding the possession of responsibility attributes by the sarpanch and panches

Perceptions	*Gender*		*Total*
	Male	*Female*	
Yes	118 54.9%	46 43.8%	164 51.3%
No	19 8.8%	9 8.6%	28 8.8%
Average	30 14.0%	21 20.0%	51 15.9%
No response	0 .0%	1 1.0%	1 .3%
Not asked*	48 22.3%	28 26.7%	76 23.8%
Total	215 100.0%	105 100.0%	320 100.0%

Pearson chi-square value 5.920.

The data in Table 5.19 makes it clear that both male and female leaders have similar kind of opinion regarding the attribute of responsibility possessed by the leaders chi-square value is 5.920 which is not significant.

Similarly, the data in Table 5.20 and chi-square value 26.098 indicates that the perceptions are independent of the castes of the leaders. In other word there is not any significant difference among leaders in their perceptions about the accountability attribute possessed by the PR leadership.

TABLE 5.20

Classification of perceptions based on the castes of the leaders regarding the possession of responsibility attributes by the sarpanch and panches

Perceptions	*Castes*						*Total*
	Farming castes	*Upper castes*	*Backward castes (A)*	*Backward castes (B)*	*Scheduled castes (A)*	*Scheduled castes (B)*	
(1)	(2)	(3)	(4)	(5)	(6)	(7)	(8)
Yes	51 51.5%	20 50.0%	17 58.6%	17 45.9%	22 43.1%	37 57.8%	164 51.3%
No	6 6.1%	6 15.0%	3 10.3%	4 10.8%	7 13.7%	2 3.1%	28 8.8%
Average	19 19.2%	7 17.5%	3 10.3%	3 8.1%	11 21.6%	8 12.5%	51 15.9%
No response	0 .0%	0 .0%	1 3.4%	0 .0%	0 .0%	0 .0%	1 .3%
Not asked*	23 23.2%	7 17.5%	5 17.2%	13 35.1%	11 21.6%	17 26.6%	76 23.8%
Total	99 100.0%	40 100.0%	29 100.0%	37 100.0%	51 100.0%	64 100.0%	320 100.0%

Pearson chi-square 26.098.

Thus, on the basis of data presented in Tables 5.18, 5.19 and 5.20 it is concluded that a simple majority of the leadership feel that local leadership possess attribute of accountability and behave in responsible manner while performing the affairs of panchayats. Further, this kind of feeling does not vary with the gender and castes of the sampled leaders. The leaders, both male and female and of different castes have almost similar kind of perceptions on this attribute of PR leadership.

The sampled leaders were also asked to rate the competence of panches/sarpanches in general. The information collected on this issue is presented in Table 5.21.

TABLE 5.21

Perceptions about the competence of the sarpanch and panches of the village

Perceptions	*Frequency*	*Valid Percent*	*Cumulative Percent*
Yes	156	48.8	48.8
No	19	5.9	54.7
Some what good	59	18.4	73.1
Not from reserved category	10	3.1	76.3
Women not competent	6	1.9	78.1
No response	5	1.6	79.7
Not asked*	65	20.3	100.0
Total	320	100.0	

The data in Table 5.21 indicates that a little less than half (48.8 per cent) of the sampled leaders found the panches and sarpanch of their village as competent. Besides them, there are 18.4 per cent of the leaders who although rated them as competent but somewhat only. Nevertheless, the leaders who called panches and sarpanches as incompetent are only 5.9 per cent and some of them stated that the reserved classes and women categories (3.1 and 1.9 per cent) of leaders are incompetent. Thus the data in table makes it clear that the majority of leaders are rated by the sampled PR leaders as competent enough to discharge their responsibilities.

TABLE 5.22

Classification of perceptions based on their gender about the competence of the panches and sarpanch of the village

Perceptions	Gender: Male	Gender: Female	Total
Yes	111 51.6%	45 42.9%	156 48.8%
No	12 5.6%	7 6.7%	19 5.9%
Somewhat good	38 17.7%	21 20.0%	59 18.4%
Not from reserved category	7 3.3%	3 2.9%	10 3.1%
Women not competent	4 1.9%	2 1.9%	6 1.9%
No response	3 1.4%	2 1.9%	5 1.6%
Not asked*	40 18.6%	25 23.8%	65 20.3%
Total	215 100.0%	105 100.0%	320 100.0%

Pearson chi -square 2.555.

The data in Table 5.22 indicates that male and female leaders do not differ in significant manner while rating the competence of panches and sarpanches. The chi-square value 2.555 also confirms it.

However, the perceptions on competence of PR leadership are different among leaders belonging to different castes as is evident from the data in Table 5.23. The data in reveals the proportion of the leaders who affirmed or who rated as some what competent differ from one caste to another caste. The chi-square value 51.378 confirms the significant difference among the various castes groups. The proportion of scheduled castes leaders who rated panches/sarpanches is higher in comparison to other castes. But it is least in proportion in case of farming castes. It is quite surprising that the proportion of farming

TABLE 5.23
Classification of perceptions based on their castes about the competence of the panches and sarpanch of the village

Perceptions	Castes						Total
	Farming castes	*Upper castes*	*Backward castes (A)*	*Backward castes (B)*	*Scheduled castes (A)*	*Scheduled castes (B)*	
(1)	(2)	(3)	(4)	(5)	(6)	(7)	(8)
Yes	42	20	13	17	29	35	156
	42.4%	50.0%	44.8%	45.9%	56.9%	54.7%	48.8%
No	4	5	3	2	3	2	19
	4.0%	12.5%	10.3%	5.4%	5.9%	3.1%	5.9%
Somewhat good	26	6	6	4	8	9	59
	26.3%	15.0%	20.7%	10.8%	15.7%	14.1%	18.4%
Not from reserved category	4	2	1	1	2	0	10
	4.0%	5.0%	3.4%	2.7%	3.9%	.0%	3.1%
Women not competent	0	2	0	0	3	1	6
	.0%	5.0%	.0%	.0%	5.9%	1.6%	1.9%
No response	1	0	3	0	0	1	5
	1.0%	.0%	10.3%	.0%	.0%	1.6%	1.6%
Not asked*	22	5	3	13	6	16	65
	22.2%	12.5%	10.3%	35.1%	11.8%	25.0%	20.3%
Total	99	40	29	37	51	64	320
	100.0%	100.0%	100.0%	100.0%	100.0%	100.0%	100.0%

Pearson chi-square 51.378.

castes, scheduled castes and backward castes (B) who do not found the leadership competent is practically similar one. The upper castes and backward castes (A) leaders' proportion is relatively higher who do not consider the village leadership up to the expected level of competence.

Therefore, the difference lies because of the group of leaders who consider the leadership as somewhat competent (26.3 per cent). It is also surprising to note that one caste leaders do not find the other castes' leaders or women as competent one.

The castes do not make one competent or incompetent rather individuals may be rated as competent or incompetent. The competence, no doubt, remains associated with social, education and economic factors, therefore, political empowerment need to be evaluated in terms of social, educational and economic perspective at least at local level. This is the proposition which need to be tested in the light of political empowerment established at PR levels.

The sampled leaders when asked to narrate their opinions about their capability to guide the developmental activities repeated almost similar pattern of responses as is there in Tables 5.21, 5.22 and 5.23. It means that majority of them opined that the PR leadership has enough capability to guide the rural development. The perceptions about this capability are not different when classified on gender basis but there is significant difference when classified on caste basis.

The majority of leaders affirmed in this study that PR leaders are capable and possess the attributes required in this level of leadership. This conclusion is based on the responses of the leaders themselves. Therefore, the information to reconfirm it, in indirect manner, was obtained during the field study by asking the question, 'Do you think that your panchayat is performing its functions in prolific manner'?

The data in Table 5.24 indicates that less than half of the leaders (42.8 per cent) evaluated the performance of their panchayat as good. The percentage is less than those who find the panch and sarpanch as competent (Table 5.21). However, about one-fourth of leaders (25.9 per cent) observed that the panchayats perform their functions in somewhat good manner, i.e. they rated the performance of panchayat as average one. The

TABLE 5.24

Perceptions about the prolific performance of the village panchayats

Perceptions	*Frequency*	*Valid Percent*	*Cumulative Percent*
Good	137	42.8	42.8
No	23	7.2	50.0
Somewhat good	83	25.9	75.9
No response	1	.3	76.3
Not asked	76	23.8	100.0
Total	320	100.0	

percentage of those who rated the competence of the sarpanch and panches as average (18.4 per cent) is lesser than those who rated the performance of panchayat as somewhat good average (25.9 per cent).

But the leaders who rated the competence and performance as good and average are equal. This means about 69 per cent are satisfied with the performance of panchayat and panches/sarpanches competence.

The leaders' responses on panchayat performance are studied with reference to the gender and castes of the sampled leaders. (Tables 5.25 and 5.26)

The data in Table 5.25 makes it clear that there is a significant difference of perceptions between sampled male and female leaders (chi-square 9.706*) regarding performance of village panchayat. The percentage of male who find the functioning of village panchayat as good is higher than the female. But the percentage who rated the village panchayat as somewhat good or average is higher among women. In total higher proportion of male leaders is satisfied from the performance of panchayats. The reasons attributed to it as male responsible for running panchayats rated their own performance as good. It is true also and many local leaders and panchayats are performing very well in the state.

Similar results are evident when leaders are classified on the basis of their castes as is evident from the data given in Table 5.26.

TABLE 5.25

Classification of perceptions about the prolific performance of the village panchayats based on their gender

Perceptions	*Gender*		*Total*
	Male	*Female*	
Good	103 47.9%	34 32.4%	137 42.8%
No	12 5.6%	11 10.5%	23 7.2%
Somewhat Good	52 24.2%	31 29.5%	83 25.9%
No response	0 .0%	1 1.0%	1 .3%
Not asked	48 22.3%	28 26.7%	76 23.8%
Total	215 100.0%	105 100.0%	320 100.0%

Pearson chi-square 9.706*.

The data in Table 5.26 and chi-square value confirms the absence of significant difference of perceptions of leaders when classified on basis of their castes.

Thus, the discussion makes to conclude, although with less force, that panchayat raj leaders are competent and perform the functions of panchayat either in a good or average manner. However, some variations in perceptions are there when compared on gender basis but not when classified on caste basis.

The sampled leaders were asked to comment on the assertion that their village panchayat perform its functions in an enthusiastic manner and with a sense of wisdom. The objective is to have an idea of sense of involvement and commitment of panchayat leaders with the gram panchayat. The data in Table 5.27 gives an account of this kind of information. The data indicates that 45.9 per cent of the leaders affirmed it saying 'yes' and 9.1 per cent simply stated as 'no'. One-fifth of the total leaders were uncertain to say anything and there is a group of

TABLE 5.26

Classification of perceptions about the prolific performance of the village panchayats based on their castes

Perceptions	*Castes*						*Total*
	Farming castes	*Upper castes*	*Backward castes (A)*	*Backward castes (B)*	*Scheduled castes (A)*	*Scheduled castes (B)*	
(1)	(2)	(3)	(4)	(5)	(6)	(7)	(8)
Good	40 40.4%	17 42.5%	13 44.8%	16 43.2%	21 41.2%	30 46.9%	137 42.8%
No	5 5.1%	3 7.5%	3 10.3%	4 10.8%	4 7.8%	4 6.3%	23 7.2%
Somewhat Good	31 31.3%	13 32.5%	7 24.1%	4 10.8%	15 29.4%	13 20.3%	83 25.9%
No response	0 .0%	0 .0%	1 3.4%	0 .0%	0 .0%	0 .0%	1 .3%
Not asked	23 23.2%	7 17.5%	5 17.2%	13 35.1%	11 21.6%	17 26.6%	76 23.8%
Total	99 100.0%	40 100.0%	29 100.0%	37 100.0%	51 100.0%	64 100.0%	320 100.0%

Pearson chi-square 21.905.

TABLE 5.27

Perceptions regarding the enthusiasm and sense of wisdom among the PR leaders while performing panchayats' functions

Perceptions	*Frequency*	*Valid Percent*	*Cumulative Percent*
Yes	147	45.9	45.9
No	29	9.1	55.0
Uncertain	64	20.0	75.0
Don't know	3	.9	75.9
Average	1	.3	76.3
Not asked	76	23.8	100.0
Total	320	100.0	

23.8 per cent respondents who were not asked to respond to this assertion.

Thus, the data lead to conclude that a majority (if percentage is taken after deducting 76 leaders from the total respondents from whom this question was not asked) of leaders possess the view point that PR leadership is energetic and sensible. In other words, many leaders in Panchayat Raj possess the attribute of commitment and remain actively involved with panchayats' activities.

These perceptions (Table 5.27) are examined with reference to the gender and castes of the leadership and tabulated in Table 5.28. The data reveals the proportion of those who affirmed and who rejected is higher among males in comparison to female. However, the proportion of those who were uncertain is quite higher among female leaders. Thus, there is significant difference between male and female leaders on this count. The chi-square value 12.571 supports the proposition that female leaders are inexperienced and consider that their panchayat does not possess the attribute of vigor and wisdom required to have a more effective leadership at village level.

Further, the data tabulated in Table 5.29 comprises of information relating to the perceptions of leaders about the

TABLE 6.28
Classification of perceptions based on their gender regarding the enthusiasm and sense of wisdom among the PR leaders

	Gender		*Total*
Perceptions	*Male*	*Female*	
Yes	109 50.7%	38 36.2%	147 45.9%
No	22 10.2%	7 6.7%	29 9.1%
Uncertain	34 15.8%	30 28.6%	64 20.0%
Don't know	1 .5%	2 1.9%	3 .9%
Average	1 .5%	0 .0%	1 3%
Not asked	48 22.3%	28 26.7%	76 23.8%
Total	215 100.0%	105 100.0%	320 100.0%

Pearson chi-square 12.571*.

attribute of enthusiasm and sense of wisdom classified on the basis of their castes does not indicate any significant difference of perceptions among the leaders belonging to different castes (chi-square 22.277).

Thus, the proposition that about half of the sampled leaders find the village panchayat as possessing necessary strength of enthusiasm and wisdom to perform the panchayat's responsibilities. It means that about half of the PR leadership have the opinion that the leadership is enthusiastic and possess the sense of wisdom. Nevertheless, the women leaders differ, however, in insignificant manner from the male leaders and relatively lesser optimistic about the presence of this attribute. The reason of difference is assigned to the fact that they themselves are confused and uncertain to take decisions when asked to do so.

TABLE 5.29

Classification of perceptions based on their castes regarding the enthusiasm and sense of wisdom among the PR leaders

Perceptions	Castes						Total
	Farming castes	*Upper castes*	*Backward castes (A)*	*Backward castes (B)*	*Scheduled castes (A)*	*Scheduled castes (B)*	
(1)	(2)	(3)	(4)	(5)	(6)	(7)	(8)
Yes	47 47.5%	17 42.5%	13 44.8%	16 43.2%	22 43.1%	32 50.0%	147 45.9%
No	8 8.1%	3 7.5%	4 13.8%	4 10.8%	5 9.8%	5 7.8%	29 9.1%
Uncertain	21 21.2%	12 30.0%	7 24.1%	3 8.1%	12 23.5%	9 14.1%	64 20.0%
Don't know	0 .0%	0 .0%	0 .0%	1 2.7%	1 2.0%	1 1.6%	3 .9%
Average	0 .0%	1 2.5%	0 .0%	0 .0%	0 .0%	0 .0%	1 .3%
Not asked	23 23.2%	7 17.5%	5 17.2%	13 35.1%	11 21.6%	17 26.6%	76 23.8%
Total	99 100.0%	40 100.0%	29 100.0%	37 100.0%	51 100.0%	64 100.0%	320 100.0%

Pearson chi-square 22.277.

The strength and performance of a panchayat is reflected from its capability of deciding its priorities. The priorities are decided in the Gram Sabha and those are said to be on paper. Therefore, this task is performed by the panchayat in general and sarpanch in particular and naturally the effectiveness to take this kind of decision depends on their competence. Hence, the sampled leaders were asked to respond to the question, "Does your panchayat know how to decide its priorities? The information obtained is presented in Table 5.30.

TABLE 5.30

Perceptions of the leaders about panchayat's capability in deciding the priorities

Perceptions	*Frequency*	*Valid Percent*	*Cumulative Percent*
Capable	147	45.9	45.9
Not capable	26	8.1	54.1
Uncertain	65	20.3	74.4
Don't know	6	1.9	76.3
Not asked	76	23.8	100.0
Total	320	100.0	

The data in Table 5.30 exhibits that 45.9 per cent of the sampled leaders stated that their panchayat is well versed with the capability to decide village priorities. It appears from the data that it is replication of responses on the enthusiasm and wisdom attribute possessed by the local leaders.

Further, these responses are classified with reference to the gender (Table 5.31) and castes (Table 5.32) of the leaders.

The data in Table 5.31 indicates that the proportion of female leaders who find the panchayat enough capable to decide priorities is lesser in comparison to men. The chi-square value 16.277 confirms the distinction of leaders based on their perception on the said issue as significant one. However, the data in Table 5.32 reveals that the perceptions of leaders of various castes do not differ from each other. Although, the proportion of SC-A, and BC-A leaders appear to be lesser in accepting that panchayat is capable to decide its priorities but

TABLE 5.31

Classification of the perceptions of the leaders based on their gender about panchayat's capability in deciding the priorities

Perceptions	*Gender*		*Total*
	Male	*Female*	
Yes Capable	110 51.2%	37 35.2%	147 45.9%
Not Capable	21 9.8%	5 4.8%	26 8.1%
Uncertain	34 15.8%	31 29.5%	65 20.3%
Don't know	2 .9%	4 3.8%	6 1.9%
Not asked	48 22.3%	28 26.7%	76 23.8%
Total	215 100.0%	105 100.0%	320 100.0%

Pearson chi-square value 16.277*.

the chi-square value 21.218 (not significant) confirms the absence of such difference of perceptions.

Thus, it confirms the proposition that many of the local leaders are competent enough to decide the village priorities (a political function to be essentially performed by elected representative in democratic world). However, this feeling is lower among female leaders in significant way but almost uniformly present among the leaders of various castes. The reason to it is attributed that women are inexperienced and not actively involved in panchayat's activities and responsibilities.

The political parties do not participate in panchayat raj election particularly at gram panchayat level in Haryana State. The Haryana Panchayat Raj Act, 1994 disallows it. There is consensus among different political parties on this issue. There are various reasons for it but one of those is that the local government is expected to deliver the service to the poor and other ignorant rural population of the state and while doing so it has to act as an instrument for administrative apparatus of the

TABLE 5.32

Classification of perceptions of the leaders based on their castes about panchayat's capability in deciding the priorities

Perceptions	*Castes*						*Total*
	Farming castes	*Upper castes*	*Backward castes (A)*	*Backward castes (B)*	*Scheduled castes (A)*	*Scheduled castes (B)*	
(1)	(2)	(3)	(4)	(5)	(6)	(7)	(8)
Capable	44 44.4%	18 45.0%	14 48.3%	15 40.5%	22 43.1%	34 53.1%	147 45.9%
Not Capable	8 8.1%	3 7.5%	4 13.8%	4 10.8%	4 7.8%	3 4.7%	26 8.1%
Uncertain	24 24.2%	10 25.0%	6 20.7%	3 8.1%	12 23.5%	10 15.6%	65 20.3%
Don't know	0 .0%	2 5.0%	0 .0%	2 5.4%	2 3.9%	0 .0%	6 1.9%
Not asked	23 23.2%	7 17.5%	5 17.2%	13 35.1%	11 21.6%	17 26.6%	76 23.8%
Total	99 100.0%	40 100.0%	29 100.0%	37 100.0%	51 100.0%	64 100.0%	320 100.0%

Pearson chi-square 21.218.

state machinery. Therefore, the political factionalism at village level may affect their lives negatively and may breed enimity in rural society.

Therefore, an effort is made to find out whether the PR leaders really are not involved in political polarization created by the political parties. They were asked to react to the assertion that it appears panches/sarpanches are more involved in politics rather than in panchayat's activities. The information obtained is presented in Table 5.33.

TABLE 5.33

Perceptions about the involvement of leaders in politics rather than in panchayat's activities

Perceptions	*Frequency*	*Valid Percent*	*Cumulative Percent*
Yes	75	23.4	23.4
No	166	51.9	75.3
Uncertain	3	.9	76.3
Not asked	76	23.8	100.0
Total	320	100.0	

The data in Table 5.33 clearly indicates that a majority of the sampled leaders (more than 51.9 per cent and even more if 23.8 per cent are excluded from the total who were not asked to respond to this assertion) negated it. However, less than a quarter of leaders (23.4 per cent) affirmed that the leaders remain involved in politics.

The information presented in Table 5.33 is also classified on the basis of their gender and castes in Tables 5.34 and 5.35 respectively.

The data in Table 5.34 and chi-square value 3.250 indicates the absence of difference among male and female leaders in their perceptions regarding their involvement in party politics in significant way. However, there is apparent difference of perception between male and female leaders on this issue. Similarly the data in Table 5.35 indicates that apparently the perceptions of backward castes-B and scheduled castes-A leaders differ very much from each other castes but chi-square

TABLE 5.34

Perceptions about the involvement of leaders based on their gender in politics rather than in panchayat's activities

	Gender		*Total*
Perceptions	*Male*	*Female*	
Yes	46 21.4%	29 27.6%	75 23.4%
No	119 55.3%	47 44.8%	166 51.9%
Uncertain	2 .9%	1 1.0%	3 .9%
Not asked	48 22.3%	28 26.7%	76 23.8%
Total	215 100.0%	105 100.0%	320 100.0%

Pearson chi-square value 3.250.

value (14.718) is not significant. It means there is more or less a uniform pattern of responses of the leaders of various castes.

Thus the majority of sampled leaders do not find most of the leaders involved in party politics rather remain involved in PRIs only. It supports an earlier conclusion of the present study itself which states that the sampled PR leaders are not regular in contesting PR elections rather they are casual leaders who do not wish to go beyond village level politics.

It is observed by many scholars that PR leadership has become more effective after 73rd constitutional amendment. The perceptions of sampled leaders in this regard are compiled in Table 5.36.

The data in Table 5.36 shows that a large majority of leaders (62.8 per cent) affirmed the positive impact saying the effectiveness of PR leadership has improved after the new panchayati raj has been introduced in the state. Further, a sizeable section (26.3 per cent) of the leaders not only affirmed but finds the leadership much better in effectiveness than the earlier one. Thus, about 90 percent of the leadership believes that the PR leadership has become more effective under new panchayati raj established after amendment.

TABLE 5.35

Classification of perceptions based on castes about the involvement of leaders in politics rather than in panchayat's activities

Perceptions	*Castes*						*Total*
	Farming castes	*Upper castes*	*Backward castes (A)*	*Backward castes (B)*	*Scheduled castes (A)*	*Scheduled castes (B)*	
(1)	*(2)*	*(3)*	*(4)*	*(5)*	*(6)*	*(7)*	*(8)*
Yes	21 21.2%	10 25.0%	8 27.6%	5 13.5%	17 33.3%	14 21.9%	75 23.4%
No	55 55.6%	23 57.5%	15 51.7%	18 48.6%	22 43.1%	33 51.6%	166 51.9%
Uncertain	0 .0%	0 .0%	1 3.4%	1 2.7%	1 2.0%	0 .0%	3 .9%
Not asked	23 23.2%	7 17.5%	5 17.2%	13 35.1%	11 21.6%	17 26.6%	76 23.8%
Total	99 100.0%	40 100.0%	29 100.0%	37 100.0%	51 100.0%	64 100.0%	320 100.0%

Pearson chi-square value 14.718.

TABLE 5.36

Perceptions regarding the positive impact of 73rd amendment on PR leadership

Perceptions	*Frequency*	*Valid Percent*	*Cumulative Percent*
Yes	201	62.8	62.8
No	5	1.6	64.4
Much better	84	26.3	90.6
No change	11	3.4	94.1
Uncertain	17	5.3	99.4
No response	2	.6	100.0
Total	320	100.0	

The perceptions of leaders are classified on the basis of their gender and castes and presented in Tables 5.37 and 5.38.

TABLE 5.37

Classification of perceptions based on gender regarding the positive impact of 73rd amendment on PR leadership

	Gender		*Total*
Perceptions	*Male*	*Female*	
Yes	139 64.7%	62 59.0%	201 62.8%
No	3 1.4%	2 1.9%	5 1.6%
Much better	64 29.8%	20 19.0%	84 26.3%
No change	6 2.8%	5 4.8%	11 3.4%
Uncertain	2 .9%	15 14.3%	17 5.3%
No response	1 .5%	1 1.0%	2 .6%
Total	215 100.0%	105 100.0%	320 100.0%

Pearson chi-square 28.310*.

TABLE 5.38

Classification of perceptions based on castes regarding the positive impact of 73rd amendment on PR leadership

Perceptions	Castes						Total
	Farming castes	Upper castes	Backward castes (A)	Backward castes (B)	Scheduled castes (A)	Scheduled castes (B)	
(1)	(2)	(3)	(4)	(5)	(6)	(7)	(8)
Yes	67 67.7%	28 70.0%	17 58.6%	18 48.6%	32 62.7%	39 60.9%	201 62.8%
No	2 2.0%	0 .0%	1 3.4%	1 2.7%	0 .0%	1 1.6%	5 1.6%
Much better	19 19.2%	11 27.5%	9 31.0%	14 37.8%	15 29.4%	16 25.0%	84 26.3%
No change	5 5.1%	0 .0%	0 .0%	0 .0%	3 5.9%	3 4.7%	11 3.4%
Uncertain	6 6.1%	0 .0%	1 3.4%	4 10.8%	1 2.0%	5 7.8%	17 5.3%
No response	0 .0%	1 2.5%	1 3.4%	0 .0%	0 .0%	0 .0%	2 .6%
Total	99 100.0%	40 100.0%	29 100.0%	37 100.0%	51 100.0%	64 100.0%	320 100.0%

Pearson chi-square 28.248.

The data in Table 5.37 reveals that the proportion of male leaders who have the opinion that the rural leadership has become more effective after amendment is much higher than the female leaders. It is also confirmed by significant value of chi-square which is 28.310.

The information pertaining to the leaders' perceptions about the impact of amendment in making the rural leadership more effective with reference to their castes tabulated in Table 5.38 chi-square value (28.248) show that the perceptions are not different in significant way among the leaders of various castes. Thus, the perceptions are independent of the caste of the leader.

The PRIs are the gateway of recruiting political leaders in mainstream politics. A study suggests that more than half of the elected representatives at all levels started their public life through PRIs.[4] Further, Dalit community has become politically more conscious of its rights and more determined to build a better future for itself and for other similarly-oppressed groups through social transformation[5] and this can happen at grassroot level. Therefore, there is an urgent need to strengthen democracy. It is believed that in addition to other dynamics, the democratic decentralization is one of the most effective instruments for enriching democratic values in the society. This means that PRIs can be a platform for the people to start their public life. In other words, the political leadership is emerging through PRIs and definitely, it will strengthen the grass democracy.

CONCLUSION

In total, the leaders found that social, educational and economic development is basic key to democratic decentralization. Further, the environment of political independence, freedom and civic society are the other conditions which can contribute in ensuring the power to the people through the ongoing process of democratic decentralization in the state.

Notes and References

1. Elhussein, Ahmed Mustafe (Jan.-March 2000). Decentralisation and Democracy in Africa—An Agenda for International Action, *IJPA*, 46(1), pp. 82-83.
2. Paoletto, Glen (2000). An Overview of Environmental Leadership presented in the Seminar on Leadership for the Local Environment, World Environment Special Event, 8-9 July, Tokyo.
3. Roy, M. Sam (1995). Emerging Panchayat Leadership and Polarisation of Political Power at Grassroot Level, *Journal of Rural Development*, 14(4), p. 355.
4. Joshi, Satyakaram (2003). Panchayat Raj Leadership in Gujarat, *IASSI Quarterly*, 21, (3 & 4), p. 84.
5. Shah, Ghanshyam (2001). Introduction: Dalit Politics in Shah, Ghanshyam (ed.), *Dalit Identity and Politics*. New Delhi: Sage Publications, p. 38.

6

Inequalities and Reservation

The rural society has been characterized by a high degree of social and economic inequalities. The inequalities are not only in terms of the use of resources rather prevailing in social, cultural, and all other aspects of life. The social and cultural inequalities are attributed to the caste system which creates a highly stratified social structure in the society.

The caste is largely endogamous groups of individuals who are invested with different social status and social meaning.[1] It is observed that, "Though there is no way by which those in a caste society can actually distinguish unfailing natural markers of difference, yet they justify caste stratification on the ground that different castes are built of different natural substances".[2] The belief based on the legacy of caste and other historical conditions of extreme inequality give rise to expectations of prejudicial treatment and hence to behaviours that tend to reproduce the inequality.[3] This belief system emphasizes and rationalizes the exploitation of the castes ranked lowest in the hierarchy. The caste system is one of many examples where, historically, social practices that created extreme inequality were attributed not to society but to nature or divinity.[4]

Besides this, in a traditional village society, the women are unequal to the men in cultural perspective. She has been serving the privileged male accepting it as her dharma. The roots of this tradition are there since several centuries. This has been continuing since past because the women are dependent on men who control social, cultural, economic and political power.

Political consciousness and participation in politics by the schedule castes and women two sections of society which are not equal to mainstream and reservation in PRIs have been made for them have traditionally been low.[5] In case of women in Haryana state it was allowed only in exceptional circumstances. It indicates that belief system in a society is responsible for creating the opportunities in social, economic and political fields. Hence, it is assumed that caste and gender of a leader have always been instrumental in shaping his/her leadership in traditional society found at village level. In other words, the leaders coming from dominant castes and scheduled castes possess different set of leadership traits. Not only this, the leadership traits of women leaders are also considered to be different from men. Therefore, an attempt has been made here to study some traits of local leadership in the above stated comparative perspective.

M.N. Srinivas states that the introduction of adult franchise and panchayat raj since independence has resulted in giving a new sense of self-respect and power to the lower castes, particularly Harijans who enjoyed reservation of seats in all elected bodies from the village panchayats to the parliament. The long-term implication of these changes is probably more important, especially in those villages where there are enough Harijans to sway the local balance of power one way or other.[6] Ashok Mehta also stated that democratic institutions with periodic elections at all levels will provide a forum for assertion of strength in large number by weaker sections.[7] It means that the local bodies have social, economic and political implications.

Similarly, a study conducted in Karnataka in 1991 concludes that apart from voting in the election most of the women did not have any experience of active politics. This was the case with 80 per cent of women of zila parishad members. For the rest, they had some political experience of varying periods, as members of the erstwhile village panchayts, taluka development boards, and two had even been MLAs. Further the study also observed that 90 per cent of the women mandal members had no prior political experience.[8] B.B. Mohanty presented the position of women leaders after amendment and found that PRIs in Maharashtra have inspired more trust in women instead men, unlike the national average as well as in many other regions.[9]

However, it is believed that in number of cases the women contested elections to retain the seat for the male members of their families and these women representatives often act as proxy for men. Now the women do not have the feeling of being the proxy of their husband rather they consider that political activity is being undertaken by the husband in close association with the wife elected to the PR office. These beliefs are tested with the help of the perceptions of sampled leaders and classifying that data on gender and caste basis.

The first proposition, put to them for their comment, was 'Social inequalities and illiteracy reduces the competence of local leadership.' The data in the shape of responses obtained from the leaders is tabulated in Table 6.1.

TABLE 6.1

Impact of social inequalities and illiteracy on the competence of local leadership

Perceptions	*Frequency*	*Valid Percent*	*Cumulative Percent*
Yes	218	68.1	68.1
No	84	26.3	94.4
Undecided	1	.3	94.7
No response	17	5.3	100.0
Total	320	100.0	

The data in Table 6.1 clearly establishes that a fair majority of leaders (68.1 per cent) affirmed the proposition presented to them. However, 26.3 per cent of them refused that social inequalities and illiteracy has any implications on the competence of rural leadership.

The responses on this proposition are classified on gender basis to find out the implication

TABLE 6.2

Classification of perceptions of impact of social inequalities and illiteracy on the competence of local leadership based on their gender

	Gender		Total
Perceptions	*Male*	*Female*	
Yes	151 70.2%	67 63.8%	218 68.1%
No	56 26.0%	28 26.7%	84 26.3%
Undecided	0 .0%	1 1.0%	1 .3%
No response	8 3.7%	9 8.6%	17 5.3%
Total	215 100.0%	105 100.0%	320 100.0%

Pearson-chi-square 5.609.

The data in Table 6.2 indicates that there is not any difference of perceptions between male and female leaders in accepting or rejecting the said proposition. No doubt there appears a difference of percentage who accepted the proposition but as chi-square value is 5.609, means the difference is insignificant one.

The responses are also classified as per the castes of the sampled leaders and tabulated in Table 6.3. The data reveals that leaders belonging to backward castes-A and scheduled castes-A possess a strong feeling that social inequalities and illiteracy reduces the competence of a local leader. The leaders belonging scheduled castes-B have relatively diluted affirmation in this regard. However, the difference of perception among the leaders of different castes is not significant as the chi-square value is 20.164.

Thus, the majority of sampled leaders affirmed the impact of social inequalities and illiteracy on the competence of leadership. It is endorsed by both male and female leaders of every caste more or less in an equal way. Thus, the inequalities

TABLE 6.3
Classification of perceptions of impact of social inequalities and illiteracy on the competence of local leadership based on their castes

Perceptions	*Castes*						*Total*
	Farming castes	*Upper castes*	*Backward castes (A)*	*Backward castes (B)*	*Scheduled castes (A)*	*Scheduled castes (B)*	
(1)	(2)	(3)	(4)	(5)	(6)	(7)	(8)
Yes	67 67.7%	27 67.5%	25 86.2%	25 67.6%	38 74.5%	36 56.3%	218 68.1%
No	28 28.3%	10 25.0%	4 13.8%	8 21.6%	9 17.6%	25 39.1%	84 26.3%
Undecided	0 .0%	0 .0%	0 .0%	0 .0%	0 .0%	1 1.6%	1 .3%
No response	4 4.0%	3 7.5%	0 .0%	4 10.8%	4 7.8%	2 3.1%	17 5.3%
Total	99 100.0%	40 100.0%	29 100.0%	37 100.0%	51 100.0%	64 100.0%	320 100.0%

Pearson chi-square 20.164.

of all kinds and illiteracy are the consummate in ensuring democratic decentralization through panchayat raj.

Another proposition of traditional leadership, i.e., the rich and resourceful dominates the working of Gram Panchayats was put to the sampled leaders. The data in Table 6.4 gives an account of information obtained during the investigation on this proposition.

TABLE 6.4

Rich and resourceful dominates the working of gram panchayats

Perceptions	*Frequency*	*Percent*	*Cumulative Percent*
Yes	121	37.8	37.8
No	189	59.1	96.9
Undecided	2	.6	97.5
No response	8	2.5	100.0
Total	320	100.0	

The data in Table 6.4 indicates that a little more than one third of the leaders (37.8 per cent) admitted the dominance of rich and resourceful in the working of gram panchayats. But, majority (59.1 per cent) denied this. Thus, the dominance of rich and resourceful is not so strong now.

The sampled leaders' perceptions on this proposition are also classified with reference to the gender and castes of the leaders and the data pertaining to these two aspects is tabulated in Tables 6.5 and 6.6 respectively.

The data in Table 6.5 and chi-square value .764 confirms that the male and female leaders do not differ in significant manner in admitting or in rejecting the dominance of rich and resourceful in the working of gram panchayats.

The data in Table 6.6 apparently reveals that the leaders belonging to scheduled castes-A and farming castes tend to favour the proposition of dominance by rich and resourceful. However, higher proportion of leaders from backward castes-B, scheduled castes-B and upper castes expressed their perceptions

TABLE 6.5

Classification of perceptions based on gender about the incidence of dominance of rich and resourceful in the working of gram panchayats

Perceptions	*Gender*		*Total*
	Male	*Female*	
Yes	79 36.7%	42 40.0%	121 37.8%
No	130 60.5%	59 56.2%	189 59.1%
Undecided	1 .5%	1 1.0%	2 .6%
No response	5 2.3%	3 2.9%	8 2.5%
Total	215 100.0%	105 100.0%	320 100.0%

Pearson chi-square .764.

against this proposition in comparison to other castes. Nevertheless the chi-square value (17.702) clearly indicates the absence of significant difference between the leaders of various castes' groups.

Third proposition put up for obtaining leaders' views in order to find out the difference of traits arising out of their belief system is that: 'the role of reserved class of leadership has sufficiently increased after the emergence of new panchayat raj'. It is in the light of observation of Shah who states that: 'the condition of Dalits at the village level continues to be vulnerable under decentralization of power. Elected representative from the Dalit community, more often than not, do not have any say in village affairs'[10]. The perceptions in this regard are presented in Table 6.7.

It is clear from the data given in Table 6.7 that a fair majority (64.1 per cent) of the sampled leaders stated that the reservation of seats in PRIs has enhanced the role of reserved classes of leaders. But, about a quarter of them did not find any difference in the role between pre-amendment and post-amendment period.

TABLE 6.6

Classification of perceptions based on castes about the incidence of dominance of rich and resourceful in the working of gram panchayats

Perceptions	*Castes*						*Total*
	Farming castes	*Upper castes*	*Backward castes (A)*	*Backward castes (B)*	*Scheduled castes (A)*	*Scheduled castes (B)*	
(1)	(2)	(3)	(4)	(5)	(6)	(7)	(8)
Yes	43 43.4%	14 35.0%	9 31.0%	11 29.7%	25 49.0%	19 29.7%	121 37.8%
No	53 53.5%	26 65.0%	17 58.6%	25 67.6%	26 51.0%	42 65.6%	189 59.1%
Undecided	0 .0%	0 .0%	1 3.4%	0 .0%	0 .0%	1 1.6%	2 .6%
No response	3 3.0%	0 .0%	2 6.9%	1 2.7%	0 .0%	2 3.1%	8 2.5%
Total	99 100.0%	40 100.0%	29 100.0%	37 100.0%	51 100.0%	64 100.0%	320 100.0%

Pearson chi-square 17.702.

TABLE 6.7

The role of reserved classes of leadership has sufficiently increased after the amendment

Perceptions	*Frequency*	*Valid Percent*	*Cumulative Percent*
Yes	205	64.1	64.1
No	81	25.3	89.4
Undecided	6	1.9	91.3
No response	28	8.8	100.0
Total	320	100.0	

The question arises who said that role has enhanced? For finding this, the data in Table 6.7 is interacted with the gender and castes of the sampled leaders.

TABLE 6.8

Classification of perceptions based on gender regarding sufficient increase in the role of reserved classes of leadership after the amendment

	Gender		*Total*
Perceptions	*Male*	*Female*	
Yes	144 67.0%	61 58.1%	205 64.1%
No	54 25.1%	27 25.7%	81 25.3%
Undecided	1 .5%	5 4.8%	6 1.9%
No response	16 7.4%	12 11.4%	28 8.8%
Total	215 100.0%	105 100.0%	320 100.0%

Pearson chi-square 9.107.

The data in Table 6.8 shows that there is significant difference of perceptions between male and female leaders in supporting the proposition that the role of reserved class of leadership has sufficiently increased after the amendment. The chi-square value 9.107 confirms the above stated conclusion.

The data in Table 6.9 is about the relationships of the perceptions of leaders on the proposition with their castes. The data in the table makes it clear that the leaders from different castes have different perceptions on this issue. The leaders belonging to upper castes and scheduled castes-A have higher proportion (75 per cent and 72.5 per cent respectively) of those who consider that there is an impact of amendment in enhancing the role of reserved class of leaders in PRIs. However, the leaders belonging farming castes and backward castes-B and backward castes-A have relatively higher proportions of those who negated the change in the role. It is also surprising to note that many leaders of these castes along with scheduled castes-B leaders did not respond to this. But, the chi-square value 19.042 indicates that the difference of perceptions on this issue is not significant one.

Thus, it is concluded that the reservation introduced by the 73rd amendment act has perceptible impact in increasing the role of reserved classes of leaders in PRIs. This is endorsed by a sizeable majority of both male and female leaders of various castes in more or less in uniform manner.

It has been assumed that the representation of scheduled castes and other poor people to the panchayati raj institutions through the mechanism of reservation will help better implementation of poverty alleviation programmes. It is observed that the poverty alleviation progammes are executed by the government itself. This has reduced the participation of panchayat and in particular the panches and sarpaches of reserved categories. It has a demoralizing impact on them, and therefore, the leaders were asked to narrate their feelings on this cultural aspect of panchayat raj.

The data given in Table 6.10 reveals that only about a quarter (26.6 per cent) leadership found a negative impact on participation of reserved class leadership when not involved in the implementation of poverty alleviation programmes. But majority of leaders (59.4 per cent) do not consider that there is any negative impact on the leadership because of governmental interventions. The reason to this state of affairs is attributed to

TABLE 6.9

Classification of perceptions based on castes regarding sufficient increase in the role of reserved classes of leadership after the amendment

Perceptions	*Castes*						*Total*
	Farming castes	*Upper castes*	*Backward castes (A)*	*Backward castes (B)*	*Scheduled castes (A)*	*Scheduled castes (B)*	
(1)	*(2)*	*(3)*	*(4)*	*(5)*	*(6)*	*(7)*	*(8)*
Yes	62 62.6%	30 75.0%	17 58.6%	18 48.6%	37 72.5%	41 64.1%	205 64.1%
No	30 30.3%	8 20.0%	8 27.6%	11 29.7%	11 21.6%	13 20.3%	81 25.3%
Undecided	0 .0%	1 2.5%	1 3.4%	1 2.7%	0 .0%	3 4.7%	6 1.9%
No response	7 7.1%	1 2.5%	3 10.3%	7 18.9%	3 5.9%	7 10.9%	28 8.8%
Total	99 100.0%	40 100.0%	29 100.0%	37 100.0%	51 100.0%	64 100.0%	320 100.0%

Pearson chi-square 19.042.

TABLE 6.10

Impact on participation of reserved class leadership when not involved in the implementation of poverty alleviation programmes

Incidence of less participation	*Frequency*	*Valid Percent*	*Cumulative Percent*
Yes	85	26.6	26.6
No	190	59.4	85.9
Undecided	14	4.4	90.3
No response	31	9.7	100.0
Total	320	100.0	

the reasonable level of involvement of panchayat and panchayat members are there in one way or the other. Some did not respond and a few of them were undecided.

The perceptions about the impact of non-involvement of reserved class leadership as per their gender are tabulated in Table 6.11.

TABLE 6.11

Classification of perceptions based on their gender about the impact of non-involvement of reserved class leadership

	Gender		*Total*
Incidence of less participation	*Male*	*Female*	
Yes	57 26.5%	28 26.7%	85 26.6%
No	138 64.2%	52 49.5%	190 59.4%
Undecided	3 1.4%	11 10.5%	14 4.4%
No response	17 7.9%	14 13.3%	31 9.7%
Total	215 100.0%	105 100.0%	320 100.0%

Pearson chi-square 17.996*.

The data in Table 6.11 indicates that there is significant difference (chi-square value 17.996) between male and female leaders in terms of rejecting the negative impact on the participation of reserved class of leadership. The proportion of female leaders who refused to accept the negative impact is lesser in comparison to male and the percentage of female leaders in the category of undecided is also higher than male leadership.

The classification of the above stated perceptions based on caste is presented in Table 6.12 and the data in the table and chi-square value 10.752 indicate that the leaders' perceptions do not differ on the above state proposition in significant sense their castes.

Thus, it is concluded that except women leaders, the perceptions of male leaders and leaders of various castes equally rejected the proposition that 'there is negative impact of non involvement of reserved class leadership on them when they are not involved in implementing poverty alleviation programmes for their community'. The indifference of perception among women may be attributed to the fact they are not involved much when decisions are being taken by the panchayat.

It is common feeling in local politics and some studies also pointed out that the reserved class of leadership has started to oppose the dominance of traditional leadership. How sampled leaders feel about it? It was asked from them and the data is presented in Table 6.13. The data in table indicates that whereas 47.2 per cent affirmed that the consciousness of opposing the traditional leadership has aroused in the reserved class of PR leadership of the state. However, a little less than them (43.1 per cent) who affirmed the proposition denied this. Others either not responded or were undecided about it.

As there is not a clear-cut trend, therefore, it is necessary that it should also be visualized in the light of gender and caste factor. The Table 6.14 and 6.15 respectively contain information in this regard.

The data in Table 6.14 and chi-square value 9.047 reveals that male leaders and female leaders differ in significant way in their feeling of opposing traditional leadership dominance in panchayat by the reserved class of leaders. The male leaders are

TABLE 6.12

Classification of perceptions based on their castes about the impact of non-involvement of reserved class leadership

Incidence of less participation	*Castes*						*Total*
	Farming castes	*Upper castes*	*Backward castes (A)*	*Backward castes (B)*	*Scheduled castes (A)*	*Scheduled castes (B)*	
(1)	(2)	(3)	(4)	(5)	(6)	(7)	(8)
Yes	27 27.3%	11 27.5%	9 31.0%	6 16.2%	12 23.5%	20 31.3%	85 26.6%
No	62 62.6%	25 62.5%	15 51.7%	22 59.5%	32 62.7%	34 53.1%	190 59.4%
Undecided	3 3.0%	2 5.0%	2 6.9%	2 5.4%	1 2.0%	4 6.3%	14 4.4%
No response	7 7.1%	2 5.0%	3 10.3%	7 18.9%	6 11.8%	6 9.4%	31 9.7%
Total	99 100.0%	40 100.0%	29 100.0%	37 100.0%	51 100.0%	64 100.0%	320 100.0%

Pearson chi-square 10.752.

TABLE 6.13

Reserved class of leadership has started to oppose traditional leadership

Incidence of opposition	*Frequency*	*Valid Percent*	*Cumulative Percent*
Yes	151	47.2	47.2
No	138	43.1	90.3
Undecided	3	.9	91.3
No response	28	8.8	100.0
Total	320	100.0	

TABLE 6.14

Classification of perceptions based on their gender of reserved class of leadership about their opposition of traditional leadership

	Gender		*Total*
Incidence of Opposition	*Male*	*Female*	
Yes	105 48.8%	46 43.8%	151 47.2%
No	95 44.2%	43 41.0%	138 43.1%
Undecided	0 .0%	3 2.9%	3 .9%
No response	15 7.0%	13 12.4%	28 8.8%
Total	215 100.0%	105 100.0%	320 100.0%

Pearson chi-square 9.047.

higher in percentage that supported the proposition and the percentage of women who did not respond is also quite higher in comparison to men. These two factors are responsible for significant difference between male and female leaders.

It is evident from the data in Table 6.15 that SC (B) and farming castes are traditional in their outlook and relatively

TABLE 6.15
Classification of perceptions based on their castes of reserved class of leadership about their opposition of traditional leadership

Incidence of opposition	*Castes*						*Total*
	Farming castes	*Upper castes*	*Backward castes (A)*	*Backward castes (B)*	*Scheduled castes (A)*	*Scheduled castes (B)*	
(1)	(2)	(3)	(4)	(5)	(6)	(7)	(8)
Yes	44 44.4%	21 52.5%	16 55.2%	20 54.1%	25 49.0%	25 39.1%	151 47.2%
No	49 49.5%	16 40.0%	11 37.9%	12 32.4%	19 37.3%	31 48.4%	138 43.1%
Undecided	0 .0%	0 .0%	0 .0%	1 2.7%	0 .0%	2 3.1%	3 .9%
No response	6 6.1%	3 7.5%	2 6.9%	4 10.8%	7 13.7%	6 9.4%	28 8.8%
Total	99 100.0%	40 100.0%	29 100.0%	37 100.0%	51 100.0%	64 100.0%	320 100.0%

Pearson chi-square 14.305.

their proportion is lesser who accept the proposition and higher in rejecting the proposition. In real sense, these are the castes, which are being replaced, because of reservation provision made there in the new panchayati raj system. However, the chi-square value (14.305) makes it clear that there are only apparent differences of perceptions between the leaders of various castes but in actual, they do not differ on the issue in significant way.

Thus the discussion concludes that the process of replacing the dominance of traditional leadership has grown as about half of them supported the proposition but this proposition is significantly supported by men and lesser by the leaders of the scheduled castes and farming castes.

The above stated proposition is interpreted in sociological perspective and stated that in traditional village society the political progress of a caste or group of castes takes place at the cost of other's dominance. It is expected that there would be a clash between a society where caste is the basic organizing principle and a Constitution which seeks to release the individual from its hold over him, what needs to be observed more carefully is that such a politics develops a new kind of anachronism which may strengthen rather than reduce a caste wars of the society.[11] It is the reality that the existing social order does not relish this special arrangement of reservation of seats for Dalit and women.[12] In other words, acquisition of political space in a community has always created a chance of conflict between the rival castes or groups. Keeping in view this fact, the sampled respondents were asked to respond on the assertion that: 'It is common thing that the reserved and non-reserved classes of local leadership are conflicting' may or may not to get hold in the gram panchayat. The data obtained during field survey is tabulated in Table 6.16.

The data in the table exhibits that a majority of the leaders (59.7 per cent) rejected the incidence of conflict between reserved and non-reserved classes of leadership. But, about one-fifth (21.6 per cent) of them reported the occurrence of conflict. It is natural and lead to conclude that there may be some conflict but it is not a common phenomenon.

The classification of responses on incidence of conflicts based on gender is presented in Table 6.17.

TABLE 6.16

Reserved and non-reserved classes of local leadership conflicts are common in gram panchayats

Incidence of conflicts	*Frequency*	*Valid Percent*	*Cumulative Percent*
Yes	69	21.6	21.6
No	191	59.7	81.3
Undecided	5	1.6	82.8
Not applicable	55	17.2	100.0
Total	320	100.0	

TABLE 6.17

Classification of responses based on their gender about the incidence of conflicts between reserved and non-reserved classes of local leadership

	Gender		*Total*
Incidence of conflicts	*Male*	*Female*	
Yes	46 21.4%	23 21.9%	69 21.6%
No	132 61.4%	59 56.2%	191 59.7%
Undecided	2 .9%	3 2.9%	5 1.6%
Not applicable	35 16.3%	20 19.0%	55 17.2%
Total	215 100.0%	105 100.0%	320 100.0%

Pearson chi-square 2.320.

The data in Table 6.17 and chi-square value (2.320) reveals that there does not present any kind of distinction between male and female leaders on this issue despite the fact that the leaders who rejected the incidence of conflicts are lesser among women in relation to male.

The data in Table 6.18 again makes one to asserts that the significant distinction of responses is not there among the

TABLE 6.18

Classification of responses based on their castes about the incidence of conflicts between reserved and non-reserved classes of local leadership

Incidence of conflicts	*Castes*						*Total*
	Farming castes	*Upper castes*	*Backward castes (A)*	*Backward castes (B)*	*Scheduled castes (A)*	*Scheduled castes (B)*	
(1)	(2)	(3)	(4)	(5)	(6)	(7)	(8)
Yes	24 24.2%	9 22.5%	7 24.1%	4 10.8%	15 29.4%	10 15.6%	69 21.6%
No	59 59.6%	25 62.5%	19 65.5%	21 56.8%	25 49.0%	42 65.6%	191 59.7%
Undecided	3 3.0%	1 2.5%	0 .0%	0 .0%	0 .0%	1 1.6%	5 1.6%
Not applicable	13 13.1%	5 12.5%	3 10.3%	12 32.4%	11 21.6%	11 17.2%	55 17.2%
Total	99 100.0%	40 100.0%	29 100.0%	37 100.0%	51 100.0%	64 100.0%	320 100.0%

Pearson chi-square 17.784.

leaders of various castes' groups (chi-square 17.784). However, it is also apparent that the scheduled castes-A and backward castes-B leaders have indifferent feelings in comparison to other castes. The proportion of the leaders in these castes who reported the incidence of conflict is relatively low (29.4 and 10.8 per cent).

Thus it is evident that these castes are either not enough empowered in numerical and political sense to send their representatives to the GP or have the attitude to live in harmony. The results are also attributed that the land owning backward castes are proportionately higher in the sample of the study as already stated. Thus it is concluded that the conflicts between reserved and non-reserved classes of leaders are not common. It is further confirmed by a direct enquiry.

Caste discrimination is another serious problem that the panchayati face. No President from scheduled castes has said that the village is free from caste discrimination.[13] Therefore, the sampled leaders were asked to give their perceptions on the proposition that 'Sarpanch belonging to a non-reserved class do not let the panches of reserved class to participate in village panchayat activities in a well mannered way'. The information obtained is tabulated in Table 6.19.

TABLE 6.19

Sarpanch of non-reserved class restricts the effective participation of panches of reserved classes in village panchayat activities

Restrictions	*Frequency*	*Valid Percent*	*Cumulative Percent*
Yes	62	19.4	19.4
No	198	61.9	81.3
Undecided	3	.9	82.2
No response	2	.6	82.8
Not applicable	55	17.2	100.0
Total	320	100.0	

The data in Table 6.19 reveals that a majority of leaders (61.9 per cent) denied any kind of restriction on reserved class of panches by the non reserved category of sarpanch. The responses are almost similar to those presented in Table 6.16. There are only 19.4 per cent of them, less than one-fourth, who found this kind of negative attitude of the sarpanch towards the panches of reserved class. Many of the sampled leaders remain undecided.

The responses on this proposition are also cross checked as per the gender and castes of the leaders. (Table 6.20 and 6.21)

TABLE 6.20

Classification of responses based on their gender on the restrictions inflicted by the sarpanch of non-reserved class on participation of panches of reserved classes in village panchayat activities

	Gender		*Total*
Restrictions	*Male*	*Female*	
Yes	37 17.2%	25 23.8%	62 19.4%
No	141 65.6%	57 54.3%	198 61.9%
Undecided	0 .0%	3 2.9%	3 .9%
No response	2 .9%	0 .0%	2 .6%
Not applicable	35 16.3%	20 19.0%	55 17.2%
Total	215 100.0%	105 100.0%	320 100.0%

Pearson chi-square 10.475*

The data in Table 6.20 and chi-square value 10.475 indicate that male and female leaders differ in their responses on the said issue in significant way. It is very surprising to note that more female leaders in comparison to male leaders pointed out the infliction of restriction on reserved class leaders. It is also evident from the data that the proportion of female leaders who rejected the incidence of restrictions is lesser than the male leaders in the sample. Therefore, the distinction between male and female appears significant one.

However, the distinction is not significant (chi-square 19.512) among leaders belonging to various castes as is clear from the Table 6.21 which indicates that the scheduled castes-A and upper castes leaders are more vocal in telling about the ill-behaviour of non-reserved class sarpanch towards reserved class of panches of the panchayat. But this is not sufficient to make distinction among various castes as significant one.

Therefore, the proposition that non-reserved class of sarpanch do not let the panches of reserved class panches to participate in village panchayat activities is not fully valid. The proposition may be changed that there may be a sarpanch in a village panchayat who may not find it proper to let the reserved class of panches to participate in village panchayat activities in a well mannered way because their participation may not suits to him or her. The members who reported ill-treatment may not be from sarpanch's group in the village rather from opposition camp in the panchayat. In reality this is not a common practice despite the fact that a sizeable proportion of scheduled castes-A leaders and female leaders sampled in this study have endorsed it.

The study of behaviour of non reserved class of leadership in PR working is not complete if the behaviour of PR officials has not taken into account. Usually allegations that the administrative officials have the tendency to dominate the elected panchayat raj in general and reserved class of leaders in particular are spellings against them. Therefore, the sampled leaders were asked to respond on the assertion that 'administrative officials also do not care much about the panches/sarpanches belonging to reserved classes'. The data is tabulated in Table 6.22.

The data in Table 6.22 reveals that 22.5 percent of leaders affirmed that administrative officials do not care much about the panches/sarpanches particularly of reserved classes. However, a majority of them (58.4 per cent) negated this kind of behaviour of administrative officials. A few of them remain undecided and a sizeable (17.2 per cent) of them did not have this kind of experience so they did not say anything on the issue.

TABLE 6.21

Classification of responses based on their castes on the restrictions inflicted by the sarpanch of non-reserved class on participation of panches of reserved classes in village panchayat activities

Perceptions	Castes						Total
	Farming castes	*Upper castes*	*Backward castes (A)*	*Backward castes (B)*	*Scheduled castes (A)*	*Scheduled castes (B)*	
(1)	(2)	(3)	(4)	(5)	(6)	(7)	(8)
Yes	20 20.2%	10 25.0%	6 20.7%	6 16.2%	12 23.5%	8 12.5%	62 19.4%
No	63 63.6%	25 62.5%	19 65.5%	19 51.4%	28 54.9%	44 68.8%	198 61.9%
Undecided	2 2.0%	0 .0%	1 3.4%	0 .0%	0 .0%	0 .0%	3 .9%
No response	1 1.0%	0 .0%	0 .0%	0 .0%	0 .0%	1 1.6%	2 .6%
Not applicable	13 13.1%	5 12.5%	3 10.3%	12 32.4%	11 21.6%	11 17.2%	55 17.2%
Total	99 100.0%	40 100.0%	29 100.0%	37 100.0%	51 100.0%	64 100.0%	320 100.0%

Pearson chi-square 19.512.

TABLE 6.22

Incidence of indifferent treatment of reserved class PR representatives by the officials

Indifferent behaviour	*Frequency*	*Valid Percent*	*Cumulative Percent*
Yes	72	22.5	22.5
No	187	58.4	80.9
Undecided	6	1.9	82.8
Not applicable	55	17.2	100.0
Total	320	100.0	

These responses (Table 6.22) are examined with the gender (Table 6.23) and castes (Table 6.24) of the leaders.

TABLE 6.23

Classification of leaders' responses on the basis of their gender about the incidence of indifferent treatment of reserved class PR representatives by the officials

	Gender		*Total*
Indifferent behaviour	*Male*	*Female*	
Yes	47 21.9%	25 23.8%	72 22.5%
No	130 60.5%	57 54.3%	187 58.4%
Undecided	3 1.4%	3 2.9%	6 1.9%
Not applcable	35 16.3%	20 19.0%	55 17.2%
Total	215 100.0%	105 100.0%	320 100.0%

Pearson chi-square 1.699.

The data in Table 6.23 and chi-square value 1.699 indicates that male and female leaders do not differ much in their perceptions about the behavioural interactions between reserved classes of leaders and administrative officials.

TABLE 6.24

Classification of leaders' responses on the basis of their castes about the incidence of indifferent treatment of reserved class PR representatives by the officials

Indifferent behaviour	*Castes*						*Total*
	Farming castes	*Upper castes*	*Backward castes (A)*	*Backward castes (B)*	*Scheduled castes (A)*	*Scheduled castes (B)*	
(1)	*(2)*	*(3)*	*(4)*	*(5)*	*(6)*	*(7)*	*(8)*
Yes	26 26.3%	8 20.0%	10 34.5%	5 13.5%	11 21.6%	12 18.8%	72 22.5%
No	58 58.6%	27 67.5%	15 51.7%	18 48.6%	29 56.9%	40 62.5%	187 58.4%
Undecided	2 2.0%	0 .0%	1 3.4%	2 5.4%	0 .0%	1 1.6%	6 1.9%
Not applcable	13 13.1%	5 12.5%	3 10.3%	12 32.4%	11 21.6%	11 17.2%	55 17.2%
Total	99 100.0%	40 100.0%	29 100.0%	37 100.0%	51 100.0%	64 100.0%	320 100.0%

Pearson chi-square 18.342.

The data in Table 6.24 indicates that the leaders who affirmed the indifferent attitude of officials towards reserved classes of leaders are relatively higher among backward castes-A leaders in proportion to the other castes' leaders. However, the chi-square value of the interactions between the sampled leaders' responses on the said issue and their castes is 18.342. It means that there is not any significant difference among the leaders' perceptions based on castes.

Thus, it is very much clear that except a few local leaders, others do not indicate the indifference of behaviour of officials towards reserved classes of leaders. Both men and women leaders belonging to all castes equally endorsed it.

The traditional leadership does not easily accept that reserved class leaders may dominate them at local panchayat level. It is empirically confirmed by asking to narrate their views on the assertion that 'the panch/sarpanch belonging to reserved class can not become a leader/s of the village, however, they may emerge as leader of their specific caste only. The responses of the sampled leaders obtained on this assertion/proposition are tabulated in Table 6.25

TABLE 6.25

Perceptions of leaders on the proposition that reserved class PR leader can not become the leader of their village

Perceptions	*Frequency*	*Valid Percent*	*Cumulative Percent*
Yes	122	38.1	38.1
No	181	56.6	94.7
Undecided	9	2.8	97.5
No response	8	2.5	100.0
Total	320	100.0	

The data in Table 6.25 testifies that although a majority (56.6 per cent) does not agree to the proposition that the panch or sarpanch of reserved class can not become the leader of the village but a large number of the leaders 122 (38.1 per cent) affirmed that this proposition is valid one.

The responses on the proposition are studied with reference to their gender and presented in Table 6.26.

TABLE 6.26

Classification of perceptions of leaders based on their gender on the proposition that reserved class PR leader can not become the leader of their village

Incidence of Opposition	*Gender*		*Total*
	Male	*Female*	
Yes	85 39.5%	37 35.2%	122 38.1%
No	127 59.1%	54 51.4%	181 56.6%
Undecided	0 .0%	9 8.6%	9 2.8%
No response	3 1.4%	5 4.8%	8 2.5%
Total	215 100.0%	105 100.0%	320 100.0%

Pearson chi-square 22.697*.

The data in Table 6.26 reveals that male and female leaders do differ in responding to the said proposition. The difference is significant one (chi-square 22.697) and women leaders are lesser than men both in accepting and rejecting the proposition. Why women's have different kind of perceptions, the enquiry could not ascertain it.

The responses on the proposition are also examined with reference to their castes and presented in Table 6.27. The data in the table explains that lesser percentage of backward castes-A and scheduled castes-A leaders have affirmed this proposition. The leaders belonging upper castes and farming castes do not indicate their willingness to find them as leaders. However, the chi-square value 22.414 indicates the absence of any significant difference among various castes' groups.

Thus, it is concluded that the proposition is not well endorsed by the sampled leadership. Therefore, it is assumed that the upper castes and farming castes do not find themselves prepared to accept reserved class of sarpanch or panch as their

TABLE 6.27

Classification of perceptions of leaders based on their castes on the proposition that reserved class PR leader can not become the leader of their village

Perceptions	*Castes*						*Total*
	Farming castes	*Upper castes*	*Backward castes (A)*	*Backward castes (B)*	*Scheduled castes (A)*	*Scheduled castes (B)*	
(1)	(2)	(3)	(4)	(5)	(6)	(7)	(8)
Yes	43 43.4%	17 42.5%	6 20.7%	14 37.8%	17 33.3%	25 39.1%	122 38.1%
No	52 52.5%	22 55.0%	20 69.0%	19 51.4%	30 58.8%	38 59.4%	181 56.6%
Undecided	2 2.0%	1 2.5%	1 3.4%	4 10.8%	1 2.0%	0 .0%	9 2.8%
No response	2 2.0%	0 .0%	2 6.9%	0 .0%	3 5.9%	1 1.6%	8 2.5%
Total	99 100.0%	40 100.0%	29 100.0%	37 100.0%	51 100.0%	64 100.0%	320 100.0%

Pearson chi-square 22.414.

village leader as stated by the upper castes and farming castes leaders.

Many leaders particularly those who are from farming castes or upper castes or other land owning castes, usually do not recognize the reserved class of panch/sarpanch as their leader. The women and Dalit leaders never behave in authoritarian manner as they have been subjugated for long. They are transparent and non-corrupt.[14] As this does not suit any one holding power in an environment of corruption and vested interests therefore it is alleged that the traditional leadership believes that reservation of office of the sarpanch has weakened the institution of gram panchayat. The respondents' views on this assertion are also obtained during field survey and tabulated in Table 6.28.

TABLE 6.28

Perceptions of leaders on the assertion that reservation of office of the sarpanch has weakened the institution of gram panchayat

Perceptions	*Frequency*	*Valid Percent*	*Cumulative Percent*
Yes	75	23.4	23.4
No	238	74.4	97.8
Undecided	4	1.3	99.1
No response	3	.9	100.0
Total	320	100.0	

The data in Table 6.28 clearly indicates that only 23.4 percent of leaders consider that the reservation of the office of sarpanch has weakened the effectiveness of gram panchayat. But a large majority of them (74.4 per cent) rejected this notion.

The perceptions tabulated in Table 6.28 are examined in the light of the gender of the leaders and presented in Table 6.29. The data in the table and chi-square value 5.201 indicates that the male and female leaders do not differ in significant manner in their perceptions on the assertion that reservation of office of the sarpanch has weakened the institution of gram panchayat.

TABLE 6.29

Classification of the perceptions based on their gender on the assertion that reservation of office of the sarpanch has weakened the institution of gram panchayat

	Gender		*Total*
Perceptions	*Male*	*Female*	
Yes	53 24.7%	22 21.0%	75 23.4%
No	160 74.4%	78 74.3%	238 74.4%
Undecided	1 .5%	3 2.9%	4 1.3%
No response	1 .5%	2 1.9%	3 .9%
Total	215 100.0%	105 100.0%	320 100.0%

Pearson chi-square 5.201.

Similarly, the perceptions tabulated in Table 6.28 are also studied with reference to the castes of the leaders and presented in Table 6.30. The data in the table indicates that relatively higher proportion of upper castes and farming castes' leaders affirmed the assertion that the reservation of office of sarpanch has weakened the institution of gram panchayat. According to them the sarpanch from reserved classes is not effective to discharge the responsibilities of the office. However, the scheduled castes and backward castes leaders rejected the assertion. It means that reserved classes of leaders assert their capability and traditional caste leaders opposed to get them their share of power in local political system. It is confirmed by the chi-square value 37.742 which indicate a clear-cut significant difference among the leaders of various castes' groups on this issue. Thus, a silent tug of war, an inevitable feature of democratic development is taking place in rural traditional society.

The panchayat leaders were also enquired to state, why the scheduled castes people vote for other castes' candidate even when their own caste's candidate is contesting for the same

TABLE 6.30

Classification of the perceptions based on their castes on the assertion that reservation of office of the sarpanch has weakened the institution of gram panchayat

Perceptions	*Castes*						*Total*
	Farming castes	*Upper castes*	*Backward castes (A)*	*Backward castes (B)*	*Scheduled castes (A)*	*Scheduled castes (B)*	
(1)	(2)	(3)	(4)	(5)	(6)	(7)	(8)
Yes	37 37.4%	14 35.0%	3 10.3%	7 18.9%	10 19.6%	4 6.3%	75 23.4%
No	60 60.6%	26 65.0%	24 82.8%	28 75.7%	40 78.4%	60 93.8%	238 74.4%
Undecided	2 2.0%	0 .0%	1 3.4%	1 2.7%	0 .0%	0 .0%	4 1.3%
No response	0 .0%	0 .0%	1 3.4%	1 2.7%	1 2.0%	0 .0%	3 .9%
Total	99 100.0%	40 100.0%	29 100.0%	37 100.0%	51 100.0%	64 100.0%	320 100.0%

Pearson chi-square 37.742.

office of the panchayat? The empirical information obtained from the sampled leaders is presented in Table 6.31.

TABLE 6.31

Scheduled castes people voting for other castes' candidate instead of their own caste's candidate

Perceptions	*Frequency*	*Valid Percent*	*Cumulative Percent*
No response	3	.9	.9
Don't know	50	15.6	16.6
Not so	78	24.4	40.9
Don't have good relations	31	9.7	50.6
Get impressed from others	2	.6	51.3
Economically not enough sound	8	2.5	53.8
Due to selfishness	8	2.5	56.3
Under pressure	8	2.5	58.8
Upper caste pressure	23	7.2	65.9
Unreserved category of leaders are more effective	11	3.4	69.4
Lack self-confidence	5	1.6	70.9
Not happy with their caste	1	.3	71.3
Depend on others	11	3.4	74.7
SC people are helpless people	14	4.4	79.1
Upper caste help the SC	16	5.0	84.1
Economic dependence on upper castes	22	6.9	90.9
Due to reputation	20	6.3	97.2
Generosity of upper castes	2	.6	97.8
Mutual relationships	7	2.2	100.0
Total	320	100.0	

The data in Table 6.31 indicates that the largest group of leaders (24.4 per cent) refused that the scheduled castes people are not doing so. They are followed by 15.6 per cent who said that they do not know about it. In other words they are not aware about the fact that the scheduled castes are voting for

TABLE 6.32

Responses of the sampled leaders based on castes regarding scheduled castes people voting for other castes' candidate instead of their own caste's candidate

Perceptions	*Castes*						*Total*
	Farming castes	*Upper castes*	*Backward castes (A)*	*Backward castes (B)*	*Scheduled castes (A)*	*Scheduled castes (B)*	
(1)	(2)	(3)	(4)	(5)	(6)	(7)	(8)
No response	1 1.0%	0 .0%	1 3.4%	0 .0%	0 .0%	1 1.6%	3 .9%
Don't know	21 21.2%	7 17.5%	10 34.5%	4 10.8%	4 7.8%	4 6.3%	50 15.6%
Not so	11 11.1%	4 10.0%	7 24.1%	10 27.0%	22 43.1%	24 37.5%	78 24.4%
Don't have good relations	7 7.1%	6 15.0%	1 3.4%	5 13.5%	7 13.7%	5 7.8%	31 9.7%
Get impressed from others	0 .0%	0 .0%	0 .0%	0 .0%	1 2.0%	1 1.6%	2 .6%
Economically not enough sound	2 2.0%	2 5.0%	2 6.9%	0 .0%	2 3.9%	0 .0%	8 2.5%
Due to selfishness	3 3.0%	2 5.0%	1 3.4%	0 .0%	2 3.9%	0 .0%	8 2.5%
Under pressure	3 3.0%	0 .0%	1 3.4%	3 8.1%	0 .0%	1 1.6%	8 2.5%

(Contd.)

Table 6.33 (Contd.)

(1)	(2)	(3)	(4)	(5)	(6)	(7)	(8)
Upper caste pressure	10	2	1	1	4	5	23
	10.1%	5.0%	3.4%	2.7%	7.8%	7.8%	7.2%
Unreserved category of	4	3	0	1	0	3	11
leaders are more effective	4.0%	7.5%	.0%	2.7%	.0%	4.7%	3.4%
Lack self-confidence	0	3	0	0	0	2	5
	.0%	7.5%	.0%	.0%	.0%	3.1%	1.6%
Not happy with their caste	1	0	0	0	0	0	1
	1.0%	.0%	.0%	.0%	.0%	.0%	.3%
Depend on others	2	0	1	2	2	4	11
	2.0%	.0%	3.4%	5.4%	3.9%	6.3%	3.4%
SC people are	8	0	1	0	2	3	14
helpless people	8.1%	.0%	3.4%	.0%	3.9%	4.7%	4.4%
Upper caste help the SC	9	2	0	0	2	3	16
	9.1%	5.0%	.0%	.0%	3.9%	4.7%	5.0%
Economic dependence	11	5	1	1	2	2	22
on upper castes	11.1%	12.5%	3.4%	2.7%	3.9%	3.1%	6.9%
Due to reputation	3	3	2	8	1	3	20
	3.0%	7.5%	6.9%	21.6%	2.0%	4.7%	6.3%
Generiosity of	1	0	0	1	0	0	2
upper castes	1.0%	.0%	.0%	2.7%	.0%	.0%	.6%
Mutual relationships	2	1	0	1	0	3	7
	2.0%	2.5%	.0%	2.7%	.0%	4.7%	2.2%
Total	99	40	29	37	51	64	320
	100.0%	100.0%	100.0%	100.0%	100.0%	100.0%	100.0%

other castes' candidate instead of their own caste candidate. Thus 40 per cent simply refused that the scheduled castes vote for their own caste candidate. Some of them may not be doing so and this kind of behaviour is because of many reasons listed in the Table 6.31 above. However, the economic dependence and pressure of upper caste is more significant one.

The majority of leaders who denied that they are voting for other castes' candidates are from scheduled castes itself as is evident from the data in Table 6.32. Moreover, the reservation and ward system clearly encouraging the caste-based voting behaviour in the panchayat's election of the state.

Notes and References

1. See Hoff, Karla and Pandey, Priyanka Belief System and Durable Inequalities : An Experimental of Indian Caste, World Bank, Pennsylvania State University, p. 3.
2. Gupta, Dipankar (2000). *Interrogating Caste: Understanding Hierarchy and Difference in Indian Society*. New Delhi: Penguin Books, p. 19.
3. See Hoff, Karla and Pandey, Priyanka, *op. cit.*
4. Sunstein, Cass R. (1995). Gender, Caste and Law in Nussbaum, Martha and Glover, Jonathan (eds), *Women, Culture and Development*, Oxford: Clarendon Press, pp. 332-59.
5. See Sudha, Pai (2001). From Harijans to Dalits: Identity Formation, Political Consciousness and Electoral Mobilsation of the Scheduled Castes in Uttar Pradesh in Shah, Ghanshyam (2001). Dalit Identity and Politics, New Delhi: Sage, pp. 258-59.
6. Srinivas, M.N. (1962). Caste in Modern India and Other Essays, Bombay: Asia Publishing House.
7. See, Report of the Committee on Panchayat Raj Institutions (Govrnment of India, (August 1978), Ministry of Agriculture and Irrigation, Department of Rural Development, New Delhi.
8. Chandersekhar, B.K. and Inbanathan, Anand (1991). Profile and Participation of Women Zila Parishad and Mandal Panchayat Members: The Case of Karnatka, *Journal of Rural Development*, 10(5), p. 581.
9. Mohanty, B.B. (2003). Panchayat Raj in Maharashtra and Orissa: An Overview, *IASSI Quarterly*, 21, (3&4)
10. Shah, Ghanshyam (2001). Introduction: Dalit Politics in Shah, Ghanshyam (ed.). Dalit Identity and Politics. New Delhi: Sage Publications, p. 37.
11. Dasgupta, Susmita (2004). The Politics of Mobilisation of the Backward Classes, Malaise, Diagnosis and Treatment in Bhosale, B.V. (ed.), Mobilisation of Backward Communities in India, New Delhi, Deep & Deep Publications (P) Ltd., pp. 74-75.

12. Palanithurai, G. (2005). Process and Performance of Gram Paṇchayat Women and Dalit Presidents, New Delhi: Concept Publishing Company, p. 362.
13. Palanithurai, G. (2005), *op. cit.*, p. 363.
14. *Ibid., op. cit.*, p. 364.

Gender Perspective

Traditional leaders based on status no longer enjoy command in village in society. The reservation mechanism has ensured berths in panchayati raj for those who never thought of it. The women are the real beneficiaries of reservation in this regard. They (women) are about half of the population but constitutes one third of the total local leadership. Incidentally, the women leaders in the present study also comprise of 32.8 percent of the total sampled rural local leaders. Tina Mathur observes that the reservation has insured women's access to the political process, the socio-cultural factors, however, constraining their effective presence and influence in the local institutions.[1] She emphasized that the reservation has created political space for women.[2] Therefore, it is believed that the reservation has helped the women to learn some what about the democratic and parliamentary political system of the society. As a result, they have started to assert their rights and their presence recognized in village politics. But the experience of reservation of seats for women on local bodies in Karnataka state has shown that there remains much to be done to make participation of women more effective.[3]

The participation of women in elections both as voters and candidates has been found to be low by various studies conducted on women empowerment. These studies have noticed that women are not independent voters; a majority of them are illiterate and make their choice on the basis of suggestions from male members of the family such as husbands and sons; they lack information and political awareness; and they are not politically conscious.[4]

Gender bias is one of the most glaring 'democracy deficits' in most democracies.[5] This is indicative of gendered conditions for political participation, which are 'intrinsic to politics'.[6] The women's subordinate position is seen as being rooted in class, gender systems and symbolic cultural practices, which for the most part, consign women to domesticity. In keeping the private out of the public sphere, women are relegated to second-class citizenship, hence their exclusion from effective participation in democratic institutions.[7] Another limitation on women's presence in democratic institutions is the gendered construction of political authority; authority has largely been associated as a male preserve. Given the multiple factors that make for women's inequality in political life, decentralization and positive discrimination is a step forward in addressing the issue.

The position of women in panchayati raj in Haryana state before 73rd amendment is far from satisfactory. They were elected or co-opted in panchayati raj only in exceptional circumstances. The amendment created a sizeable political space in PRIs for them. It appears that rural women particularly who are poor and illiterate were not socially and culturally prepared to contest election of these institutions in the state. They did not have social and economic independence of any kind to participate in village politics. Therefore, the men come forward and projected their wives as candidates for the office of panches/sarpanch on the seats reserved for women in the panchayat. Probably, the practice still continues but studies pointed out that the reservation has its own impact.

Therefore the belief that reservation has helped the political and social empowerment of the women leadership in Haryana state needs empirical validation. The empirical data for this purpose in the present study is collected through a set of propositions/assertions put to the sampled leaders. The information so obtained is discussed and inferences are drawn to testify the belief about the women leadership. First of all, the proposition that: 'No doubt the women are not real representative but their election in panchayat has essentially bringing a social change; was put to the sampled leaders for their comments. The data in this regard is presented in Table 7.1 given below.

TABLE 7.1

Women are not real representatives but essentially bringing a social change

	Frequency	*Valid Percent*	*Cumulative Percent*
Yes	264	82.5	82.5
No	48	15.0	97.5
Undecided	8	2.5	100.0
Total	320	100.0	

The data in Table 7.1 clearly shows that an overwhelming majority (82.5 percent) agreed to the proposition that it is true that women are not real representatives but their election in panchayat has essentially bringing a social change in the rural society. However, 15 percent of the total sampled respondents disagreed to this fact.

The data in Table 7.2 reveals the classification of leaders' perceptions on gender basis on the proposition stated above. It is evident the data and chi-square value .307 that there is not any significant difference of perception between male and female leaders. In other words, out of total 48 leaders who disagreed to the proposition, 33 are male and 15 are females, i.e. almost in the proportion in which they are present in the sample.

Similarly the information in Table 7.3 indicates that the leaders who denied the proposition are distributed in all caste groups and their proportion is relatively higher (more than the average) among backward castes-B, scheduled castes-A and backward castes-A. The reason to this may be attributed to the

TABLE 7.2

Classification of sampled leaders perceptions based on their gender on the proposition that women are not real representatives but essentially they are bringing a social change

Perceptions	*Gender*		*Total*
	Male	*Female*	
Yes	176 81.9%	88 83.8%	264 82.5%
No	33 15.3%	15 14.3%	48 15.0%
Undecided	6 2.8%	2 1.9%	8 2.5%
Total	215 100.0%	105 100.0%	320 100.0%

Pearson chi-square .307.

social backwardness of these castes. However, the difference of perceptions is not significant among the sampled leaders of various castes as chi-square value is 12.831.

Thus, most of the sampled leaders (82.5 per cent) including men and women and across all castes agree that no doubt the women are not real representatives but their election in panchayats has essentially bringing a social change. Thus, the process of social development has become much vigorous because of women participation in panchayats. It is expected that more meaningful participation of women may help in bringing desired transformation in the rural society in the time yet to come.

Women's inequality in the political sphere has been explained differently in various studies. therefore women particularly elected for the office of sarpanch or as member of panchayat samities are considered as much empowered as panchayati raj leaders particularly in comparison to women panch of a gram panchayat. it is being said that they (women sarpanch and women PS member) consider themselves as representatives of their voters, is it true? this question lead to put up a proposition that women elected as sarpanch or

TABLE 7.3

Classification of sampled leaders perceptions based on their castes on the proposition that women are not real representatives but essentially they are bringing a social change

Perceptions	*Castes*						*Total*
	Farming castes	*Upper castes*	*Backward castes (A)*	*Backward castes (B)*	*Scheduled castes (A)*	*Scheduled castes (B)*	
(1)	(2)	(3)	(4)	(5)	(6)	(7)	(8)
Yes	84 84.8%	37 92.5%	23 79.3%	27 73.0%	37 72.5%	56 87.5%	264 82.5%
No	14 14.1%	3 7.5%	5 17.2%	9 24.3%	11 21.6%	6 9.4%	48 15.0%
Undecided	1 1.0%	0 .0%	1 3.4%	1 2.7%	3 5.9%	2 3.1%	8 2.5%
Total	99 100.0%	40 100.0%	29 100.0%	37 100.0%	51 100.0%	64 100.0%	320 100.0%

Pearson chi-square 12.831.

member panchayat samiti consider themselves as representatives of their voters.

TABLE 7.4
Women elected as sarpanch or PS member are real representatives of their voters

Real representatives	*Frequency*	*Valid Percent*	*Cumulative Percent*
Yes	172	53.8	53.8
No	123	38.4	92.2
Undecided	25	7.8	100.0
Total	320	100.0	

The data in Table 7.4 indicates that a majority of the leaders (53.8) consider that the women leaders elected as sarpanch or member panchayat samiti consider themselves as representatives of their voter. However, there is a sizeable percentage (38.4 percent) of the leaders who disagreed to the said proposition. Above 8 percent of the leaders were undecided when asked to respond.

The responses on the above stated proposition are crossed with their gender, castes and positions and information is presented in Tables 7.5, 7.6 and 7.7.

The data in Table 7.5 indicates a significant distinction of perception on the proposition between male and female leaders (chi-square 22.785). It is evident that 72.4 percent of women consider that they (women sarpanch/member PS) are the representative of their voters but the percentage of men who endorsed women as representative of their voters is 44.7. It is also important to note that the percentage of men who disagreed to the proposition is quite higher in comparison to women percentage. Thus the men are not ready to accept women as PR leader but they wish to be leader at least at the PR level mentioned in the proposition.

The data in Table 7.6 indicates the difference of perceptions among the leaders from various castes. This difference is more apparent in case of leaders' negative perceptions or among those who rejected this proposition. As for example 54.1 percent

TABLE 7.5

Classification of leaders' perceptions based on gender on the proposition that women elected as sarpanch or PS member are real representatives of their voters

Real representatives	*Gender*		*Total*
	Male	*Female*	
Yes	96 44.7%	76 72.4%	172 53.8%
No	101 47.0%	22 21.0%	123 38.4%
Undecided	18 8.4%	7 6.7%	25 7.8%
Total	215 100.0%	105 100.0%	320 100.0%

Pearson chi-square 22.785*.

of backward castes-B and 41.2 percent of scheduled castes-A and 40 percent of upper caste do not favour the proposition (average proposition of leaders, who do not favour the proposition is 38.4 percent). However the chi-square value 10.635 confirms the absence of significant difference of perceptions on this issue.

The data in Table 7.7 indicates clear distinction of perceptions between gram panchayat leaders including sarpanches and PS leaders. The chi-square value 26.605 confirms this. The data reveals that much more PS leaders consider the sarpanch and PS leaders as representatives of their voters in comparison to gram panchayats leaders.

Thus, the proposition that women who are sarpanches/ members PS are considered representatives of their voters is accepted by 53.8 percent of the sampled leaders. Further, more women representatives in comparison to men recognize themselves as leaders of their voters. The male leaders in general and the leaders belonging to backward castes-B, scheduled caste-A and upper castes leaders' views (although not in significant manner) are not much supportive to the proposition. In other words, the women elected as sarpanch or

TABLE 7.6

Classification of leaders' perceptions based on castes on the proposition that women elected as sarpanch or PS member are real representatives of their voters

Real representatives	*Castes*						*Total*
	Farming castes	*Upper castes*	*Backward castes (A)*	*Backward castes (B)*	*Scheduled castes (A)*	*Scheduled castes (B)*	
(1)	*(2)*	*(3)*	*(4)*	*(5)*	*(6)*	*(7)*	*(8)*
Yes	54 54.5%	22 55.0%	19 65.5%	15 40.5%	25 49.0%	37 57.8%	172 53.8%
No	39 39.4%	16 40.0%	6 20.7%	20 54.1%	21 41.2%	21 32.8%	123 38.4%
Undecided	6 6.1%	2 5.0%	4 13.8%	2 5.4%	5 9.8%	6 9.4%	25 7.8%
Total	99 100.0%	40 100.0%	29 100.0%	37 100.0%	51 100.0%	64 100.0%	320 100.0%

Pearson chi-square 10.635.

TABLE 7.7

Classification of leaders' perceptions based on positions on the proposition that women elected as sarpanch or PS member are real representatives of their voters

Perceptions	Positions								Total
	PS leaders before 73rd amendment	*PS leaders after 73rd amendment (1st election)*	*PS leaders after 73rd amendment (2nd election)*	*PS leaders after 73rd amendment (3rd election)*	*GP leaders before 73rd amendment*	*GP leaders after 73rd amendment (1st election)*	*GP leaders after 73rd amendment (2nd election)*	*GP leaders after 73rd amendment (3rd election)*	
(1)	(2)	(3)	(4)	(5)	(6)	(7)	(8)	(9)	(10)
Yes	2 50.0%	15 50.0%	46 73.0%	18 60.0%	12 44.4%	19 38.8%	36 50.7%	24 52.2%	172 53.8%
No	2 50.0%	15 50.0%	16 25.4%	10 33.3%	12 44.4%	25 51.0%	29 40.8%	14 30.4%	123 38.4%
Undecided	0 .0%	0 .0%	1 1.6%	2 6.7%	3 11.1%	5 10.2%	6 8.5%	8 17.4%	25 7.8%
Total	4 100.0%	30 100.0%	63 100.0%	30 100.0%	27 100.0%	49 100.0%	71 100.0%	46 100.0%	320 100.0%

Pearson chi-square 26.605*.

members PS considers themselves as representative of their voters is partially valid and extent of validation is relatively lower among male and gram panchayat leaders.

The above stated proposition pertains to the women sarpanch and PS members and not to the panches of gram panchayats. Therefore, another proposition, relating to the position of women panches, that the women panches can provide leadership to the women of their village was put before the sampled leadership and data in this regard is presented in Table 7.8.

TABLE 7.8

Perceptions of the sampled leadership on the proposition that the women panches can provide leadership to the women of their village

Perceptions	*Frequency*	*Valid Percent*	*Cumulative Percent*
Yes	117	36.6	36.6
No	190	59.4	95.9
Undecided	13	4.1	100.0
Total	320	100.0	

The data in Table 7.8 clearly indicates that only 36.6 per cent of leaders expressed their affirmation to the said proposition. However, a majority (59.4 per cent) of them declined to agree with this kind of optimism about women leadership at village panchayat level. About four percent of the leaders did not respond or remain undecided.

The perceptions tabulated in Table 7.8 are cross-examined with the gender and castes of the sampled leaders in Tables 7.9 and 7.10 respectively.

It is very motivating to note from the data in Table 7.9 that women leaders are confident that women panches at village panchayat level can lead their sisters in the village. It is evident from the proportion of women who favoured the proposition and quite higher in comparison to male leaders of the sample. The chi-square value is also highly significant (29.004) which

TABLE 7.9

Classification of perceptions based on gender of the leadership on the proposition that the women panches can provide leadership to the women of their village

Perceptions	*Gender*		*Total*
	Male	*Female*	
Yes	57 26.5%	60 57.1%	117 36.6%
No	149 69.3%	41 39.0%	190 59.4%
Undecided	9 4.2%	4 3.8%	13 4.1%
Total	215 100.0%	105 100.0%	320 100.0%

Pearson chi-square 29.004*.

means that male and female leaders significantly differ in their perceptions from each other. Thus, the men do not find the women capable to lead the society may be because of sociological and cultural factors.

The data in Table 7.10 shows the difference of perceptions of the leaders belonging to different castes. The proportion of leaders who considers that women can lead the other women at village level is lower among backward castes and scheduled castes. However, the difference of perceptions is not significant among the leaders of various castes' groups as chi-square value is 17.595.

Thus, there is only a beginning and about third of the sampled leaders accepted that elected women leaders have potentiality to lead rural women folk. This proposition is favoured more by women in comparison to men. Thus, the proposition that elected women leaders may be able to lead the rural women folk is valid up to some extent only.

The women in villages are socially and economically very much dependent on their family. In other words, independent existence of women in rural society of the state is unthinkable. She (woman) is in real sense indivisible part of the family.

TABLE 7.10

Classification of perceptions based on castes of the leadership on the proposition that the women panches can provide leadership to the women of their village

Perceptions	Castes						Total
	Farming castes	*Upper castes*	*Backward castes (A)*	*Backward castes (B)*	*Scheduled castes (A)*	*Scheduled castes (B)*	
(1)	*(2)*	*(3)*	*(4)*	*(5)*	*(6)*	*(7)*	*(8)*
Yes	38 38.4%	19 47.5%	8 27.6%	12 32.4%	17 33.3%	23 35.9%	117 36.6%
No	60 60.6%	21 52.5%	18 62.1%	24 64.9%	28 54.9%	39 60.9%	190 59.4%
Undecided	1 1.0%	0 .0%	3 10.3%	1 2.7%	6 11.8%	2 3.1%	13 4.1%
Total	99 100.0%	40 100.0%	29 100.0%	37 100.0%	51 100.0%	64 100.0%	320 100.0%

Pearson chi-square 17.595.

Therefore, their present status is because of their family or their husband who is head of the family and owner of all kinds of social, economic and political resources of the family. Naturally, the credit to be elected in PRIs is assigned to the family or the husband as the case may be. This was probed and information from all sampled leaders on the assertion that the women do not consider them as real representatives. They give credit to their family or husband for their election in panchayats.

TABLE 7.11

Perceptions of leaders on the assertion that credit for election of women in panchayats goes to their family or husband

Perceptions	*Frequency*	*Valid Percent*	*Cumulative Percent*
Yes	267	83.4	83.4
No	51	15.9	99.4
Undecided	2	.6	100.0
Total	320	100.0	

The data in Table 7.11 indicates that an overwhelming majority of 83.4 percent endorsed the assertion that credit for election of women in panchayats goes to their family or husband. It is attributed to the fact that the women do not have any kind of independence which separates her identity from the family or husband. Moreover, it is also not desirable in panchayat politics. But a few of them (15.9 per cent) said that the role of family is not as much as it should be, therefore, they did not give credit to their family or husband.

The perceptions of sampled leaders regarding the credit for successful election of women in panchayats are examined with their gender and castes.

The data in Table 7.12 reveals that male leaders' proportion is higher than female leaders in supporting the proposition that women do not consider themselves as local leader in real sense and they give credit of their elections to their family/husband. The chi-square value 16.647 confirms the significant difference

TABLE 7.12

Classification of perceptions of leaders based on their gender on the assertion that credit for election of women in panchayats goes to their family or husband

Perceptions	*Gender*		*Total*
	Male	*Female*	
Yes	191 88.8%	76 72.4%	267 83.4%
No	22 10.2%	29 27.6%	51 15.9%
Undecided	2 .9%	0 .0%	2 .6%
Total	215 100.0%	105 100.0%	320 100.0%

Pearson chi-square 16.647*.

between male and female groups of leaders on the said assertion relating to the women leadership in panchayati raj.

However, the data in Table 7.13 reveals different results (when classified on castes basis). It is evident from the data that the leaders belonging to backward castes-A are indifferent and did not support the assertion that credit of successful election of women candidate in panchayati raj is attributed to the family or husband. The chi-square value 12.468 underlines the fact that the leaders from various castes groups do not differ significantly in their perceptions on the said assertion.

Thus, it is clear that the women do not consider themselves as leader of the village or their ward. Rather, they attribute the credit for their election in panchayat to their family/husband. It is equally supported by all castes leaders and more strongly by male leaders in comparison to female leaders. The reason, in rural politics the family is indivisible unit and claim of individuality separate from family means non-utilization of social, economic and political resources which are essentially required to be successful in panchayati raj election.

The election of gram panchayat has become a family affair in most of the cases if not all. The candidate may be the male member or female member of the family. Thus the family is a

TABLE 7.13

Classification of perceptions of leaders based on their castes on the assertion that credit for election of women in panchayats goes to their family or husband

Perceptions	Castes						Total
	Farming castes	Upper castes	Backward castes (A)	Backward castes (B)	Scheduled castes (A)	Scheduled castes (B)	
(1)	(2)	(3)	(4)	(5)	(6)	(7)	(8)
Yes	84 84.8%	35 87.5%	20 69.0%	30 81.1%	44 86.3%	54 84.4%	267 83.4%
No	15 15.2%	4 10.0%	9 31.0%	6 16.2%	7 13.7%	10 15.6%	51 15.9%
Undecided	0 .0%	1 2.5%	0 .0%	1 2.7%	0 .0%	0 .0%	2 .6%
Total	99 100.0%	40 100.0%	29 100.0%	37 100.0%	51 100.0%	64 100.0%	320 100.0%

Pearson chi-square 12.468.

political unit in gram panchayat election and not an individual in practical sense. Moreover, the women have come forward to contest panchayat's election to retain the family position in village politics when the ward or office of sarpanch is reserved for women candidate. In other words the reservation of seats in panchayats has made them to serve as *ad hoc* arrangement for their husband or family. The silent authorization given to male member of the family to sit in meetings of the gram panchayats has strengthened this practice. Now the village people do not differentiate between male and female member contesting election or who is formally contesting election of the panchayat? They (villagers) take it as it is the male member of the family who is the real contestant in the election.

In the light of above stated facts the sampled leaders were asked to express their response on the assertion that women consider themselves as an *ad hoc* arrangement for their family in village politics. The data in Table 7.14 gives an account of those responses.

TABLE 7.14

Responses of the sampled leaders on the assertion that women consider themselves as an *ad hoc* arrangement for their family in village politics

Responses	*Frequency*	*Valid Percent*	*Cumulative Percent*
Yes	171	53.4	53.4
No	133	41.6	95.0
Undecided	16	5.0	100.0
Total	320	100.0	

The data in Table 7.14 illustrates that the responses of the leaders are almost equally divided as 53.4 per cent agreed and 45.6 per cent disagreed to the assertion that women consider themselves as an ad hoc arrangement for their family in village politics. The remaining 5 per cent could not decide what to say?

The responses on the assertion that women consider themselves as *ad hoc* arrangement for their family are cross examined with their gender and castes and pertinent information is tabulated in Tables 7.15 and 7.16.

TABLE 7.15

Classification of responses of the leaders based on their gender on the assertion that women consider themselves as an *ad hoc* arrangement for their family in village politics

	Gender		*Total*
Responses	*Male*	*Female*	
Yes	120 55.8%	51 48.6%	171 53.4%
No	81 37.7%	52 49.5%	133 41.6%
Undecided	14 6.5%	2 1.9%	16 5.0%
Total	215 100.0%	105 100.0%	320 100.0%

Pearson chi-square 6.070*.

The data in Table 7.15 and chi-square value 6.070 indicates a significant difference between male and female leaders in their perception on the assertion that women consider themselves as an *ad hoc* arrangement for their family in village politics. It is evident that women constitute lesser proportion (48.6 percent) of leaders in relation to men (55.8 percent) in supporting the assertion.

It is also evident from the data that the percentage of women who do not consider themselves as *ad hoc* arrangement is higher than those who consider so. The women who do not consider themselves as *ad hoc* nominee of the family are from those families whose family members had not contested any panchayat election before them. It indicates that they are not an *ad hoc* arrangement for the family as they (women) are the first person from their families to contest panchayat election and in this way the assertion is partially correct.

The data in Table 7.16 shows that the responses of the leaders of various castes differ from each other but up to some

TABLE 7.16

Classification of responses of the leaders based on their castes on the assertion that women consider themselves as an *ad hoc* arrangement for their family in village politics

Responses	*Castes*						*Total*
	Farming castes	*Upper castes*	*Backward castes (A)*	*Backward castes (B)*	*Scheduled castes (A)*	*Scheduled castes (B)*	
(1)	*(2)*	*(3)*	*(4)*	*(5)*	*(6)*	*(7)*	*(8)*
Yes	49 49.5%	20 50.0%	17 58.6%	24 64.9%	27 52.9%	34 53.1%	171 53.4%
No	46 46.5%	18 45.0%	10 34.5%	12 32.4%	18 35.3%	29 45.3%	133 41.6%
Undecided	4 4.0%	2 5.0%	2 6.9%	1 2.7%	6 11.8%	1 1.6%	16 5.0%
Total	99 100.0%	40 100.0%	29 100.0%	37 100.0%	51 100.0%	64 100.0%	320 100.0%

Pearson chi-square 10.868.

extent only. The backward castes leaders have higher percentage (than the average of the total sample) of leaders who approved the assertion that women consider themselves as an *ad hoc* arrangement of their family in village politics. The data also suggests that the leaders belonging to farming castes and upper castes are lesser motivated to support this proposition. The chi-square value (10.868) also denotes the absence of significant difference in leaders' responses based on castes.

Thus, the assertion that women consider themselves as an *ad hoc* arrangement for their family in village politics is partially correct. The perception on the said assertion indicates that it is significantly more favoured by men in relation to women. The women who do not consider themselves as *ad hoc* nominee of the family are from those families whose family members had not contested any panchayat election before them. This assertion is more or less equally valid for the leaders of various castes groups.

The present study do not approve that the women are *ad hoc* arrangement for their families. Therefore the proposition that 'the women cannot consider themselves as real representative at GP level' needs empirical clarification. The sampled leaders' perceptions in this regard are presented in Table 7.17.

TABLE 7.17

Perceptions of the sampled leaders on the proposition that the women cannot consider themselves as real representative at GP level

Perceptions	*Frequency*	*Valid Percent*	*Cumulative Percent*
Yes	160	50.0	50.0
No	146	45.6	95.6
Undecided	14	4.4	100.0
Total	320	100.0	

The data in Table 7.17 reveals that 50 percent of the sampled leaders have approved the proposition that the women cannot consider themselves as real representative at GP level. However, almost about another half (45.6 percent) did not agree to this proposition. A few of them (4.4 percent) remain undecided. Thus, like earlier about half of leaders consider that the belief that women cannot be real representative at GP level is not correct.

The perceptions of leaders on the proposition that the women cannot consider themselves as real representative at GP level are classified based on their gender and castes and presented in Tables 7.18 and 7.19.

TABLE 7.18

Classification of perceptions of the leaders based on their gender on the proposition that the women cannot consider themselves as real representative at GP level

	Gender		*Total*
Perceptions	*Male*	*Female*	
Yes	119 55.3%	41 39.0%	160 50.0%
No	87 40.5%	59 56.2%	146 45.6%
Undecided	9 4.2%	5 4.8%	14 4.4%
Total	215 100.0%	105 100.0%	320 100.0%

Pearson chi-square 7.626*.

The data in Table 7.18 clearly indicates that the men and women leaders are well apart (with male being higher in their percentage) in their perceptions on the proposition that the women cannot consider themselves as real representative at GP level. The chi-square value 7.626 confirms the significant difference of perceptions between male and female leaders of the study.

The data in Table 7.19 shows that scheduled castes-B and upper castes leaders' proportion supporting the proposition is relatively higher (59.4 percent and 52.5 percent respectively and

TABLE 7.19

Classification of perceptions of the leaders based on their castes on the proposition that the women cannot consider themselves as real representative at GP level

Perceptions	*Castes*						*Total*
	Farming castes	*Upper castes*	*Backward castes (A)*	*Backward castes (B)*	*Scheduled castes (A)*	*Scheduled castes (B)*	
(1)	*(2)*	*(3)*	*(4)*	*(5)*	*(6)*	*(7)*	*(8)*
Yes	49 49.5%	21 52.5%	12 41.4%	19 51.4%	21 41.2%	38 59.4%	160 50.0%
No	47 47.5%	19 47.5%	15 51.7%	15 40.5%	26 51.0%	24 37.5%	146 45.6%
Undecided	3 3.0%	0 .0%	2 6.9%	3 8.1%	4 7.8%	2 3.1%	14 4.4%
Total	99 100.0%	40 100.0%	29 100.0%	37 100.0%	51 100.0%	64 100.0%	320 100.0%

Pearson chi-square 9.606.

average of the sample is 50.0 percent). Further, the proportion of leaders who rejected the proposition is higher among the backward castes-A and scheduled castes-A leaders. However, the chi-square value 9.606 is not significant hence the difference of perceptions based on castes is not significant.

Thus, it is quite clear that women are not considered as real representatives at village panchayat level by about half of the sampled leaders. Further, the proportion of leaders having this belief is significantly higher among men in contrast to women. Surprisingly, the leaders of all castes are almost in equal proportion in accepting and rejecting the said proposition.

The women represent proxy leadership. They themselves are not contesting elections, unable to mobilize support in their favour, dependent on male family members for their mobility and to go outside in accompany with the family members and their interactions in meetings are either by their family member or as instructed or guided by their family members. Therefore, to find out the real position the sampled leaders are asked to respond to the proposition that 'the women leaders take directions from their husband/family members for panchayat works'. The data obtained is presented in Table 7.20.

TABLE 7.20

Perceptions of sampled leaders on the proposition that the women leaders take directions from their husband/ family members for panchayat works

Perceptions	*Frequency*	*Valid Percent*	*Cumulative Percent*
Yes	270	84.4	84.4
No	39	12.2	96.6
Undecided	11	3.4	100.0
Total	320	100.0	

The data in Table 7.20 indicates that it appears that every one is endorsing the proposition as 84.4 percent affirmed to it. There is only 12.2 percent of the sample who rejected this proposition. A small percentage (3.4 percent) is undecided.

The perceptions to the proposition that women leaders are directed by their husband or family members are cross-examined with their gender and castes.

TABLE 7.21

Classification of perceptions based on gender of the leaders on the proposition that the women leaders take directions from their husband/family members for panchayat works

	Gender		*Total*
Perceptions	*Male*	*Female*	
Yes	186 86.5%	84 80.0%	270 84.4%
No	24 11.2%	15 14.3%	39 12.2%
Undecided	5 2.3%	6 5.7%	11 3.4%
Total	215 100.0%	105 100.0%	320 100.0%

Pearson chi-square 3.276.

The data in Table 7.21 indicates that the sampled male and female leaders do differ on the proposition that they (women) take directions from their husband/families to perform panchayat functions but only an in apparent manner as chi-square value 3.276 is not significant one. Similarly, the data in Table 7.22 reveals that the perceptions on the propositions are more or less similar and chi-square value 11.763 is highly insignificant.

Thus, it is concluded that women leaders take directions from their husband/family members in discharging panchayat functions. The pattern of responses is uniform in both sexes and among the leaders of various castes' groups. It confirms the proposition that the women leaders take directions from their husband/family members for panchayat works.

It is said that the women were not social and culturally prepared to assume the role of PR leadership when the new legislation has reserved seats for them. But they were excited to

TABLE 7.22

Classification of perceptions based on castes of the leaders on the proposition that the women leaders take directions from their husband/family members for panchayat works

Perceptions	*Castes*						*Total*
	Farming castes	*Upper castes*	*Backward castes (A)*	*Backward castes (B)*	*Scheduled castes (A)*	*Scheduled castes (B)*	
(1)	*(2)*	*(3)*	*(4)*	*(5)*	*(6)*	*(7)*	*(8)*
Yes	81 81.8%	32 80.0%	23 79.3%	31 83.8%	44 86.3%	59 92.2%	270 84.4%
No	16 16.2%	7 17.5%	5 17.2%	4 10.8%	3 5.9%	4 6.3%	39 12.2%
Undecided	2 2.0%	1 2.5%	1 3.4%	2 5.4%	4 7.8%	1 1.6%	11 3.4%
Total	99 100.0%	40 100.0%	29 100.0%	37 100.0%	51 100.0%	64 100.0%	320 100.0%

Pearson chi-square 11.763.

find their place in PRIs. Therefore, the process of assimilation and adaptation of women panchayat leaders might be slow. In addition to this, the active participation and direct involvement of women leaders for discharging responsibilities in a highly traditional and conservative rural society of the state is naturally encountered with number of social, economic and cultural obstructions.

The studies also indicate that women are not capable to discharge the responsibilities assigned to them as panch or sarpanch in the panchayat. Therefore, another proposition depicting the capabilities of women leaders 'women would not be able to perform panchayat functions' was put to the sampled leaders for their comments. The information collected from the leaders is tabulated in Table 7.23.

TABLE 7.23

The perceptions of the sampled leaders on the proposition that women would not be able to perform panchayat functions

Perceptions	*Frequency*	*Valid Percent*	*Cumulative Percent*
Yes	100	31.3	31.3
No	201	62.8	94.1
Undecided	19	5.9	100.0
Total	320	100.0	

The data in Table 7.23 reveals that 31.3 per of the leaders are of the opinion that women would not be able to perform panchayat functions. But, a fair majority of (62.8 percent) of leaders rejected this kind proposition put to them. About 6 percent of them were undecided on this issue.

The perceptions of sampled leaders comprising Table 7.23 are examined with the gender and castes of sampled leaders and data to this effect is tabulated in Tables 7.24 and 7.25

The data in Table 7.24 and chi-square value (1.942) illustrates that there is not any significant difference between male and female leaders on the said proposition.

TABLE 7.24

Classification of the perceptions of the sampled leaders based on their gender on the proposition that women would not be able to perform panchayat functions

	Gender		*Total*
Perceptions	*Male*	*Female*	
Yes	68 31.6%	32 30.5%	100 31.3%
No	137 63.7%	64 61.0%	201 62.8%
Undecided	10 4.7%	9 8.6%	19 5.9%
Total	215 100.0%	105 100.0%	320 100.0%

Pearson chi-square 1.942.

The data in Table 7.25 makes it clear that the leaders from farming castes and scheduled castes-B have relatively higher proportion (37.4 and 37.5 per cent respectively) of leaders who consider that the women leaders would not be enough competent to discharge panchayat functions. Naturally, their proportion is lower in rejecting the proposition. However, the chi-square value 10.884 which is less than significant value confirms the absence of significant difference of perceptions among various castes' leaders.

Thus, it is concluded that after three panchayat elections and 12 years of reforms and reservation in the state, a majority of leaders consider the women leaders that they would be able to discharge the functions of panchayats entrusted to them. Further, more or less uniform pattern of responses among the leaders of both sexes and various castes emphasize the significance of the change in attitude towards women leadership of the state.

The women leaders particularly at village level could not become independent of their families and social customs. They are not politically aware and the political wisdom is a very distant dream for them. Moreover, the local politics was the exclusive domain of men till reservation for them was carved

TABLE 7.25

Classification of the perceptions of the sampled leaders based on their castes on the proposition that women would not be able to perform panchayat functions

Perceptions	*Castes*						*Total*
	Farming castes	*Upper castes*	*Backward castes (A)*	*Backward castes (B)*	*Scheduled castes (A)*	*Scheduled castes (B)*	
(1)	(2)	(3)	(4)	(5)	(6)	(7)	(8)
Yes	37 37.4%	9 22.5%	7 24.1%	11 29.7%	12 23.5%	24 37.5%	100 31.3%
No	59 59.6%	30 75.0%	19 65.5%	23 62.2%	34 66.7%	36 56.3%	201 62.8%
Undecided	3 3.0%	1 2.5%	3 10.3%	3 8.1%	5 9.8%	4 6.3%	19 5.9%
Total	99 100.0%	40 100.0%	29 100.0%	37 100.0%	51 100.0%	64 100.0%	320 100.0%

Pearson chi-square 10.884.

out. The practice of co-option was there but that was administered by the sarpanch by co-opting own relative or a poor women who could put up her thumb impression without asking what is it? Therefore the women do not have any political experience before the amendment in 1992. Therefore the direction and dependence on family members by women leader at village level is natural. Moreover, what is wrong in taking the directions from husband/family members? The women in traditional society, practicing *purdah* system cannot come out at par with male local leaders. Therefore, the system is definitely likely to stay if not for long.

The policy-makers have this realization and therefore they had gone for their reservation. Local politics is a group activity and leader remains in regular and direct contact with the people voted for him/her all the time. In such situation, how it can be insulated from a husband or family member?

But the question whether the women leaders elected after constitutional amendment have been able to acquire the requisite political understanding? To find out the answer of this question the sampled leaders were asked to give their perceptions on the assertion that the political understanding has started to grow among the women leaders after they were elected in panchayats. Their perceptions are presented in Table 7.26.

TABLE 7.26

Perceptions of sampled leaders on the assertion that the political understanding has started to grow among the women leaders

Perceptions	*Frequency*	*Valid Percent*	*Cumulative Percent*
Yes	256	80.0	80.0
No	60	18.8	98.8
Undecided	4	1.3	100.0
Total	320	100.0	

It is evident from the data in Table 7.26 that an overwhelming majority of sampled leaders (80 percent) affirmed the proposition that the political understanding has started to grow among the women leaders. There are only 19 percent of the sampled leaders who did not approve this proposition put to them.

These perceptions presented in Table 7.26 are studied with reference to their gender and castes and information to this effect is given in Tables 7.27 and 7.28.

TABLE 7.27

Classification of perceptions of the leaders based on their gender on the assertion that the political understanding has started to grow among the women leaders

	Gender		*Total*
	Male	*Female*	
Yes	177 82.3%	79 75.2%	256 80.0%
No	38 17.7%	22 21.0%	60 18.8%
Undecided	0 .0%	4 3.8%	4 1.3%
Total	215 100.0%	105 100.0%	320 100.0%

Pearson chi-square 9.038*.

The data in Table 7.27 indicates a significant difference between male and female leaders. The chi-square value 9.038 also makes it clear that women and men are significantly different from each other and the proportion of leaders who supported this proposition is higher among males in comparison to females.

Further, the classification of the said perceptions based on castes of the leaders is presented in Table 7.28 and the data in the Table reveals that proportion of support to this proposition is much higher than the average of the sample among the leaders belonging farming castes and scheduled castes-B (85.9 and 84.4 percent respectively). However, the chi-square value 9.440 denotes that the significant difference of perceptions is not there among the leaders of various castes' groups.

TABLE 7.28

Classification of perceptions of the leaders based on their caste on the assertion that the political understanding has started to grow among the women leaders

Perceptions	*Castes*						*Total*
	Farming castes	*Upper castes*	*Backward castes (A)*	*Backward castes (B)*	*Scheduled castes (A)*	*Scheduled castes (B)*	
(1)	(2)	(3)	(4)	(5)	(6)	(7)	(8)
Yes	85 85.9%	32 80.0%	22 75.9%	27 73.0%	36 70.6%	54 84.4%	256 80.0%
No	14 14.1%	7 17.5%	7 24.1%	9 24.3%	14 27.5%	9 14.1%	60 18.8%
Undecided	0 .0%	1 2.5%	0 .0%	1 2.7%	1 2.0%	1 1.6%	4 1.3%
Total	99 100.0%	40 100.0%	29 100.0%	37 100.0%	51 100.0%	64 100.0%	320 100.0%

Pearson chi-square 9.440.

CONCLUSION

Thus, it is concluded that the election of women in panchayats has generated the beginning of the process of political understanding among them is valid up to a great extent. The endorsement to this proposition is much among men than women leaders of panchayat raj.

NOTES AND REFERENCES

1. Mathur, Tina (2003). Women in Panchayati Raj Institutions: Reservation and Participation. *Dynamics of Public Administration*, 13-14, (1-2), Jan.-Dec. 2003, p. 88.
2. *Ibid*.
3. *Ibid*.
4. Luckham, R. and Goetz, A.M. (2000). Democratic Institutions and Politics in Contexts of Inequality, Poverty and Conflict. Working Paper 104, Brighton, Institute of Development Studies quoted in Mathur, Tina, *op. cit.*
5. Phillips (1993). In Goetz and Hasim quoted in Mathur, Tina (2000), *Ibid*.
6. Mathur, Tina (2003). *op. cit*.
7. Luckham, R. and Goetz, A.M. (2000), *op. cit*.

Role Performance

The political system is defined as 'consisting of interacting roles, structures, and subsystems, and of underlying psychological propensities which affect these interactions'.[1] Further, the functioning of any system may be viewed on different levels. One of these levels is the capability of the system and it means the way it (system) performs as a unit in its environment.[2] The second level of functioning is conversion processes, or functions, which are defined as the ways systems transform inputs into outputs. It involves the ways in which demands and supports are transformed into authoritative decisions and are implemented.[3] The third level is known as system maintenance and adaptation.[4]

The political system may facilitate economic growth and it can impede or prevent economic development.[5] When political systems acquire this kind of capability (promoting or preventing growth) it means that political development has taken place. In other words the political development is pre-requisite for economic growth and in present case it is the rural development. The political development also involves primarily the role of citizenry and their new standards of loyalty and involvement. It is political awakening to make people active and committed citizens. It entails expanded popular participation. It means mass participation for a diffusion of decision-making, and participation brought some influence on choice and decision.[6] It is also believed that political development is a capacity either to control social change or be controlled by it.[7] Thus, the political development is an important factor which determines the role performance of panchayat leaders.

The rural leadership is an institution evolved and established for managing village affairs. It is also termed as local political system at the local village level. The panchayat comprises of a structure which means it has to perform a set of the observable activities assigned to it legitimately and with appropriate authority of coercion and command in a defined boundary of specified activities. In general the panchayats are entrusted with the responsibility of rural development which is a process of uplifting social, economic and cultural levels of the poor people living in villages.

It is also observed that people participation ensures effectiveness in realizing rural development in the country. Naturally, to ensure effective participation in hierarchical rural society there is an urgent need of a representative leadership at village level. This need is being fulfilled since past through the Panchayati Raj Institutions in India. These institutions have been made representative of requisite level after 73rd amendment act and the task of rural development is assigned to these more representative panchayats and the panchayati raj leadership.

Further, the delivery of development functions largely influenced upon by the courage, responsibility and imagination on the part of local leadership,[8] in addition to the availability of requisite resources for development. In real sense the leadership must be quick to respond to changing circumstances and be ready to assume new functions as they arise. It means in addition to political development, an optimum level of competence and capability in rural leadership is essential for discharging panchayats' responsibilities. The people adjudge local leaders' capacity to perform the functions assigned to them. The gram sabha meetings and periodic elections are the means through which they measure their leaders' performance and capacity.

The local leaders while discharging functions come across many kinds of institutional and non-institutional factors which either facilitate or prevent their efforts in achieving the objective of rural development. Therefore, the role performance depends on the capability of the leader how he or she converts the input into output by utilizing and facilitating the resources and overcoming the obstacles. The 73rd amendment has assigned a list of functions and carrying out those requires time and a reasonable level of ability. Therefore, the need for evaluating the role performance of a panchayat leader has become more significant as that will help in devising the ways and means to establish capable and competent Panchayati Raj leadership.

Therefore, an effort is made to find out the ability of sampled leadership required to perform the functions entrusted to them. For this purpose, the sampled leaders were asked a set of questions—whether they may be able to perform certain functions or not? Each question asked from sampled leadership has four options, i.e. Yes/No/Difficult/Impossible. The leaders were asked to choose any one of the said options. Further, 76 sampled leaders were not included in the sample as they were interviewed only after 15 days of their election in panchayats and had not performed any role till then.

The first question: Have you constructed school/road/street/panchayat ghar/drinking water facility, etc. while sarpanch or panch in village panchayat? The information obtained is presented in Table 8.1.

TABLE 8.1

Responses of construction of school/street/etc. by the village leaders in the village

	Frequency	*Valid Percent*	*Cumulative Percent*
Yes	223	91.4	91.4
No	19	7.8	99.2
Difficult	2	.8	100.0
Total	244	100.0	

The data in Table 8.1 illustrates that 91.4 per cent of leaders have performed all or some of the above stated functions while they are/were in panchayats. There were only 7.8 per cent who denied that they did not do that. Thus there is involvement of almost all the leaders in panchayat functions. But the kind of involvement varies from leader to leader. The leaders involvement in above stated activities start from suggesting to do a work or asking to do a particular activity, suggesting how to do it, supervising and sanctioning budget for it. It is true most of the technical details concerning these activities are attended by specialists of Block Development Office but the sarpanch in particular and panches in general get these done in the village.

The responses of the sampled leaders in Table 8.1 are studied with reference to their gender and castes and presented in Table 8.2 and 8.3.

TABLE 8.2

Classification of responses of the leaders based on the gender about their involvement in construction of school/ street/etc. by the village leaders in the village

	Gender		*Total*
Perceptions	*Male*	*Female*	
Yes	158 94.6%	65 84.4%	223 91.4%
No	9 5.4%	10 13.0%	19 7.8%
Difficult	0 .0%	2 2.6%	2 .8%
Total	167 100.0%	77 100.0%	244 100.0%

Pearson chi-square 8.844*.

The data in Table 8.2 indicates that the proportion of women leaders' responses about their involvement in construction of school/street/etc. is significantly lower than men. The chi-square value 8.844 is significant and confirms the difference of the responses.

The data in Table 8.3 reveals that there is not any kind of difference among leaders of various castes in this regard. The leader of every caste has remained involved in these activities. The chi-square value 8. 760 also do not indicate any difference among the leaders of various castes.

Thus almost every one is involved in panchayat's activities of constructing school, streets, roads, panchayat ghar, dispensary and drinking water facilities etc. The women leaders are significantly lesser involved than the male leaders but there is not any such difference among the leaders of various castes.

The present panchayat system has its origin in Panch Parmeshwar or Nyaya Panchayats of the earlier times. These to resolve panchayats of earlier times used to settle the disputes and conflicts of village people within the village itself. The panchayats were having social sanctions to deliver justice and execute those judicial pronouncements. Although, the present panchayati raj and legal system have not endowed the power in this regard but the panchayats still resolve some social disputes. To find out leaders' involvement and inclination to solve social and small disputes, they were asked: Have you settled local disputes? The answers to this question of the leaders are tabulated in Table 8.4.

The data in Table 8.4 indicates that every one did not have this kind of experience but a majority of local leaders (77.5 per cent) have the taste of this role. The data also reveals that 19.7 per cent of leaders did not involve in such matters in any way.

Who are not involved? Or who do not have inclination towards this kind of role? To find out the answer the responses of leaders are classified on the basis of their gender and castes and information is tabulated in Tables 8.5 and 8.6.

The data in Table 8.5 indicates that the proportion of male leaders (83.2 per cent) involved much in dispute resolution in comparison to female leaders (64.9 per cent). The chi-square value 10.347* also confirms the difference between men and women leaders as significant. Moreover, the female actually do not participate in dispute resolution process because of social reason, rather their husbands participated in such activities if permitted. Therefore, whosoever responded affirmative does

TABLE 8.3

Classification of responses of the leaders based on the castes about their involvement in construction of school/street/etc. by the village leaders in the village

Perceptions	*Castes*						*Total*
	Farming castes	*Upper castes*	*Backward castes (A)*	*Backward castes (B)*	*Scheduled castes (A)*	*Scheduled castes (B)*	
(1)	(2)	(3)	(4)	(5)	(6)	(7)	(8)
Yes	70 92.1%	31 93.9%	23 95.8%	22 91.7%	36 90.0%	41 87.2%	223 91.4%
No	5 6.6%	2 6.1%	0 .0%	2 8.3%	4 10.0%	6 12.8%	19 7.8%
Difficult	1 1.3%	0 .0%	1 4.2%	0 .0%	0 .0%	0 .0%	2 .8%
Total	76 100.0%	33 100.0%	24 100.0%	24 100.0%	40 100.0%	47 100.0%	244 100.0%

Pearson chi-square 8.760.

TABLE 8.4

Responses of the leaders regarding their involvement in settling local disputes

	Frequency	*Valid Percent*	*Cumulative Percent*
Yes	189	77.5	77.5
No	48	19.7	97.1
Difficult	7	2.9	100.0
Total	244	100.0	

TABLE 8.5

Classification of responses of the leaders based on their gender regarding their involvement in settling local disputes

	Gender		*Total*
	Male	*Female*	
Yes	139 83.2%	50 64.9%	189 77.5%
No	25 15.0%	23 29.9%	48 19.7%
Difficult	3 1.8%	4 5.2%	7 2.9%
Total	167 100.0%	77 100.0%	244 100.0%

Pearson chi-square 10.347*.

not mean she herself participated in panchayat activities rather her family member has participated in this.

The data in Table 8.6 clearly indicates that there is not any significant difference among leaders of different castes and chi-square value 7.807 confirms the absence of such difference in significant sense.

Thus, it is concluded that a large majority of the leaders from various castes do participate in dispute resolution but the participation of men in such activity is significantly higher than

TABLE 8.6
Classification of responses of the leaders based on their castes regarding their involvement in settling local disputes

	Castes						*Total*
	Farming castes	*Upper castes*	*Backward castes (A)*	*Backward castes (B)*	*Scheduled castes (A)*	*Scheduled castes (B)*	
(1)	(2)	(3)	(4)	(5)	(6)	(7)	(8)
Yes	61	27	18	18	28	37	189
	80.3%	81.8%	75.0%	75.0%	70.0%	78.7%	77.5%
No	12	6	4	5	11	10	48
	15.8%	18.2%	16.7%	20.8%	27.5%	21.3%	19.7%
Difficult	3	0	2	1	1	0	7
	3.9%	.0%	8.3%	4.2%	2.5%	.0%	2.9%
Total	76	33	24	24	40	47	244
	100.0%	100.0%	100.0%	100.0%	100.0%	100.0%	100.0%

Pearson chi-square 7.807.

women because of social reasons. The dispute resolution activity usually invites the persons from each caste.

The leaders must have the capacity to call a meeting of people or their colleague to discuss a matter of local significance. This trait of capacity is assessed with the help of responses of the leaders on the assertion that 'leaders can call the meeting of villagers and can discuss the issues relating to village'. The information obtained from the sampled leaders is presented in Table 8.7.

TABLE 8.7

Responses of leaders on the assertion that they can call people in a meeting and can discuss the issue related to the village

	Frequency	*Valid Percent*	*Cumulative Percent*
Yes	194	79.5	79.5
No	33	13.5	93.0
Difficult	16	6.6	99.6
Impossible	1	.4	100.0
Total	244	100.0	

The data in Table 8.7 shows that a large majority (79.5 per cent) are enough capable to discharge the role of calling meeting and to discuss village affairs. It is considered as an easy affair in a village but organizing a Gram Sabha is a very difficult task to perform. However, 13.5 per cent refused to have this kind of competence. Thus, although the majority of leaders can perform this function of panchayat which may mean that they have some supporters or peers having faith in their leadership and participate with their leader in common cooperative activities.

As per the practice, the responses obtained from the local leaders on the issue stated above is studied with reference to the gender and caste of the leaders and The data is tabulated in Tables 8.8 and 8.9.

The data in Table 8.8 indicates that men (85.0 per cent) and women (67.5 per cent) leaders differ from each other in their responses on the capability of possessing the capability of

TABLE 8.8

Classification of responses based on the gender of the leaders on the assertion that they can call people's meeting and can discuss the issue related to the village

	Gender		*Total*
	Male	*Female*	
Yes	142 85.0%	52 67.5%	194 79.5%
No	15 9.0%	18 23.4%	33 13.5%
Difficult	9 5.4%	7 9.1%	16 6.6%
Impossible	1 .6%	0 .0%	1 .4%
Total	167 100.0%	77 100.0%	244 100.0%

Pearson chi-square 11.666*.

calling meetings and discussing village affairs. The chi-square value 11.666 confirms this distinction in significant way.

The inability to do so is more among women (23.4 per cent) leaders in comparison to male (9.0 per cent) leadership. Another thing, which is necessary to point out that the women, cannot call the people to such meetings particularly of the males. Further, whatever the women do in this regard they do it through their husbands. However, they can ask the women to assemble. This ability also depends upon the issue to be discussed.

The data in Table 8.9 reveals that there is a difference of responses regarding this ability when the sampled leaders are classified on caste basis. The data in table indicates that the leaders belonging to upper castes, farming castes and backward castes-A are relatively more confident about their ability to do so. But, the chi-square value 14.853 clearly indicates the absence of significant difference in the responses among the leaders of various castes on the said assertion.

Thus, it is concluded that a good majority of leaders have the peers in the village that can assemble to discuss the common

TABLE 8.9

Classification of responses based on the castes of the leaders on the assertion that they can call people's meeting and can discuss the issue related to the village

	Castes						*Total*
	Farming castes	*Upper castes*	*Backward castes (A)*	*Backward castes (B)*	*Scheduled castes (A)*	*Scheduled castes (B)*	
(1)	(2)	(3)	(4)	(5)	(6)	(7)	(8)
Yes	66 86.8%	27 81.8%	18 75.0%	16 66.7%	33 82.5%	34 72.3%	194 79.5%
No	8 10.5%	4 12.1%	3 12.5%	5 20.8%	6 15.0%	7 14.9%	33 13.5%
Difficult	1 1.3%	2 6.1%	3 12.5%	3 12.5%	1 2.5%	6 12.8%	16 6.6%
Impossible	1 1.3%	0 .0%	0 .0%	0 .0%	0 .0%	0 .0%	1 .4%
Total	76 100.0%	33 100.0%	24 100.0%	24 100.0%	40 100.0%	47 100.0%	244 100.0%

Pearson chi-square 14.853.

things with their representatives when asked to do so by their leader. However, the traits of this ability are definitely higher among male leaders in comparison to female leaders. The caste of the leader although does not distinguish in significant way but it appears apparently that the dominating castes' leaders have an edge over the others in this regard. The discussions in these meetings have always been informal in nature. It is evident from the fact that the leaders are claiming this ability in them but not successful in holding formal Gram Sabha meeting which means informal assembly is preferred.

Now the panches in a panchayat are the representative of their ward. Many of them are illiterate or lesser educated. They may or may not be associated with the political set-up of the local and regional political system. They may hesitate to be acquainted or do not set opportunity to get acquainted with bureaucratic system engaged in rural development. In such situation, it may be difficult for these representatives to mobilize resources for the village activities. Therefore, the local leader in general and sarpanch of a village in particular is expected that he/she must be a person who can mobilize the requisite resources for panchayat's functions or village welfare/development activities. Hence, the sampled leaders were asked to respond on the proposition that 'he/she can mobilize resources for village development from government and non-governmental agencies'. The information in the form of responses of the leaders on the issue are presented in Table 8.10.

TABLE 8.10

Responses of the leaders on the proposition that they can mobilize resources for village development from government and non-governmental agencies

	Frequency	*Valid Percent*	*Cumulative Percent*
Yes	163	66.8	66.8
No	34	13.9	80.7
Difficult	35	14.3	95.1
Impossible	12	4.9	100.0
Total	244	100.0	

The data in Table 8.10 shows that 66.8 per cent leaders affirmed this that they can mobilize resources for the panchayat's developmental activities. About 14 per cent refused that they are not capable to do these responsibilities. Another 14.3 per cent said that the mobilization of resources is quite difficult task. A few (4.9 per cent) said it is impossible for them.

Thus, it is clear from the data that more than half of the sampled leaders find themselves enough capable to mobilize resources for their panchayat. Who are capable and who are not? The answer to this question is derived by examining the responses comprising Table 8.10 with the gender and castes of the leaders and relevant information is presented in Tables 8.11 and 8.12.

TABLE 8.11

Classification of responses based on the gender of the leaders on the proposition that they can mobilize resources for village development from government and non-governmental agencies

	Gender		*Total*
	Male	*Female*	
Yes	121 72.5%	42 54.5%	163 66.8%
No	20 12.0%	14 18.2%	34 13.9%
Difficult	20 12.0%	15 19.5%	35 14.3%
Impossible	6 3.6%	6 7.8%	12 4.9%
Total	167 100.0%	77 100.0%	244 100.0%

Pearson chi-square 7.946*.

The data in Table 8.11 reveals that men and women differ in accepting the proposition that the capability of mobilizing financial resources for their panchayat. It is obvious also as women encounter many kinds of social obstacles in doing that. Not only this, the women leaders who accepted it, are saying as their husband/family members are influential in getting this things done. The proportion of women leaders who simply declined to possess the ability to mobilize resources (18.2 per cent) and who said it is quite difficult (19.5 per cent). Thus, female leaders are not empowered to mobilize resources. The chi-square value 7.946 also distinguishes the two groups of leaders in significant manner in their responses on the proposition.

Similarly, the Table 8.12 gives details of classification of sampled leaders based on their castes and their responses regarding ability to mobilize resources from governmental and non-governmental resources.

The data in Table 8.12 indicates that the responses of the sampled leaders from various castes differ from each other on the proposition in discussion. The leaders from farming castes, upper castes and scheduled castes-B are more confident that they or panchayat leadership has the requisite ability to moblize resources for panchayat. It indicates that the leaders from these castes are relatively more empowered. However, the chi-square value 20.523 does not indicate any significant difference in responses of the leaders from various castes' groups.

Thus, it is clear that mobilizing funds for panchayat's activity is difficult task for many of the leaders but more than half of the local leaders are capable to do that. Further, this capability is perceived in much proportion among male leaders in significant manner and also among leaders from upper castes and farming castes and scheduled castes-B leaders but not in significant way.

Next proposition is relating to the attribute of personal quality of the leader to motivate and encourage the people for cooperative effort and to achieve the common goal. It was a very common practice in the village society in past. The leadership role of undertaking cooperative efforts depends on this attribute of the leader. Therefore, sampled leaders were asked to answer the whether they can motivate the villagers to contribute labour, gift money, etc. for the common purpose. The answers obtained in this regard are tabulated in Table 8.13.

The data in Table 8.13 illustrates that 68 per cent of them readily agreed that they are capable to motivate the people to contribute towards common goal. However, 23.8 per cent

TABLE 8.12

Classification of responses based on the castes of the leaders on the proposition that they can mobilize resources for village development from government and non-governmental agencies

	Castes						*Total*
	Farming castes	*Upper castes*	*Backward castes (A)*	*Backward castes (B)*	*Scheduled castes (A)*	*Scheduled castes (B)*	
(1)	*(2)*	*(3)*	*(4)*	*(5)*	*(6)*	*(7)*	*(8)*
Yes	58 76.3%	24 72.7%	13 54.2%	13 54.2%	22 55.0%	33 70.2%	163 66.8%
No	11 14.5%	3 9.1%	3 12.5%	5 20.8%	9 22.5%	3 6.4%	34 13.9%
Difficult	5 6.6%	6 18.2%	6 25.0%	5 20.8%	5 12.5%	8 17.0%	35 14.3%
Impossible	2 2.6%	0 .0%	2 8.3%	1 4.2%	4 10.0%	3 6.4%	12 4.9%
Total	76 100.0%	33 100.0%	24 100.0%	24 100.0%	40 100.0%	47 100.0%	244 100.0%

Pearson chi-square 20.523.

TABLE 8.13

Responses of the leaders regarding possession of capability to motivate villagers for contributing labour and gifting money for common purpose

	Frequency	*Valid Percent*	*Cumulative Percent*
Yes	166	68.0	68.0
No	58	23.8	91.8
Difficult	20	8.2	100.0
Total	244	100.0	

indicate their disability when asked to answer the question in this regard. A small section (8.2 per cent) stated that it is a difficult task for them. The responses are almost similar to the earlier proposition concerning the ability to mobilize the resources (Table 8.10). Therefore, these responses are also treated with the gender and castes of the leaders. The data about this kind of classification is presented in Table 8.14 and 8.15.

TABLE 8.14

Classification of responses based on the gender of the leaders regarding possession of capability to motivate villagers for contributing labour and gifting money for common purpose

	Gender		*Total*
	Male	*Female*	
Yes	117 70.1%	49 63.6%	166 68.0%
No	38 22.8%	20 26.0%	58 23.8%
Difficult	12 7.2%	8 10.4%	20 8.2%
Total	167 100.0%	77 100.0%	244 100.0%

Pearson chi-square 1.209.

The data in Table 8.14 and chi-square value 1.209 makes it clear that there is not any significant difference between male and female leaders concerning their answer to the question that they can motivate the people to contribute for the common purpose. However, it is again reminded that the spouses of women leaders perform this kind of functions on their behalf.

The data in the Table 8.15 reveals that the proportion of leaders from farming castes followed by upper castes and scheduled castes-A is higher in comparison to other castes' groups is higher. It means that the leaders from these castes feel relatively much empowered to perform the role of motivating people to contribute for common purposes. However, the chi-square value 10.864 denotes the absence of any significant difference in their responses on the issue.

Thus, it is concluded that more than half of the leaders found that they could motivate and encourage their village fellow to contribute labour, gift money and other for a common purpose. However, the male leaders and leaders from farming castes, upper castes and scheduled castes-B feel relatively much empowered than others in this regard but not significantly different from other castes' leaders.

The local leadership led the society. The leaders are the agent of change in traditional society. Therefore, the social awareness level of leadership is very important for socio-cultural, economic and political progress of rural society. Further this progress is very much essential to build up a good citizenship. It is not only essential for social life but also required to ensure democratic value-based good governance in the country. Therefore, it becomes necessary to find out the capability of the local leadership in making the society well aware about the prevalent social evils. The sampled leaders were asked to answer the question could you make the village people aware about the prevailing social evils present in the society? Their answers are presented in Table 8.16.

The data in the Table makes it clear that 69.7 per cent leaders simply stated that they possess the ability to educate people of their village about prevailing social evils in the society. Some of them said that they are already doing it. A sizeable section of 11.5 per cent leaders perceived it, as a difficult task and 18.9 per cent do not find themselves able to do that. Thus,

TABLE 8.15

Classification of responses based on the castes of the leaders regarding possession of capability to motivate villagers for contributing labour and gifting money for common purpose

	Castes						*Total*
	Farming castes	*Upper castes*	*Backward castes (A)*	*Backward castes (B)*	*Scheduled castes (A)*	*Scheduled castes (B)*	
(1)	(2)	(3)	(4)	(5)	(6)	(7)	(8)
Yes	58 76.3%	23 69.7%	16 66.7%	15 62.5%	20 50.0%	34 72.3%	166 68.0%
No	13 17.1%	6 18.2%	6 25.0%	7 29.2%	16 40.0%	10 21.3%	58 23.8%
Difficult	5 6.6%	4 12.1%	2 8.3%	2 8.3%	4 10.0%	3 6.4%	20 8.2%
Total	76 100.0%	33 100.0%	24 100.0%	24 100.0%	40 100.0%	47 100.0%	244 100.0%

Pearson chi-square 10.864.

TABLE 8.16

Responses of the leaders about their ability to make people aware about prevailing social evils in the society

	Frequency	*Valid Percent*	*Cumulative Percent*
Yes	170	69.7	69.7
No	46	18.9	88.5
Difficult	28	11.5	100.0
Total	244	100.0	

like earlier proposition about 70 per cent of sampled leaders stated that the panchayat leadership possesses the ability to educate their followers in the village about the prevailing social evils.

The responses of Table 8.16 are classified as per the gender and castes of the sampled leadership and tabulated in Tables 8.17 and 8.18 respectively.

TABLE 8.17

Classification of responses based on the gender of the leaders about their ability to make people aware about prevailing social evils in the society

	Gender		*Total*
	Male	*Female*	
Yes	119 71.3%	51 66.2%	170 69.7%
No	32 19.2%	14 18.2%	46 18.9%
Difficult	16 9.6%	12 15.6%	28 11.5%
Total	167 100.0%	77 100.0%	244 100.0%

Pearson chi-square 1.873.

The data in Table 8.17 and chi-square value 1.873 shows that the proportion of male and female leaders have more or less similar responses to the question asked from them.

TABLE 8.18
Classification of responses based on the castes of the leaders about their ability to make people aware about prevailing social evils in the society

	Castes						*Total*
	Farming castes	*Upper castes*	*Backward castes (A)*	*Backward castes (B)*	*Scheduled castes (A)*	*Scheduled castes (B)*	
(1)	(2)	(3)	(4)	(5)	(6)	(7)	(8)
Yes	54 71.1%	25 75.8%	15 62.5%	17 70.8%	22 55.0%	37 78.7%	170 69.7%
No	13 17.1%	4 12.1%	5 20.8%	4 16.7%	13 32.5%	7 14.9%	46 18.9%
Difficult	9 11.8%	4 12.1%	4 16.7%	3 12.5%	5 12.5%	3 6.4%	28 11.5%
Total	76 100.0%	33 100.0%	24 100.0%	24 100.0%	40 100.0%	47 100.0%	244 100.0%

Pearson chi-square 9.241.

The data in Table 8.18 makes it evident that the proportion of leaders from the scheduled castes-B, upper castes and farming castes is higher than the other castes particularly scheduled castes-A and backward castes-B. The results are on expected pattern as the political cohesiveness among the scheduled castes-B is found to be highest in comparison to other castes. But, the difference of responses among various castes' groups is not significant as the chi-square value is 9.241.

Thus, it is concluded that about seventy percent of the leaders responded that they possess the ability to educate people of their village about prevailing social evils in the society and it is equally true for both male and female sampled leadership. It is also observed that the proportion of leaders from the scheduled castes-B, upper castes and farming castes is higher than the other castes particularly scheduled castes-A and backward castes-B. The results are on expected pattern as the political cohesiveness among the scheduled castes-B is found to be highest in comparison to other castes. But the difference of responses among the leaders of various castes is not significant.

The leader without followers is unimaginable. Therefore, the leader must have the ability to influence the people to the level they become his/her followers. The panchayat leader needs the mass support of his or her people to impress upon a viewpoint in the panchayat. Moreover, the involvement of people in panchayat by the leader makes him/her successful as the support of the people is real strength in democratic institutions. It is believed that most of the leaders lack this kind of mass support and are not able to hold Grama Sabha, a statutory requirement of the panchayat raj. Therefore, the leaders were asked to state: Do they possess the ability to motivate village people to participate in panchayat activities? The data obtained from them is tabulated in Table 8.19.

The data in the table indicates that a large majority (74.2 per cent) of them can motivate the people to participate in panchayat's activities. A sizeable proportion of sampled leaders (12.3 per cent) found this task as difficult one and 13.5 percent indicated their inability to do this.

The responses of the leaders on their ability to motivate people for participating panchayat activities are classified to find out the reality who can motivate much and who is

TABLE 8.19

Leaders' responses on the possession of ability by them to motivate people to participate in panchayat activities

	Frequency	*Valid Percent*	*Cumulative Percent*
Yes	181	74.2	74.2
No	33	13.5	87.7
Difficult	30	12.3	100.0
Total	244	100.0	

incapable to do that? The information in this regard is presented in Table 8.20 and 8.21.

TABLE 8.20

Classification of leaders' responses based on the gender on possessing the ability by them to motivate the people to participate in panchayat activities

	Gender		*Total*
	Male	*Female*	
Yes	137 82.0%	44 57.1%	181 74.2%
No	15 9.0%	18 23.4%	33 13.5%
Difficult	15 9.0%	15 19.5%	30 12.3%
Total	167 100.0%	77 100.0%	244 100.00

Pearson chi-square 17.201*.

It is evident from the data in Table 8.20 that there is significant difference in male and female leaders' responses on possessing the ability to motivate the people to participate in panchayat activities by them. The chi-square value 17.201 is highly significant and hence indicates that women leaders as a distinct class is less empowered in this regard in comparison to male leaders.

TABLE 8.21

Classification of leaders' responses based on their castes on possessing the ability by them to motivate the people to participate in panchayat activities

	Castes						*Total*
	Farming castes	*Upper castes*	*Backward castes (A)*	*Backward castes (B)*	*Scheduled castes (A)*	*Scheduled castes (B)*	
(1)	(2)	(3)	(4)	(5)	(6)	(7)	(8)
Yes	59 77.6%	23 69.7%	17 70.8%	19 79.2%	25 62.5%	38 80.9%	181 74.2%
No	10 13.2%	4 12.1%	4 16.7%	3 12.5%	8 20.0%	4 8.5%	33 13.5%
Difficult	7 9.2%	6 18.2%	3 12.5%	2 8.3%	7 17.5%	5 10.6%	30 12.3%
Total	76 100.0%	33 100.0%	24 100.0%	24 100.0%	40 100.0%	47 100.0%	244 100.0%

Pearson chi-square 6.521.

The data in Table 8.21 reveals that the responses of the leaders from scheduled castes-B, backward castes-B and farming castes are although higher than the other castes' leaders but not significant as chi-square value is 6.521.

Thus, it is concluded that a large majority of leaders (74.2 percent) stated that they possess the attributes of motivating people to participate in village panchayat activities. This kind of feeling is significantly higher among men in comparison to women leadership. Similarly, the leaders from scheduled castes-B, backward castes-B and farming castes are although better placed than others in this sense but not in significant way.

Organizing people is another attribute of leadership. Therefore, the leaders were probed to find out their capacity to organize people. They were made to answer the question: 'Can you organize an association or union of people' in your village? The data obtained from sampled leaders is tabulated in Table 8.22.

TABLE 8.22

Responses of leaders on their capacity to organize an association or union of people

	Frequency	*Valid Percent*	*Cumulative Percent*
Yes	103	42.2	42.2
No	75	30.7	73.0
Difficult	64	26.2	99.2
Impossible	2	.8	100.0
Total	244	100.0	

The data in Table 8.22 indicates that 42.2 per cent of the leaders feel that they have the capacity to organize an association or union of people. About one fourth (26.2 per cent) consider that organizing people in formal association is a difficult task. However, 30.7 per cent simply stated that they do not possess this trait of leadership.

The responses of leaders about their own organizing capacity are examined with reference to their gender and castes and information is presented in Tables 8.23 and 8.24 respectively.

TABLE 8.23

Classification of Responses of Leaders based on their Gender about their Capacity to Organize an Association or Union of People

	Gender		Total
	Male	*Female*	
Yes	74 44.3%	29 37.7%	103 42.2%
No	50 29.9%	25 32.5%	75 30.7%
Difficult	41 24.6%	23 29.9%	64 26.2%
Impossible	2 1.2%	0 .0%	2 .8%
Total	167 100.0%	77 100.0%	244 100.0%

Pearson chi-square 2.152.

The data in Table 8.23 and chi-square value 2.152 clearly indicates that except some apparent difference there is not any significant distinctiveness between male and female leaders sampled for this study. Similarly, the data in Table 8.24 reveals that the group of leaders of various castes' groups has expressed the possession of this trait differently. It indicates that the scheduled castes-A, backward castes both A and B groups are having lower proportion of leaders who feel that they can organize people in establishing a group or an association.

Thus it is concluded that about 42 percent of leaders feel that they are endowed with the ability to organize people at village level. But a significant proportion of them (about 58 per cent) stated they can not build up the association or union of village people or it is difficult task to perform for them. The data also suggests that apparently the women lag behind men

TABLE 8.24

Classification of responses of leaders based on their castes about their capacity to organize an association or union of people

	Castes						*Total*
	Farming castes	*Upper castes*	*Backward castes (A)*	*Backward castes (B)*	*Scheduled castes (A)*	*Scheduled castes (B)*	
(1)	*(2)*	*(3)*	*(4)*	*(5)*	*(6)*	*(7)*	*(8)*
Yes	39 51.3%	14 42.4%	8 33.3%	8 33.3%	11 27.5%	23 48.9%	103 42.2%
No	21 27.6%	7 21.2%	10 41.7%	8 33.3%	16 40.0%	13 27.7%	75 30.7%
Difficult	16 21.1%	11 33.3%	6 25.0%	8 33.3%	13 32.5%	10 21.3%	64 26.2%
Impossible	0 .0%	1 3.0%	0 .0%	0 .0%	0 .0%	1 2.1%	2 .8%
Total	76 100.0%	33 100.0%	24 100.0%	24 100.0%	40 100.0%	47 100.0%	244 100.0%

Pearson chi-square 15.621.

and the leaders from scheduled castes-A, backward castes both A and B groups are relatively worse than other castes in this regard but not in significant manner.

There is another activity and that pertains to the entertainment of the village people. It relates to organize Bhajans or Saang (local form of dance, drama or entertainment) in the village. The leaders were asked: 'Do they have the capacity to organize Bhajan or Saang like activities in the village?' The objective behind this is to find out the ability of organizing cultural activities in the village in direct sense but to find out the capacity to take initiative with a simple non-partisan, non-factional but a common activity.

TABLE 8.25

Responses of sampled leaders about their capacity to organize bhajan or saang like activity in the village

	Frequency	*Valid Percent*	*Cumulative Percent*
Yes	99	40.6	40.6
No	116	47.5	88.1
Difficult	29	11.9	100.0
Total	244	100.0	

The data in Table 8.25 presents a picture of responses relating to the organizing and initiative taking capacity of leaders. The data indicates that 40.6 per cent feel that they can organize Bhajan or Saang like activity in the village. Although 11.9 per cent found it a difficult activity but it is very much disappointing to find that 47.5 percent simply denied that they do not possess this kind of capacity. Thus the majority of sampled leaders are not having the attribute of organizing an event or not ready to take initiative for a non-partisan, non-factional but a common activity.

The responses of leaders about the capacity of organizing an event are examined with reference to their gender and castes and information is presented in Tables 8.26 and 8.27 respectively.

TABLE 8.26

Classification of responses of sampled leaders based on their gender about their capacity to organize bhajan or saang like activity in the village

	Gender		*Total*
	Male	*Female*	
Yes	71 42.5%	28 36.4%	99 40.6%
No	81 48.5%	35 45.5%	116 47.5%
Difficult	15 9.0%	14 18.2%	29 11.9%
Total	167 100.0%	77 100.0%	244 100.0%

Pearson chi-square 4.347

It is evident from the data in Table 8.26 that the proportion of male leaders who can get this kind of things done and also who find themselves unable to do it, is higher than female but definitely not in significant manner(chi-square value 4.347 is not significant). The higher proportion of women rated this task as a difficult one therefore they are also not to be said as those possessing the attribute of taking initiative to undertake an activity. It is also to note that the women alone can not perform this job. Their husbands perform this for them.

The data in Table 8.27 indicates that the proportion of leaders from backward castes (both groups) who feel that they have the capacity to organize Bhajan or Saang like activity in the village is lowest in the sample. But the chi-square value 10.100 indicates the lack of significant difference in their responses of the leaders of various castes' groups.

Thus, it is stated that only a sizeable proportion (40.6 per cent) of local leaders possesses the trait of taking initiative to do something common in the village. The others particularly women and leaders from backward castes (both groups) are having relatively lower proportion of leaders endowed with this attribute of organizing an event in the village.

TABLE 8.27

Classification of responses of sampled leaders based on their gender about their capacity to organize bhajan or saang like activity in the village

	Castes						*Total*
	Farming castes	*Upper castes*	*Backward castes (A)*	*Backward castes (B)*	*Scheduled castes (A)*	*Scheduled castes (B)*	
(1)	(2)	(3)	(4)	(5)	(6)	(7)	(8)
Yes	33 43.4%	19 57.6%	5 20.8%	7 29.2%	17 42.5%	18 38.3%	99 40.6%
No	35 46.1%	11 33.3%	16 66.7%	13 54.2%	18 45.0%	23 48.9%	116 47.5%
Difficult	8 10.5%	3 9.1%	3 12.5%	4 16.7%	5 12.5%	6 12.8%	29 11.9%
Total	76 100.0%	33 100.0%	24 100.0%	24 100.0%	40 100.0%	47 100.0%	244 100.0%

Pearson chi-square 10.100.

Lastly, the panchayat raj leadership also performs certain political functions and therefore they must have certain political inclination. Therefore, the sampled leaders were asked: 'Can you canvass for a political leader contesting election'? The objective to ask this question is to find out the political standing of a local leader, his/her inclination in politics and courage to associate with a political philosophy and willingness to integrate village politics with mainstream political system of the area or state. The responses of the sampled leaders are tabulated in Table 8.28.

TABLE 8.28

Responses of the sampled leaders regarding their readiness to canvass for a political leader contesting election

	Frequency	*Valid Percent*	*Cumulative Percent*
Yes	104	42.6	42.6
No	114	46.7	89.3
Difficult	26	10.7	100.0
Total	244	100.0	
Grand Total	320		

The data in Table 8.28 makes it clear that 42.6 per cent of the leaders have accepted that they can canvass for a political leader. However, 46.7 per cent, more than those who can canvass refused that they can not do it. About eight per cent stated canvassing as a difficult task which means that they are not willing to do it.

Thus, 42.6 per cent leadership possess a level of political standing and inclination for politics and enough courage to associate with a political philosophy and willing to integrate with mainstream political system of the area or the state.

The responses of the leadership on their readiness to canvass are studied in gender and caste contexts of the sampled leadership. The information so classified on these two characteristics is presented in Tables 8.29 and 8.30 respectively.

TABLE 8.29

Classification of responses of the sampled leaders based on their gender regarding their readiness to canvass for a political leader contesting election

	Gender		*Total*
	Male	*Female*	
Yes	82 49.1%	22 28.6%	104 42.6%
No	77 46.1%	37 48.1%	114 46.7%
Difficult	8 4.8%	18 23.4%	26 10.7%
Total	167 100.0%	77 100.0%	244 100.0%

Pearson chi-square 22.339*.

The dated in Table 8.29 and chi-square value 22.339 indicate a strong and significant difference of proportion of responses between male and female leaders particularly in accepting that they can canvas for a political leader contesting election and stating that this task of canvassing for a particular leader is quite difficult one. The leaders who observed canvassing a difficult task are not ready to canvass for a leader.

The data in Table 8.30 indicates that the proportion of leaders from backward castes (both groups) and scheduled castes-A is relatively lower regarding the leadership readiness to canvass for a political leader contesting election. In other words, leaders from farming castes, upper castes and scheduled castes-A feel relatively much empowered to canvass for a leader. However, the chi-square value 11.377 indicates that the difference of responses on the said issue is not significant.

Thus, it is concluded that 42.6 per cent of the sampled leadership possess a level of political standing and inclination for politics and willing to integrate with mainstream political system of the area or the state. In other words, a majority of local leaders contest panchayat elections for their social and local interest instead of political reasons. Further, the men are significantly ahead of women and farming castes, upper castes

TABLE 8.30

Classification of responses of the sampled leaders based on their castes regarding their readiness to canvass for a political leader contesting election

	Castes						*Total*
	Farming castes	*Upper castes*	*Backward castes (A)*	*Backward castes (B)*	*Scheduled castes (A)*	*Scheduled castes (B)*	
(1)	*(2)*	*(3)*	*(4)*	*(5)*	*(6)*	*(7)*	*(8)*
Yes	37 48.7%	15 45.5%	9 37.5%	9 37.5%	19 47.5%	15 31.9%	104 42.6%
No	32 42.1%	12 36.4%	12 50.0%	11 45.8%	17 42.5%	30 63.8%	114 46.7%
Difficult	7 9.2%	6 18.2%	3 12.5%	4 16.7%	4 10.0%	2 4.3%	26 10.7%
Total	76 100.0%	33 100.0%	24 100.0%	24 100.0%	40 100.0%	47 100.0%	244 100.0%

Pearson chi-square 11.377.

and scheduled castes-A leaders are although relatively more advanced to other castes leaders but not in significant manner.

Notes and References

1. Almond, Gabriel A. and Powell Jr, G. Bingham (1976). Comparative Politics—A Development Approach, New Delhi: Oxford and IBH Publishing Comp., p. 25.
2. *Ibid.*, p. 28.
3. *Ibid.*, p. 29.
4. *Ibid.*, p. 29.
5. *Ibid.*, p. 42.
6. Pye, Lucian W. (1966). Aspects of Political Development, New Delhi: Amerind Publishing Co., p. 33.
7. *Ibid.*, p. 39.
8. Darshankar, A.Y. (1979). Leadership in Panchayat Raj, Jaipur: Panchsheel Prakashan, p. 125.

9

Conclusions and Suggestions

The social and cultural inequalities traditional rural society are attributed to the caste system which creates a highly stratified social structure in the society. The legacy of caste and other historical conditions of extreme inequality give rise to expectations of prejudicial treatment and hence to behaviours that tend to reproduce the inequality. This belief system emphasizes and rationalizes the exploitation of the castes ranked lowest in the hierarchy.

The women are considered lesser in status to the men in cultural perspective. She has been serving the privileged male accepting it as her dharma. The roots of this tradition are there since several centuries. This has been continuing since past because the women are dependent on men who control social, cultural, economic and political powers. The Preamble of our constitution promises social, economic and political equity to all men and women in the country. The nation has always strived for this noble goal in one way or the other. The 73rd Constitutional Amendment Act, 1992 and in particular the reservation provision made therein is one of such sincere efforts for pursuing political equity at panchayati raj level in the country. Therefore, an attempt has been made here to find out the role of new panchayati raj in alleviating the political standing of the women and scheduled castes leadership *vis-à-vis* the dominant traditional leadership at gram panchayat level in the Haryana state.

CONCLUSIONS

It is found in the study that from first panchayats, election onwards (after 73rd amendment), the percentage of younger leaders has gone upwards. In simple words, the proportion of younger people is increasing in the panchayati raj leadership. They have started to dominate the rural political life. Moreover, the proportion of the young female PR leaders is higher than the younger male panchayati raj leaders. The proportion of leaders having educational level (above matriculation) is relatively significantly higher among the leaders of younger age groups. It is also found that the leaders belonging to Backward Castes (A) and Scheduled Castes (A) are very traditional and electing least percentage of the younger leaders in comparison to middle aged and elder aged who constitute 82.7 per cent of them. The sampled leaders' age groups are not significantly differentiated on the basis of their estimated annual incomes and thus they have been from the families having different income levels. Thus, young leaders from smaller sizes of families are joining panchayati raj institutions. They (young leaders) are relatively better educated than the traditional leadership.

It is evident from the study that a majority of the sampled leaders (55.9 per cent) are from the families having up to six members. Some of the leaders (17.2 per cent) are even from smaller families of 3-4 members. However, the percentage of leaders who belong to bigger families (9-10 members) are 32.8 per cent and large families (more than 10 members) 11.3 per cent. Thus, earlier belief that big joint families dominate the village leadership is fading in the state. In actual, the sizes of families in villages are decreasing owing to social transformation taking place there and leaders from those small families are joining local panchayat politics. There is variation of proportion of representation of leaders belonging different sizes of family. The farming castes and scheduled castes are at least apparently ahead of others castes' leaders in context with their belongingness to large sized families. Further, it is also concluded from the study that the variations of family sizes based on gender and educational levels are not real but an apparent one. Thus, an analysis of the sizes of families with gender, castes, educational achievements, and incomes reveals that most active family size (in term of their representation in PRIs) is 5-6 members, i.e. average family size (38.4 per cent) followed by the bigger size, i.e. 9-10 members (32.8 per cent).

The study concludes that panchayati raj leadership comprises of leaders belonging to various castes in the village and it is due to the reservation provisions, numerical strength and delimitation of wards. It is observed that every caste having enough electors to elect a panch in the village has been able to send its representative to gram panchayat. There is a strong caste consciousness among the various castes of the village to make sincere efforts to send their representatives to the gram panchayat and the reservation provision has strengthened this feeling in a significant sense. Further, it is evident from the data that the women of all castes could get elected in panchayats but due to reservation alone and the socio- economic and attitudinal characteristics have not influenced the election of women particularly at gram panchayat and panchayat samiti levels. It is also revealed by the study that the leaders from various castes' groups are significantly different in terms of land possession and their estimated annual incomes. The leaders belonging farming castes, upper castes, and backward castes (B) are relatively well-off in economic sense unlike scheduled castes and other castes leaders. Thus, the caste is an indispensable factor in deciding the election of a person to the panchayati raj institutions.

Education facilitates progress to an individual. Its need particularly in village leadership is essentially significant as the rural society is characterized with illiteracy and social backwardness. But an overwhelming majority (84.7 per cent) of leaders is either illiterate or educated up to matriculation level. It is also found that higher the educational level, lesser the percentage of women leaders. More specifically, there are only five women in the sample strength of 105 women leaders, who are educated higher than the matriculation level. Similarly, the upper castes, farming castes, and backward castes (B) leaders are relatively more educated in comparison to other caste leaders in significant manner. It is quite surprising to note that the educational achievements of the sampled panchayati raj leaders are independent of their family sizes and income levels. Thus, educated leadership at gram panchayat level is a goal, which is not likely to be achieved in near future but some castes may likely to provide educated leaders to these panchayati raj institutions.

The sampled leaders are engaged in the occupations related to agriculture only. However, a large percentage of them (41.6 per cent) do not possess any kind of land holdings. It means that many of them are agricultural labourers. It is also found that the big farmers and erstwhile big farmers are still active in village politics and constitute a sizeable section of leadership. Further, about 31.6 percent of the leaders are having annual incomes below Rs. 25,000 which means that they are very poor and live below poverty line and most of these people are from scheduled castes (both groups) and backward classes (A) group. Further, a group of 32.8 per cent of the leadership is relatively rich and possesses fairly bigger sizes of land holdings (more than 5 acres). Moreover, they are from upper castes, farming castes and backward castes (B). Thus the study concludes that the leaders belonging to farming and business occupations and residing in villages are not only holding offices in local institutions but also capable to influence the village politics. The poor are also representing and participating in panchayati raj institutions but all because of their castes' support, legal and constitutional provisions. Thus, the panchayati raj has given an opportunity to the so far neglected people of society to rise to the position of leadership

It is found in the study that a large majority (84.1 per cent) of leaders are first timer in panchayati raj politics. Therefore, they are termed as representatives rather than leaders. The reason, they are not contesting elections again and again to become regular politician. This habit is similar both in male and female leaders. Further, the leaders from the upper castes followed by farming castes and backward castes (B) are relatively more regular and permanent leaders in comparison to other castes' leaders. It is also observed that a new trend that the new enactment has its impact in arousing interest among rural people of different castes to come forward for contesting elections of gram panchayat and panchayat samiti elections. However, the difference in this habit of contesting elections in continuous manner between the leaders of different castes is not significant one. It is also concluded that the regularity of contesting elections does not differ in significant way with the educational levels and income levels of the sampled leaders. Thus, most of the village leaders do not make effort to establish themselves as regular and permanent political leader of the village or the area around their village.

It is also found in the study that there are only a few PR leaders who are contesting PR elections almost on regular basis and most of them are contesting election for the office of the sarpanch. It is evident from the data that only 13.1 per cent contested the election for this position and out of this, 10.6 per cent contested once and they won that election. The data indicates that on an average basis, there have been one or less than one person in each village (total villages surveyed) are (8), who have keen interest in village politics and they are regularly contesting the election of sarpanch. No doubt, the reservation provision has an adverse influence on such kind of dominance of individuals in village politics as that has disrupted the continuity to contest the election. Nevertheless, in such situation also they motivated a candidate from reserved caste or made their wife to contest the election. Thus, the reservation has widened the scope for those candidates who in the absence of which had not thought of contesting sarpanch's election even as a proxy candidate. Thus, there has been much democratization at local levels in general and office of sarpanch in particular after 73rd constitutional amendment act. Further, the women do not contest sarpanch's election unless to be the proxy of their husband or family. Further, the percentage of leaders who contested the election of sarpanch more than once is relatively higher among farming castes. The scheduled castes (both A and B groups) followed them. However, the regularity of contesting election for the office of the sarpanch does not vary with position, educational levels of the sampled leaders.

It is found in the study that in total 188 candidates contested the election for the office of panch in a gram panchayat. Out of these 131 are men and 57 are women. Further, the percentage of such leaders who contested elections for the office of panch more than once is only 15, i.e. 4.6 per cent. However, in case of panch the continuity of contesting election for the position of panches in gram panchayats is higher among scheduled castes (A), followed by upper castes, scheduled castes (B), backward castes (A) and farming castes. It means that upper castes and scheduled castes (A) are having stable leadership in terms of contesting panches' election. Further, the frequency to contest election for the position of panch is influenced by the educational and income levels in significant way. Thus, the attitude of village leaders to contest panch's election is different from the election of sarpanch.

It is evident from the data that out of 129 sampled leaders (total sampled PS leaders are 90) who reported that they contested PS election only seven stated that they have done it more than once. Further, it is also clear from the data that out of those who contested PS election, 87 are men and 47 women. The leaders from various castes have different levels of frequency of contesting PS elections. In simple words, some of the reserved class PS leaders (a very limited number) have adopted the political life on regular basis and contesting local elections every time they get the opportunity. The regularity of contesting election is not showing any trend in context with their annual income except a few poor persons who belong reserved classes and become full time political worker at village level or in the area. They may or may not have any affiliation with political parties but remain engaged to help their people in one way or the other. This becomes their profession. But the data is not enough to make reasonable level of generalized statement in this regard. It appears (as the study does not have relevant empirical information on this aspect) that the regularity to contest PS election is not very attractive and a few of the poor reserved classes of leaders who are not much educated have contested the elections more than once. Thus, the conclusions relating to the regularity in contesting local elections in this study suffer from certain limitations. The leaders, who reported regularity is in real sense, have adopted it in inheritance or who have assimilated themselves in party politics of the state. The low percentage of these leaders is because young leaders have just begun their career in politics and contested for the first time or so

The reservation has provided a wider opportunity to develop much democratic and participative local leadership at gram panchayat and panchayat samiti levels as most of the sampled leaders joined the local institutions for the first time. Therefore, they consider that they have not acquired the role of political worker. This kind of feeling is significantly higher among women (61.9 per cent) in comparison to men (46.5 per cent). In castes' context, the leaders who perceive themselves in political workers' role is higher among farming castes followed by scheduled castes (B), upper castes and backward castes (A) and scheduled castes (A). In addition, the backward castes (A) are relatively less developed in political sense in comparison to backward castes (B).

It is also concluded from the data that farming castes, backward castes (B) and upper castes are politically active and backward castes (A) and scheduled castes as a whole find themselves lesser active castes in the sampled villages. Further, the perception that they have acquired the role of political worker more or less increases with the rise in educational levels of the sampled leaders. The education is considered as responsible factor facilitating the assimilation of panchayati raj leader infused in localized mainstream politics of the state. Thus it is concluded that big farmers and many of those who get the local politics in inheritance, reservation introduced by new panchayat raj, willingness to promote political interests and concern for development/welfare activities are the motivating factors for sampled rural leaders to take local politics as political career.

The majority of the sampled leaders (55.3 per cent) perceived village life as an inactive life. This kind of perception is significantly different among male and female and gram panchayat and panchayat samiti leaders, and also between various educational and income levels. It is also found that the leaders of various castes (except backward castes (B). and scheduled castes (B)) affirmed the inactiveness of life in villages and the percentages of gram panchayat leaders, who denied the inactive life in villages, is also lesser than the panchayat samiti leaders holding such perception. Further, relatively much educated leaders considers that there is inactiveness in village life and it decreases with the increase in income levels. However, there is no significant difference in their perceptions on this issue among the leaders of various income levels.

The study concludes that there are only a few castes which are politically active and possess the requisite resources required to be successful in local politics. It is also believed in rural society that the resourceful people dominate in PRIs and numerical strength is instrumental in deciding the nature of leadership at village level. Many times, it is argued that the sarpanch belonging to upper castes only be successful. It means that the caste plays an important role in decision-making process of PRIs. The reservation system introduced particularly after 73rd constitutional amendment has facilitated the representation of SC/women and naturally that has elevated their status in politics in particular and society in general. In this context, it is concluded that a large majority (63.4 per cent) of the rural leadership stated that all castes have their independent role in electing gram panchayat leaders. Further, the percentage of male leaders (60.5 per cent) holding this opinion is lesser than the female leaders (69.5 per cent). Similarly, the gram panchayat leaders in comparison to panchayat samiti leaders have higher proportion that holds this view point. However, the leaders of various castes' groups have responded differently and the percentage of those who consider that all the castes are independent in electing their representatives but it is lowest (35.3 per cent) among SC (A) representatives indicating their inability to compete with other castes of their respective villages. In context with the educational levels, it is found that the senior secondary passed leaders are at the lowest (53.3 per cent) and graduate leaders are at the highest level (75 per cent) on this continuum who stated that all castes have independent role in local elections.

The study reveals that the PS leaders before 73rd amendment were used to be rich, influential, party worker and having closeness with the mainstream political leadership of the state. Similarly, in case of gram panchayat leaders, most of them used to be rich and big landlords, active in politics, influential and closely related to mainstream political leaders and bureaucrats. But, the panchayat samiti leaders elected after amendment are from the different classes of people, no doubt, maximum of them are rich, influential and active in politics instead of closely related with mainstream political leadership of the state. In case of gram panchayat leaders, it is found that they are now coming from all classes of rural people and the dominance of earlier dominant class has diluted to the extent that the base of recruiting leaders in local politics has widened to include more common and poor people. Thus it is interred that the panchayati raj institutions have become more and more popular and broadbased.

Thus above stated inference is based upo the fact percentage (30.3 per cent) of leaders is either big landlords or political active or influential persons of the village/area or persons having relationships in state bureaucracy. Similarly another 16.9 percent are either rich persons or influential or party workers or close to a political leader or active in politics. Besides this, a group of 8.4 per cent of the sampled leaders stated that they are from the mainstream of the society and having relationships with political leaders or bureaucrats or local influential persons. Further, the male leaders are more resourceful than the female in significant way and the leaders of various castes differ in terms of resources possessed by them. It is also concluded that a large percentage of leaders who are illiterate, primary and middle passed are not very resourceful. Therefore, it is concluded that the most important resource to reserve a berth in rural local political system is the caste, hierarchical level of the caste and numerical strength of the caste in the village concerned. The upper castes and land-owning castes leaders are more resourceful in social, economic and political sense therefore they still have holds on the panchayati raj institutions in the state. But it has diluted over the years as is evident from the fact that 32.8 per cent and 31.9 per cent of the sampled leaders agreed and disagreed respectively to the proposition that resourceful and influential persons alone are influencing the election and working of panchayats in the state. The analysis of data also holds that there is no difference of opinion on the basis of gender, castes and educational level regarding the dominance of resourceful and morally sound persons in local democratic system except in an apparent manner.

It is concluded on the basis of data that only about one third of the sampled leaders endorsed the proposition that numerical strength of a specific caste is an active and contributory factor, which decides the composition and nature of village leadership. In real sense, the instrumentality of numerical strength in deciding the composition of village leadership is undermined by the reservation provision and ward system introduced after reforms. However, the sampled leaders who are either literate or graduate and who belong to the scheduled castes (A) group of castes are much (50 percent or more) in favour of this belief. Thus, the numerical strength is one of the factors which decide the composition of gram panchayat or the nature of gram panchayat leadership.

It is quite clear from the study that a simple majority (55 per cent) of leadership denied that caste plays an important role in decision making process of a panchayat. There is only less than a quarter (23.8 per cent) who affirmed this. In this way, the caste is not so significant in decision-making process of the panchayats. Further, the farming castes and scheduled castes (A) leaders recognize this role of caste much more in comparison to other castes' leaders. It is argued that backward castes and scheduled castes (B) have realized their political potential and asserting to negate the dominance of traditional castes in panchayati raj. The data in the study also establishes that higher the level of education of the leader, lesser the recognition of the role of caste in local political system leaving some exceptions. Thus although only about a quarter of the sampled leaders believe that caste plays an important role in decision-making process of a panchayat but the leaders of different gender, castes and educational levels differ in their perceptions on this issue.

More explicitly, is found in the study that about 53 per cent of the sampled leaders stated that role of caste is not instrumental in decision-making process of panchayat. However, more leaders from scheduled castes (A) and farming castes' leaders support the proposition that contribution to the decision of a panchayat depend on the caste of the leader in relation to scheduled castes (B) and backward castes leaders. Moreover, the affirmation of the role of caste in decision making decreases and denial increases as one move from illiterate to higher educational level. But, there is discontinuity to this generalized statement in case of primary and secondary passed leaders. Thus, the caste of a leader is significant in terms of the contribution of the leader towards the panchayat decision but the education and political empowerment of leaders is diminishing the role of castes in decision-making process of a panchayat.

The study concludes that a large majority (73.4 per cent) of the sampled leadership affirmed that, 'the reservation of seats in PRIs for scheduled castes and women has elevated their respect in society'. This perception is independent of the variables like castes, gender and educational level. In other words, both male and female leaders and of all castes and educational levels perceive that the reservation of seats in PRIs has elevated the respect of scheduled castes and women in society. Further, the unanimous elections are favoured by almost all of the sampled leaders. There is no difference in this liking among men and women and the leaders from different castes and the leaders of different education levels.

The study concludes that the majority of those who are literate enough to read newspaper have this habit. It simply means leaders are interested to get acquainted with about their surroundings. As expected there is significant difference between male (51.6 per cent) and female (16.2 per cent and those are also the leaders of panchayat samities) leaders on this attributes. Further, the leaders from the upper castes, followed by backward castes and farming castes have relatively higher proportion of leaders having newspaper reading habit. But, only 17.5 per cent of them affirmed the utility of newspaper reading habit in understanding local governance and another 14.1 per cent consider that this habit helps in developing wisdom to run the affairs of PRIs. The proportion of leaders supporting the said proposition is higher among male, upper castes and farming castes' leaders and the panchayat samiti leaders. The female, scheduled castes and GP leaders are relatively backward in this context.

It is clear from the study that 89.1 per cent of the sampled leaders desire that sarpanch must be an educated person. Further, both male and female leaders understand the efficacy of education as they like an educated person to be the sarpanch of their village. The proportion of leaders who favoured this proposition are higher among educated leaders and lower in case of farming castes and scheduled castes (B) and illiterates. Thus, it is concluded that the people expect that persons having requisite level of education or understanding are the successful local leaders.

The study further concludes that a simple majority of the leaders (54.1 per cent) expected that the srapanch must be a mature in age, followed by another 20.6 per cent who stated that they expected that elder persons must be their sarpanch in the village. It is important to note that about 25 per cent of leaders are elders there in the sample. It means that even the sampled elders preferred for young and mature person to be the sarpanch of the village. Further, the data establishes that the perceptions of male and female leaders do not differ in significant manner on the issue of what should be the preferred age of the sarpanch of the village? It is interesting to state that majority of them wish to find that a mature person in the age group of 36-50 years should be the sarpanch of a village.

Similarly, the leaders from backward castes (A) and upper castes followed by scheduled castes (A) and others rated mature leaders as their preference for the office of the sarpanch of the village. It is also interesting to find that the sampled leaders belonging to scheduled castes (33.3 and 31.3 percent) and backward castes (B) (32.4 percent) are higher in comparison to other castes leaders (average is 25.3 percent) who preferred young leadership. The elders are preferred much by the backward castes and farming castes in comparison to other castes' leaders. However, the chi-square value (22.729) confirms that the caste-based difference of perceptions is an apparent one and not enough significant to draw valid conclusion. Thus, an educated and mature person is preferred as the sarpanch of the village.

A large majority (86.3 per cent) of leadership likes to have a sarpanch who must be a person able to provide moral leadership. This liking is uniform across the gender and castes of the leadership.

The study reveals that a simple majority (51.3 per cent) of the leadership feels that local leadership possess the attribute of accountability and behaves in responsible manner while performing the affairs of panchayats. Further, this kind of feeling does not vary with the gender and castes of the sampled leaders. The leaders, both male and female and of different castes have almost similar kind of perceptions on this attribute of panchayati raj leadership. Thus, the panchayat leaders behave in responsible manner but it is not true for all.

The data in the study makes it clear that the majority of leaders rated the panchayat leaders as competent enough to discharge their responsibilities. Further, the male and female leaders do not differ in their perceptions in significant way while rating the competence of panches and sarpanches. However, the perceptions on the said proposition differ from one caste to another caste in significant manner. The proportion of scheduled castes' leaders who rated panches/sarpanches as competent is higher and least in case of farming castes. But, at the same time, a majority of sampled leaders (68.1 per cent) affirmed the impact of social inequalities and illiteracy on the competence of leadership. It is endorsed by both male and female leaders of every caste more or less in an equal way. Thus, the inequalities of all kinds and illiteracy are the hindrances in ensuring democratic decentralization through panchayat raj.

It is somewhat surprising to find that less than half of the leaders (42.8 per cent) evaluated the performance of their panchayat as good. It is lesser than the proportion of those who found the panches and sarpanches as competent. Further, about one-fourth of leaders (25.9 per cent) stated that their panchayat perform its functions in somewhat good manner, i.e. they rated the performance of panchayat as average one. Thus, about 69 per cent are satisfied with the performance of panchayat and panches/sarpanches competence. It is also found that male in comparison to female leaders are satisfied from the performance of panchayats.

Thus, the discussion above makes to conclude although with less force, that panchayat raj leaders are competent and perform the functions of panchayat either in a good or average manner. However, some variations in perceptions are there when compared on gender basis but not when classified on caste basis.

It is concluded that about half of the sampled leaders (45.9 per cent) are possessing necessary strength of enthusiasm and wisdom to perform the panchayat's responsibilities. Nevertheless, the women leaders differ in significant manner from the male leaders and relatively lesser optimistic about the presence of such attributes. But, the perceptions of leaders across castes do not differ from each other in significant sense. Thus, majority of panchayati raj leaders are not energetic, enthusiastic and sensible enough to satiate the expectation even of the sampled leadership.

It is also concluded by the study that many of the local leaders (45.9 percent) are competent enough to decide the village priorities (a political function to be essentially performed by elected representative in democratic world). However, this feeling is lesser among female leaders in significant way but almost uniformly present among the leaders of various castes. The reason to it may be attributed that women are inexperienced and not actively involved in panchayat's activities and responsibilities.

The study also establishes the proposition that a simple majority of sampled leaders do not find most of the leaders involved in party politics rather remain involved in PRIs only. It supports an earlier conclusion of the present study itself which states that the sampled panchayati raj leaders are not regular in contesting panchayati raj elections rather they are casual leaders who do not wish to go beyond village level politics.

The proposition that 'the effectiveness of panchayati raj leadership has improved after the new panhayati raj has been introduced in the state, it is endorsed by a large majority (89.1 per cent) of leaders and equally supported by the leaders across various castes. However, the proportion of male leaders who supported this proposition is much higher than the female leaders. Thus, all male leaders consider a change in role performance of panchayats.

As stated earlier also, about one-third of sampled leadership has admitted the dominance of rich and resourceful in the working of gram panchayats. But, majority (59.1 per cent) of them denied this. In other words, the dominance of rich and resourceful is not so strong now. Further, the perceptions in this regard are not different when considered on gender and caste basis. The information in the study also reveals that a fair majority (64.1 per cent) of the sampled leaders consider that the reservation of seats in PRIs has enhanced the role of reserved classes of leaders. In other words, the reservation introduced by the 73rd amendment act has perceptible impact in increasing the role of reserved classes of leaders in PRIs. This is endorsed by a sizeable majority of both male and female leaders of various castes in more or less in similar manner.

The study also indicates that 47.2 per cent of the leadership is of the opinion that consciousness of opposing the traditional leadership has aroused in the reserved class of panchayati raj leadership of the state. Further, the higher percentage of male in comparison to female leadership supported this proposition. Thus, the process of replacing the dominance of traditional leadership has grown and reservation has contributed to this process in significant way. However, this proposition is significantly supported by women leaders and lesser by the leaders of the scheduled castes and farming castes.

A majority of the leaders (59 per cent) rejected the incidence of conflict between reserved and non reserved classes of leadership. But, about one-fifth (21.6 per cent) of them reported the occurrence of such conflicts. Further, the responses on this are almost equally distributed between male and female leaders and across various castes. A majority of leaders (61.9 per cent) contradicted that 'sarpanch belonging to a non-reserved class do not let the panches of reserved class to participate in village panchayat activities in a well mannered way. Thus, the conflicts between reserved and non-reserved classes of leaders are not common and the proposition that non-reserved class of sarpanch does not let the panches of reserved class to participate in village panchayat activities is not fully valid. It may be restated as 'there may be a sarpanch in a village panchayat who may not find it proper to let the reserved class of panches to participate in village panchayat activities in a well mannered way' because of certain prevailing conditions The members who reported ill-treatment may not be from sarpanch's group in the village rather from opposition camp in the panchayat. In reality this is not a common practice despite the fact that it is endorsed by enough number of scheduled castes (A) leaders and female leaders sampled in this study.

It is concluded in the study that a majority (56.6 per cent) of the sampled leaders do not agree to the proposition that the panch or sarpanch of reserved class can not become the leader of the village. Not only this, a large majority of them (74.4 per cent) rejected this notion that reservation of office of the sarpanch has weakened the institution of gram panchayat. It is suggested by the data that the upper castes and farming castes leaders do not find themselves prepared to accept reserved class of sarpanch or panch as their village leader and expressed that the reservation has weakened the institution of gram panchayat. There is a silent tug of war between reserved and non-reserved classes of leaders to assert their position in gram panchayat, which is a feature of democratic development taking place in rural traditional society.

The proposition that the women are not real representatives but their election in panchayats is essentially bringing a social change in rural society, is endorsed by 82.5 per cent of the sampled leaders. However, the women who are sarpanch/members PS are considered themselves as real representatives of their voters (accepted by 53.8 percent of the sampled leaders). It is also evident that more women representatives in comparison to men recognize themselves as leaders of their voters. The male leaders in general and the leaders belonging to backward castes-B, scheduled caste-A and upper castes leaders' views (although not in significant manner) are not much supportive to the proposition. Besides this, the representation of women in panchayati raj institutions is only a beginning and about one third of sampled leaders accepted that elected women leaders have the potentiality to lead rural women folk. This proposition is favoured more by women in comparison to men but almost equally across the castes of the leaders. Further, the women are not considered as real representatives at village panchayat level by about half (53.4 per cent) of the sampled leaders. Thus the women in panchayats may be able to bring the social change in the village but they are the real local leaders till now.

The women do not consider themselves as leader of the village or their ward. Rather, they attribute the credit for their election in panchayat to their family/husband. It is equally supported by all castes leaders and more strongly by male leaders in comparison to female leaders. The reason, in rural politics the family is indivisible unit and claim of individuality separated from family means that the social, economic and political resources of the family are not utilized which are essentially required to be successful in panchayati raj election. The women leaders (endorsed by 84.4 per cent) take directions from their husband/family members in discharging panchayat functions. The pattern of responses is uniform in both the genders and among the leaders of various castes' groups.

It is also revealed by the study that after three panchayat elections and 12 years after the reforms and reservation in the state, a majority of leaders (62.8 per cent) consider the women leaders that they would be able (in future) to discharge the functions of panchayats entrusted to them. Thus, there is a change in attitude towards women leadership of the state and that is also both among men and women and the leadership comprises of all castes.

It is established in the study that 91.4 per cent of leaders have performed many of the functions entrusted to panchayats while in PRIs. Thus there is involvement of almost all the leaders in panchayat functions. But the kind of involvement varies from leader to leader. The leaders involvement in above stated activities start from suggesting to do a work or asking to do a particular activity, suggesting how to do it, supervising and sanctioning budget for it. It is true most of the technical details concerning these activities are attended by specialists of Block Development Office but the sarpanch in particular and panches in general get these done in the village. However, the women leaders are significantly lesser involved than the male leaders but there is not any such difference among the leaders of various castes. Similarly, it is concluded that a large majority of the leaders (77.5 per cent) stated that they participate in dispute resolution but the participation of men in such activity is significantly higher than women because of social reasons.

The study concludes that a good majority of leaders have the peers in the village that can assemble on invitation from their leader to discuss the common things with their representative. However, the traits of this ability are definitely higher among male leaders in comparison to female leaders. The caste of the leader although does not distinguish them on this variable in significant way but it appears apparently that the dominating castes' leaders have an edge over the others in this regard. Further, the discussions in these meetings have always been informal in nature.

It is clear from the study that mobilizing funds for panchayat's activities is difficult task for many of the leaders but more than half of the local leaders (66.8 per cent) are capable to do that. Similarly more than half of the leaders (68 per cent) found that they could motivate and encourage their village fellow to contribute labour, gift money and other for a common purpose. Further, this capability is perceived to be possessed significantly much more by male leaders and also by the leaders belonging to upper castes and farming castes and scheduled castes-B leaders in comparison to other castes but not in significant way.

The study makes it clear that a large majority of leaders (74.2 per cent) stated that they possess the attributes of motivating people to participate in village panchayat activities. This kind of feeling is significantly higher among men in comparison to women leadership. Similarly, the leaders from scheduled castes (B), backward castes (B) and farming castes are although better placed than others in this sense but not in significant way. The study also concludes that about 70 percent of the leaders responded that they possess the ability to educate people of their village about prevailing social evils in the society and it is equally true for both male and female sampled leadership. It is also observed that the proportion of leaders from the scheduled castes-B, upper castes and farming castes is higher than the other castes particularly scheduled castes-A and backward castes-B. But, leaders from backward castes (both groups) are having relatively lower proportion of leaders endowed with this attribute of organizing an event in the village.

It is also concluded that about 42 percent of leaders feel that they are endowed with the ability to organize people at village level. But a significant proportion of them (about 58 per cent) stated that they can not build up the association or union of village people or it is difficult task to be performed by them. The data also suggests that apparently the women lag behind men and the leaders from scheduled castes (A) and backward castes both A and B groups are relatively worse than other castes in this regard but not in significant manner.

It is difficult for the sampled leaders to canvass for a political leader as is evident from the data. Only 42.6 per cent leadership accepts that they can canvass for a political leader and 8 percent consider it a difficult task. Thus about 50 percent of them possess a level of political standing and inclination for politics and willing to integrate with mainstream political system of the area or the state. In other words, a majority of local leaders contest panchayat elections for their social and local interest instead of political reasons. Further, the men are significantly ahead of women and farming castes, upper castes and scheduled castes (A) leaders although relatively more advanced to other castes leaders but not in significant manner.

It is concluded in the study that majority of leaders (59.4 per cent) do not consider that there is any negative impact on the leadership because of governmental interventions. The reason to this state of affairs is attributed to the reasonable level of involvement of gram panchayat and panchayat samiti members in mainstream politics in one way or the other. Further it is also clear that except women leaders, the perceptions of male leaders and leaders of various castes equally rejected the proposition that 'there is negative impact of non-involvement of reserved class leadership on them when they are not involved in implementing poverty alleviation programmes for their community'. The reason is attributed that women are not involved much when decisions in panchayat are being taken by the panchayat. Thus, the non-involvement of women leaders in panchayati raj activities gets testified in an indirect way.

SUGGESTIONS

It is considered that the local leaders are appropriate persons along with the officials to tell how the democratic decentralization can be strengthened in the state. Therefore the sampled leaders were asked to give their suggestions for strengthening democratic decentralization in the state. The suggestions are tabulated in Table 10.1 given below.

TABLE 10.1

Sampled leaders suggestions for strengthening democratic decentralization in the state

	Frequency	*Valid Percent*	*Cumulative Percent*
Educated and rights' conscious people	33	10.3	10.3
Educated + social and economically developed people	3	.9	11.3
Education + freedom from inhibition	11	3.4	14.7
Education awareness of rights + prosperity	17	5.3	20.0
Education + prosperity + absence of inhibitions	13	4.1	24.1
Education + awareness + prosperity + freedom	101	31.6	55.6
Many reasons	15	4.7	60.3
People should be educated	47	14.7	75.0
Awareness of rights and responsibilities	62	19.4	94.4
Based on social + economic development	4	1.3	95.6
Independence of thoughts	8	2.5	98.1
Others	3	.9	99.1
Uncertain	3	.9	100.0
Total	320	100.0	

It is evident from the data obtained from the that there are sampled leaders which indicate that there are many ways to strengthen democratic decentralization in the state. The maximum proportion of them (31.6 per cent) is of the opinion that the educational and economic development, political awareness along with freedom will enrich the democracy. Another, 19.4 per cent said that the awareness of rights and responsibilities can help it in significant manner. The third larger group of leaders (14.7 per cent) emphasized the need of educational development as that will enlighten the people and help in establishing civic society. A section of leaders (10.3 per cent) stated that educated and rights conscious people are the assets of democratic decentralization. In total, the leaders found that social, educational and economic development is basic key to democratic decentralization and political independence, freedom and empowerment of civic society are the other conditions which can contribute in an effective way to strengthen the democratic decentralization in the state in particular.

Bibliography

(i) Books and Papers

Agarwal, Bina (ed.) (1988). Structures of Patriarchy: State, Community and Household in Modernising Asia, New Delhi: Indian Association for Women's Studies.

Ahuja Ram (1999). Society in India. Jaipur : Rawat Publications.

Airan, J.W. (ed.) (1969). The Nature of Leadership, Bombay: Lalwani Publishing House.

Aiyar, Mani Shankar (2002). Panchayati Raj: The Ways Forward. *Economic and Political Weekly*, 37 (31), August 3, 2002.

Allport, F.H. (1924). Social Psychology, Boston: Houghton Miffin, p. 41.

Almond Gabriel and James S. Coleman (1960). The Politics of Developing Areas, Princeton: Princeton University Press.

Bachenherimer, R. (1959), 'Elements of Leadership in an Andhra Village in Richard L. Park and Irene Tinker (eds.), Leadership and Political Institutions in India, Princeton, NJ : University Princeton Press, pp. 445-52.

Balaramulu Ch. and Raghavender Rao (1995). Political Leadership in Panchayati Raj: A Study of Mandal Praja Parishad Leadership in Andhra Pradesh, *Administrative Change*, 22(2), Jan.-June 1995, p. 173.

Bardhan, Kalpana (1985). Women's Work, Welfare and Status: Forces of Tradition and Change in India, *Economic and Political Weekly*, 20(50), and (51-52), December 14 and December 21-28.

Barnabas, A.P. (1958). Characteristics of 'Lay Leaders' in Extension Work. *Journal of the M.S. University*, Baroda.

———, (1969). Social Change in a North Indian Village, New Delhi: Indian Institute of Public Administration.

Barnard, C.L. (1948). Organization and Mànagement, Cambridge Mass: Harvard University Press.

Bathla, Harbhagwan (1994). Panchayati Raj and Political Parties—An Empirical Study of Grassroot Level in Haryana, Kurukshetra: Nirmal Book Agency.

Baxi, Upendra (1987). Participatory Justice: A Unique of Nyaya Panchayats in Karnataka in Mathew, George (Ed.), Panchayat Raj in Karnataka Today, New Delhi: Institute of Social Sciences.

Bearls, R. (1959). Leadership in a Mysore Village in Park, Richard L. and Tukker, Irene (eds.). Leadership and Political Institutions in India, Princeton: Princeton University Press.

Bellows, Roger (1959). Creative Leadership, Prentice Hall.

Beteille, Andre (1965). Caste, Class and Power: Changing Pattern of Stratification in a Tanjore village, Berkeley: University of California Press.

Bhargava, B.S. (1977). Emerging Leadership in Panchayati Raj System,. Bangalore, Institute for Social and Economic Change.

———, (1979). Panchayati Raj System and Political Parties, New Delhi: Ashish Publishing House.

Bhargava, B.S. and Samal, K. (1996). Panchayati Raj System in Orissa: Problems and Prospects in Mahajan, V.S. (ed.). Agriculture, Rural Development and Panchayati Raj: National level Strategies and Policies, New Delhi: Deep and Deep Publication (P) Ltd.

Bhatnagar, S. (1974). Rural Local Government in India, New Delhi: Light and Life Publishers.

Bhattacharya, Mohit and Dutta, Prabhat K. (1991). Governing Rural India, New Delhi: Uppal Publishing House.

Biddle, William W. (1953). The Cultivation of Community Leaders, New York: Harper and Bros. Publishers.

Biju, M.R. (1998). Dynamics of New Panchayati Raj System: Reflections and Retrospections, New Delhi: Manas Publishing.

Blair, Harry W. (1996). Democracy, Equity and Common Property Resource Management in the Indian Subcontinent, *Development and Change*, 27(3), July.

Brecher Michael (Ed.) (1969). Political Leadership in India, New York: Frederick A. Prager Publishers.

Burman, Roy B.K. (1995). Self-Government in Tribal Areas and the Seventy third Amendment in State Panchayat Acts: A Critical Review (Annexure), New Delhi: Voluntary Action Network.

Carole, Pateman (1970). Participation and Democratic Theory, Cambridge: Cambridge University Press.

Chander, Subhash (1995). Rural Power Structure in Haryana: A Study of Three Panchayat Samitis of Thanesar Sub-Division, (Distt. Kurukshetra), Ph.D Thesis (Unpublished), Department of Political Science, Kurukshetra University, Kurukshetra.

Chandersekhar, B.K. and Anand, Ibanathan (1991). Profile and Participation of Women Zila Parishad and Mandal Panchayat Members : The Case of Karnataka, *Journal of Rural Development,* 10(5) : 578-79.

Choudhry, D.S. (1984). Emerging Rural Leadership in an Indian State: A Case Study of Rajasthan. Rohtak: Manthan Publications, p. 52.

Dasgupta, Susmita (2004). The Politics of Mobilisation of the Backward Classes—Malaise, Diagnosis and Treatment in Bhosale, B.V. (ed.). Mobilisation of Backward Communities in India, New Delhi: Deep and Deep Publications, pp. 74-75.

Datta Prabhat (1992). The Second Generation Panchayats in India, Calcutta: Calcutta Book House.

Dey, S.K. (1960).Community Development, Allahabad: Kitab Mahal.

———, (1960). Community Development, Vol. II, Allahabad: Kitab Mahal.

———, (1964). Community Development: A Bird's Eye View, New York: Asia Publishing House.

———, (1962). Nilokheri, Asia Publishing House.

———, (1961). Panchayati Raj, Bombay: Asia Publishing House.

———, (1969). Power to the People, New Delhi: Orient Longman.

Dhaka, Rajvir S. (Jan. 2002). Panchayat Raj Institutions in Haryana: A Field Study, Kurukshetra, pp. 46-48.

Dhillon, H.S. (1955). Leadership and Groups in South Indian villages, New Delhi: Planning Commission.

Doob, C.B. (1988), Sociology: An Introduction, New York: Holt, Rinehart and Winston.

Dreze, Jean and Sen, Amartya (1999). India: Economic Development and Social Opportunity. New Delhi: Oxford University Press.

Dube, S.C. (1967). India's Changing Village. Bombay: Allied Publishers.

Dube, Leela (1988). On the Construction of Gender: Hindu Girls in Patrilineal India, *Economic and Political Weekly,* 23(18), April 30.

Dutta, Prabhat K. (1993). The Second Generation Panchayats in India, Calcutta: Calcutta Book House.

Fernades, Aureliano (1999). Reconnecting Sabha to Gram in Strengthening Village Democracy. Hyderabad: NIRD.

Fiedler Fred E. (1958). Leaders' Attitude and Group Effectiveness, Urbana: University of Illinois Press.

Francis, C. (1993). Rural Development, People's Participation and the Role of NGOs, *Journal of Rural Development,* Hyderabad: NIRD.

Fund, A. and E.O. Wright (2001). Deepending Democracy: Innovations in Empowered Local Governance, *Politics and Society,* 29(1).

Gabriel A. Almond and Powell Jr., G. Bingham (1976). Comparative Politics : A Development Approach. New Delhi: Oxford and IBH Publishing Company.

Gahalan, Virender Kumar (2004). The Administrative Culture in Panchayati Raj Institutions : A Comparative Study of two Districts in the State of Haryana, unpulished Ph.D. Thesis, Department of Public Administration, Kurukshetra University, Kurukshetra.

Gandhi, Rajiv (1989). Strengthening the Roots of Local Self-Government, New Delhi: Government of India.

Ganesh, L.S. (ed.), (1997). Autonomous District Council, New Delhi: Om Sons Publications.

Gangrade, K.D.: (1974). Emerging Patterns of Leadership: A Comparative Study of Leadership and Social Structure; Delhi: Rachna Publications.

Geventa, J. (2002), Towards Participatory Governance, Currents, 28, pp. 29-35.

Goldsmith, Mike (1990). Local Autonomy—Theory and Practice in King, D. and Pierre, J. (eds.). Challenges of Local Government; London: Sage, p. 20.

Government of India (1965). Emerging Pattern of Rural Leadership in Southern Asia. Hyderabad: NICD.

———, (1955). Leadership and Groups in a South Indian Village.

Government of Karnataka (1999). Guidelines for the conduct of Grama Sabhas, Bangalore: Dept. of Rural Development and Panchayat Raj.

Gupta, Dipankar (2000). Interrogating Caste: Understanding Hierarchy and Difference in Indian Society, New Delhi: Penguin Books, p. 19.

Hoff Karla and Pandey, Priyanka. Belief System and Durable Inequalities An Experimental of Indian Caste. World Bank: Pennsylvania State University, p. 3.

House, R.J. (2004). Culture, Leadership, and Organizations: The GLOBE Study of 62 Societies, Thousand Oaks: Sage Publications, p. 15.

Hutton, J.H. (1969). Castes in India, Oxford University Press.

Inamdar, N.R. (1970), Functioning of Village Panchayats, Popular: Bombay.

———, (1991). Panchayati Raj Leadership: Emerging Dimensions. *Journal of Rural Development*, 10(5), September, pp. 561-73.

Institute of Social Sciences, Occasional Paper Series-6 (1989). Social Background of Zila Parishad Members in Karnataka, New Delhi.

———, Occasional Paper Series-7, (1990). Karnataka: Mandal Panchayat Members, Social Background, New Delhi.

Jain, S.P. (1976). Panchayat Raj in Assam, Hyderabad: National Institute of Community Development.

Jathar, R.V. (1964). Evolution of Jathar, Evolution of Panchayati Raj in India, Dharwar: J.S.S. Institute of Economic Research.

Jean, Dreze and Sen, Amartyha (1995). India—Economic Development and Social Opportunity, Oxford University Press.

Jha, Shree Nagesh (1972). Leadership and Local Politics, Bombay.

———, (1979). Leadership and Local Politics : A Study of Meerut District in Uttar Pradesh, 1923-73, Mumbai : Popular Prakashan.

Jha, Shikha (2002). Strengthening Local Governments: Rural Fiscal Decentralization in India, *Economic and Political Weekly*, 37 (26), June 29, 2002.

Jhamtani, Anita (1995). Rural Women: The Powerless Partners in Development, Kurukshetra, 42.

John, Harris (2000). The Dialectics of Decentralisation, *Frontline*, June 24-July 7.

Joshi, Satyakam (2003). Panchayat Raj Leadership in Gujarat, *IASSI Quarterly*, 21(3 and 4), pp. 79-91.

Joshi, S.D. and Mitragotri, N.P. (2000). Maharasthra in Status of Panchayati Raj in the States and Union Territories of India, Mathew George (Gen. Ed.), New Delhi: Institute of Social Sciences, Concept Publishing Company.

Kerlinger, F.N. (1967). Foundations of Behavioural Research; New Delhi: Surjeet Publication.

Ketter, J.P (1996). Leading Change, Harvard Business School Press, pp. 25-158.

Khan, Iltiza (1969). Government in Rural India, New Delhi : Asia Publishing House.

Khatkhate, Deena R. (1990). Profile of Leadership in a Developing Society, *Economic and Political Weekly*, 24 Nov.

Koontz, H. and O'Donnel, G. (1955). Principles of Management, New York: McGraw Hill Quoted in Srivastava, R.S. (January-June 1996), *Prashasnika*, 28(1).

Kothari, Rajni (Ed.) (1970). Caste in Indian Politics, New Delhi: Orient Longman.

———, (August, 1989). Decentralization: The Real Issue, *Seminar*, No. 360.

———, (1996). Decentralised Governance in Asian Countries in Aziz, Abdul and Arnold David D. (eds.). Delhi: Sage.

Kotter, John P. (1996). Leading Change, Boston: Harvard Business School Press.

Krech, David and Crutch-field, Richard S. (1948). Theory and Problems of Social Psychology, New York: McGraw Hill.

Lalini, V. (1991). Rural Leadership in India: A Study of Emerging Trends in Democratic Authoritarian Rural Leadership, New Delhi: Gyan Publishing House.

Lamprecht, Jurg: (Dec. 1996). What an individual is a leader of its group? An evolutionary concept of distance regulation and leadership, *Social Science Information*, 35 (4), p. 597.

Likert, R. (1967). The Human Organization: Its Management and Value. New York: McGraw Hill.

Luckham R. and Goetz, A.M. (2000). Democratic Institutions and Politics in Contexts of Inequality, Poverty and Conflict. Working Paper 104. Brighton: Institute of Development Studies.

Maheshwari, Shriram (1979). New Perspective on Rural Local Government in India: The Asoka Mehta Committee Report, *Asian Survey*, 19(2).

Mahi Pal, (2002). A People-Oriented Panchayati Raj Framework, *Economic and Political Weekly*, 37(8), February 23.

Malik, A.S. (1990). National Planning and Women Development: A Specific Study of Tribal Village Lakheria in Banswara District in Rajasthan; *Maharishi Dayanand University Research Journal* (Arts); 5(1).

———, (2005). Local Self Government at Village Level—An Assessment; *The Indian Journal of Political Science*; 66(4) Oct.-Dec., pp. 773-92.

———, (2005), Caste Based Discrimination and Gram Panchayats in Haryana State; *Journal of Haryana Studies*; Vol. 37, 2005.

———, (2007), Village Leadership—A Study of their Economic Status, *The Indian Journal of Political Science*, Vol. LXVIII, No. 1, January-March 2007, pp. 93-102.

Malik, A.S. and Yadav, Pushpender (2008). Social and Educational Characteristics of Village Leadership in Haryana, *South Asian Survey*, 15:2 (2008), 289-306.

Malik, Ajmer Singh (1996), Scheduled Castes Development Perspective—A Review of Policy and Administration in Singh, Mohinder (ed.), Social Policy and Administration in India.

Mander, Harsh (January, 1999). Towards Direct Democracy: The Legal Empowerment of Gram Sabha, Kurukshetra, 48 (1).

Manor, James (1999). The Political Economy of Democratic Decentralization. Washington DC: The World Bank.

Mathew, George and Nayak, Ramesh, C. (July 6, 1996). Panchayati Raj at Work: What it means for the Oppressed, *Economic and Political Weekly*, Bombay, 31(27)

Mathew, George (1994). Orissa leads the way in Panchayati Raj: From Legislation to Movement, New Delhi: Concept.

———, (1996). Panchayats in a Death Trap, Chennai: *The Hindu*, June 14.

Mathur, P.C. (1981). Local Politics, in *ICSSR Survey of Research in Political Science,* Vol. II (Political Process), New Delhi: Allied Publishers.

———, (1995). The Constitutional Panchayats of India: Some Emerging Jurico-Philosophical Issues in Jain, S.P. and Thomas W. Hochgesang (eds.). Emerging Trends in Panchayati Raj (Rural Local Self-government) in India, Hydrabad: National Institute of Rural Development: Konrad Adenauer Foundation.

———, (1991). Political Dynamics of Panchayati Raj—The Institutional Pendulum of Devolution and Retraction 1959-90 with special reference to Rajasthan, New Delhi: Konark.

Mathur, Tina (2003). Women in Panchayati Raj Institutions: Reservation and Participation, Dynamics of Public Administration, 13-14(1-2), Jan.-Dec.

Mehta, S.R. (1972). Emerging Pattern of Rural Leadership, New Delhi: Wiley Eastern.

Mehta, Sushila (1971). Social Conflict in Village Communities, Delhi: S. Chand.

Mehta, Udhay (1978). The Impact of Panchayati Raj on Rural India in Desai, A.R. (ed.), Rural Sociology in India, Bombay: Popular Prakashan.

Miglani, D.C. (1993). Politics and Rural Power Structure: Emerging Trends, New Delhi: Deep and Deep Publications.

Mill, J.S. (1931) Representative Government, London: Everyman; Wilson E.H. (1948). Essays in Local Government, Oxford: Blackwell and Jones G. and Stewart J. (1985). The case for Local Government, London: Allen and Unwin.

Mishra, S.N. (June 1997). Participatory Planning, Kurukshetra, 45 (9).

Mishra, S.N. (1977). Pattern of Emerging Leadership in Rural India, Patna: Ashish Publications.

Mishra, Suresh (2002). New Trends in Community Initiatives: Panchayats in Action, *Journal of Rural Development*, 21 (3), pp. 395-410.

Mishra, S.N. and Mishra, Sweta (April 1995). Future of Panchayati Raj after 73rd Constitutional Amendment Act, Kurukshetra.

Mishra, S.N. (1986). Panchayati Raj, Bureaucracy and Rural Development, New Delhi: Indian Institute of Public Administration.

Mishra, Sweta (1994). Democratic Decentralization in India: Study in Retrospect and Prospect, New Delhi: Mittal Publications.

Mohanty, B.B. (2003). Panchayat Raj in Maharashtra and Orissa: An Overview; *IASSI Quarterly*; 21(3&4), pp. 92-125.

Mustafe Ahmed Elhussein (2000). Decentralisation and Democracy in Africa—An Agneda for International Action, *IJPA*, 46(1) Jan-March, pp. 82-83.

Narain, Iqbal and Mathur, P.C. (1967). Panchayati Raj in Rajasthan—A Case Study of Jaipur District in Jacob, George (ed.) Readings in Panchayati Raj, Hyderabad: National Institute of Rural Development.

Narain, Iqbal, and Pande, K.C. *et. al.* (1970). Panchayati Raj Administration: Old Controls and New Challenges. New Delhi: Indian Institute of Public Administration.

Natraj, V.K. (2000), Political Decentralization and Development Models. *Economic and Political Weekly*, 35 (25), June 24.

Omvedt, Gail, (1987). Women and Maharashtra Zila Parishad, *Economic and Political Weekly*, 47(21).

Opler, Morris Edward (1959). Component, Assemblage and theme in Cultural Integration and Differentiation, *American Anthropologist*, 61(6) : 955-64.

Orenstein, H. (1959). Leader and caste in a Bombay village in Park, Richard L. and Tunker, Irene (eds.). Leadership and Political Institutions in India, Princeton: Princeton University Press.

Orenstein (1959), Leadership and Caste in a Bombay Village in R.L. Park and I. Tinker (eds.), Leadership and Political Institutions in India, Madras.

Oscar, Lewis (1958). Village Life in Northern India: Studies in a Delhi Village, New York: Random House.

Palanithurai, G. (2005). Process and Performance of Gram Panchayat women and Dalit Presidents, New Delhi: Concept Publishing Company.

———, (1999). Gram Sabha: A Civil Society at the Bottom paper presented at a National Conference on Gram Sabha, July 28-29, *NIRD*, Hyderabad.

———, (1994). Empowering People for Prosperity: A Study in New Panchayati Raj System, New Delhi: Kanishka Publishers.

Pandya, H.J. (1974). Leadership in Panchayati Raj—Its Composition and Changing Pattern (Mimeographed), Department of Public Administration, South Gujarat Univ. Surat.

Paoletto, Glen (2000). An Overview of Environmental Leadership paper presented in the Seminar on Leadership for the local environment, World Environment Special Event, 8-9 July Tokyo.

Patel, Priyadavan (1988). Politics of Local Power, Local Institutions and 'Powerless' people", *Indian Journal of Political Science*, July-September.

Patil, R.B. (2003). Constitutional Amendment and Changing Panchayati Raj Institutions: A Study of Empowerment of Women and Scheduled Castes in Kolhapur District, *IASSI Quarterly*, 21(3 and 4).

Philip Atkinson (1999). Without Leadership there is no Change. Management Services, August, p. 9.

La Piere, R.T. and Farnsworth, R.R. (1936), Social Psychology, New York: McGraw Hill Book Company.

Praharaj, G.S. : Dimensional Role of the Rural Leaders in Relation to their Socio-Psychological Characteristics, pp. 139-45.

Prasad, V. Sivalinga (1981), Panchayats and Development, New Delhi, Light and Life.

PRIA (2001). State of Panchayats: A Participatory Perspective.

———, (2001). Parallel Bodies and Panchayati Raj Institutions: Experiences from States.

Raghavulu, C.V and Naryana, E.A. (Jan-March 1991). Reforms in Panchayati Raj: A Comparative Analysis of Andhra Pradesh, Karnataka and West Bengal, *Indian Journal of Public Administration*.

Rajiv Gandhi Foundation, Task Force on Panchayati Raj (1999). Road blocks to the Institutions of Self-government, New Delhi.

Rao, C.V.H. (1965). Emerging Leadership in Panchayati Raj. Kurukshetra, Vol. 13, 1964-65.

Reddy, G. Ram (1982). Panchayati Raj and Rural Development in Andhra Pradesh, India in Uphoff, Norman T. (ed.) Rural Development and Local Organisation in Asia, Vol. 1, New Delhi: Macmillan.

———, (1967). Pattern of Panchayati Raj in India, Delhi: Macmillan.

Reddy, M. Gopinath (2003). Status of Decentralised Local Bodies: Post-73rd Amendment Scenario, *Economic and Political Weekly*, 38 (12-13), March 22.

Robert, Putnam (1997). Making Democracy Work, New Jersey: Princeton University Press.

Rogers, J.L. (Summer 1992). Leadership Development for the 90's: Incorporating Emergent Paradigm Perspectives, *NASPA Journal*, pp. 243-51.

Rosan, Ned A. (1969). Leadership Change and Work Group Dynamics, New York: Cornell University Press.

Roskill, S.W. (1964). The Art of Leadership. London: Collins.

Ross, M.G. and Hendry, C. E. (1957). New Understandings of Leadership, New York Association Press.

Ross Murray G. and Hendry, Charles, E. (1958). New Understanding of Leadership, New York, Association Press.

Rost, J.C. (1991). Leadership in the 21st Century, New York: Praeger.

———, (1993). Leadership Development in the New Millennium, *The Journal of Leadership Studies*, November, pp. 91-110.

Roy, M. Sam (1995). Emerging Panchayat Leadership and Polarisation of Political•Power at Grassroot Level, *Journal of Rural Development*, 14(4).

Roy, M.N. (1952). Democracy and Party Politics, *Radical Humanism*, April 22.

Sahay, B.N. (1969). Dynamics of Leadership, New Delhi: Bookhive.

Sastrys, K.R., Vittal, C.P. and Ramachandraiah, G. (1995). Panchayati Raj in Andhra Pradesh: An Analytical Study, Panchayati Raj Institutions in Select States—An Analytical Study, Hyderabad: National Institute of Rural Development.

Sen, Lalit K. (1976). Awareness of Community Development in India, Hyderabad, National Institute of Rural Development.

Shah, Ghanshyam (2001). Introduction: Dalit Politics in the book Dalit Identity and Politics; Ghanshyam Shah (ed.) New Delhi; Sage Publications; pp. 17-43.

———, (1997). Office without *defacto* Power: A Study of Social Justice Committee in Gujarat in Shah, Ghanshyam (ed.) *Social Transformation in India*. Vol. 2, Jaipur: Rawat.

Sharma, Surjan Singh (1978). Pattern of Emerging Rural Leadership : A Case Study of village Panchayat Presidents in a Block in Uttar Pradesh, *Journal of Social and Economic Studies*, 6(1), pp. 165-79.

Sharma, Sudesh (1976). Panchayati Raj in India: A Study of Reforms at Centre and State level since Independence, New Delhi: Trimurti.

Sharpe, I.J. (1970). Theories of Local Government, *Political Studies*, 18, pp. 153-74.

Shiviah, M. (1991). Panchayat Raj, Development and Development Performance : An Institution Building Perspective. *Journal of Rural Development*, 10(5), pp. 515-41.

Shiviah, M., *et al.* (1986). Panchayati Raj Elections in Andhra Pradesh: 1981, A Study in Institution Building for Rural Development, Hyderabad: NIRD.

Shiviah, M. (1986). Panchayati Raj: A Policy Perspective, Hyderabad: NIRD.

Shrivastava, T.N. (2002). Local Self-Government and the Constitution, *Economic and Political Weekly*, 37(10).

Shukla, N.K. (1976). Social Structure of an Indian Village. New Delhi: Cosmo Publications.

Singh, Avtar (1973). Leadership Patterns and Village Strucutre, Jullundur: Sterling Publishers.

Singh, Hargian (1985). Panchayati Raj Administration in Haryana, Gurgaon: Indira Publications.

Singh, Hoshiar and Malik, A.S. (2001). Socio-Economic Development of Scheduled Castes in India, Jaipur: Aalekh Publishers.

———, (1998). The Scheduled Castes and Scheduled Tribes (Prevention of Atrocities) Act, 1989: An Analysis in Barthwal, C.P. (ed.) *Social Justice in India*, Lucknow: Bharat Prakashan.

———, (1998). Women Participation in Panchayat Raj in, R.P. Joshi (ed.). Constitutionalisation of Panchayati Raj—A Reassessment, Jaipur: Rawat Publications.

Singh, Mohinder (2002). Role of Chairpersons of Samities: A Study in Haryana, *Dynamics of Public Administration*, 11-12, (1-2), pp. 1-7.

Singh, Partap (1983). Caste as Determinant of Rural Leadership: A Case Study of Haryana. *The Indian Political Science Review*, 27(2), July, pp. 157-62.

Singh, Ranbir (2002). Haryana Panchayati Raj—Creating Political Awareness, Kurukshetra, Jan., p. 44.

Singh, Yogendra (1969). Changing Power Structure of Village Community: A Case Study of Six Villages in Eastern U.P. in Desai, A.R. (ed.). Rural Sociology in India, Bombay: Popular Prakashan.

Singh, Harjinder (1969). Village Leadership, New Delhi: Sterling Publishing House.

Singh, Mohinder (2003). Strategies for Empowering Women in Panchayati Raj, Dynamics of Public Administration, 13-14(1-2), pp. 30-37.

Singh, S.K. (1993). 73rd Constitutional Amendment: An Analytical Framework, *The Administrator*, 38(4), October-December.

Singh, S.S. and Mishra, S.N. (1993). Legislative Framework of Panchayati Raj in India. New Delhi: Intellectual Publishing House.

Sirsikar, V.M. (1970). The Rural Elite in a Developing Society, New Delhi: Orient Longman.

Sirsikar, V.M. (1973). Sovereigns Without Crowns, Bombay: Popular Prakashan.

Sivanna, N. (1998). Decentralised Governance and Planning in Karnataka: A Historical Review, *Social Change,* 28(1).

Special Number on Decetnralization (1973). *Indian Journal of Public Administration,* 19(3).

Srinivas, M.N. (1962). Caste in Modern India and Other Essays, Bombay: Asia Publishing House.

———, (1977). The Changing Position of Indian Women, *Man,* 12(2), August.

Srivastava, S.K. (1965). Directed Social Change and Rural Leadership and Rural Leadership in India, Dube, S.C. (ed.). *Emerging Pattern of Rural Leadership in South Asia.*

Sunstein, Cass R. (1995). Gender, Caste and Law in Nussbaum, Martha and Glover (eds.). Jonathan Women, *Culture and Development,* Oxford: Clarendon Press, pp. 332-59.

Syed, A. (1966), The Political Theory in American Local Government. New York: Random House.

Dahl, R.A. (1967). The city in the future of democracy. *American Political Science Review,* 61(4), pp. 953-70.

Tandon, R. (2002). Linking Citizenship, Participation and Accountability: A Perspective for PRIA, *IDS Bulletin,* Vol. 33.

Tannerbaum, Robert, Weschler Irving R. and Massarik Fred (1961). Leadership and Organisation, New York: McGraw Hill.

Tead, Ordway (1935). The Art of Leadership. New York: McGraw Hill.

Terry, George (1960). The Principles of Management, Homewood Ill: Richard Irwin Inc.

Urwick, L.F. (1957). Leadership in Twentieth Century, London: Sir Issac Pitman and Sons Ltd.

Vasant, Desai (1990). Panchayati Raj: Power to the People, Bombay: Himalaya Publishing House.

Verma, B.M. (1990). Decentralisation in Administration, New Delhi: Uppal Publishing House.

Vidhyarthi, L.P. (Ed.) (1967). Leadership in India, Bombay: Asia Publishing House.

Vyasulu, Vinod (2001). Decentrlaization, Democratization and Local Finances After 73rd Constitutional Amendment, Bangalore: CBPS.

Vyasulu, Vinod (2003). Panchayats, Democracy and Development, New Delhi: Rawat Publications.

(ii) Reports

Government of Andhra Pradesh (Hyderabad 1960); High Power Committee on the Reorganisation of Panchayat Samiti/ Blocks and Allied Matters, Panchayati Raj Development, Report (Hyderabad 1964); Andhra Pradesh Congress Legislature Party Committee on Panchayati Raj (Convener, J. Vengal Rao) (Hyderabad, 1968); Government of Andhra Pradesh High Power Committee on Panchayati Raj (Chairman : C. Narasimham), Report (Hyderabad, 1972); State Committee on Panchayati Raj Institutions, Reports (Chairman : C. Narasimham) Hyderabad, 1981.

Government of Andhra Pradesh, High Power Committee on Panchayati Raj (Chairman: B.V.R. Vikttal), Hyderabad: Government of Andhra Pradesh, 1992.

Government of Andhra Pradesh, Report of the High Power Committee on Panchayati Raj, 1972 (C. Narasimham).

Government of Andhra Pradesh, Report on Panchayati Raj (Chairman: C. Narashimhan), Hyderabad, Government of Andhra Pradesh, 1972.

Government of Andhra Pradesh, Report on Panchayati Raj (Chairman: C. Narashimham), Hyderabad: Government of Andhra Pradesh, 1981.

Government of Andhra Pradesh, The Andhra Pradesh Panchayati Raj Act, 1994, Hyderabad: Government of Andhra Pradesh, 1994.

Government of India, "Provision of the Panchayats (Extension to the Scheduled Areas) Act, 1996: Gazette of India, Extraordinary Part II, Section 1, New Delhi: Government of India, December 24, 1996.

Government of India, Census 1991, Haryana Village and Town Directory, New Delhi: Government of India.
Government of India, Committee on Plan Projects: Study Team (Chairman: Balwantrai Mehta), New Delhi: Planning Commission, 1957.
Government of India, Constitution of India, New Delhi: 1994.
Government of India, Ministry of Agriculture, Department of Rural Development, Report of the Committee to Review the Existing Administrative Arrangement for Rural Development and Poverty Alleviation Programme, New Delhi, 1985.
Government of India, Ministry of Rural Development, 1999, Swaranajayanti Gram Swarozgar Yojana, Guidelines, New Delhi.
Government of India, Report of the Committee on Panchayati Raj Institutes (Chairman: Ashok Mehta), New Delhi: Government of India, 1978.
Government of India, Report of the Team for the Study of Community Projects and National Extension Service (Chairman: Balwantrai Mehta), New Delhi: Government of India, 1958.
Government of India: "The Constitution (Seventy-third Amendment) Act, 1992", Gazette of India, Extraordinary, Part II, Section 1, New Delhi: Government of India, April 20, 1993.
Government of Kerala, Committee on Decentralisation of Power (Final Report), 1997, Trivandrum.
Government of Mysore, Report of the Committee on Panchayati Raj, 1963 (Kondaji Basappa).
Government of Orissa, Orissa Gram Panchayat (Amendment) Act, 1994, Bhubaneshwar, 1994.
Government of Orissa, Orissa Gram Panchayat (Amendment) Act, 1994, Bhubaneshwar, 1997.
Government of Orissa, Orissa Gram Panchayat (Amendment) Act, 1991, Bhubaneshwar, 1991.
Government of Orissa, Orissa Zila Parishad (Amendment) Act, 1993, Bhubaneshwar, 1993.
Government of Orissa, Orissa Zila Parishad (Amendment) Act, 1997, Bhubaneshwar, 1997.

Government of Orissa, Orissa Zila Parishad Act, 1991, Bhubaneswar, 1991.

Government of Rajasthan, Report of High Power Committee on Panchayati Raj (Chairman: Girdharilal Vyas), Jaipur: Government of Rajasthan, 1973.

Government of Rajasthan, Report of the Study Team on Panchayati Raj (Chairman: Sadiq Ali), Jaipur: Government of Rajasthan, 1964.

Government of Rajasthan, Rajasthan First State Finance Commission Report, Jaipur: Government of Rajasthan, 1995.

State Planning Board, Government of Kerala, 1999, *Economic Review,* 1998, Trivandrum, Government Press.

Some more committees: Sadiq Ali Team of Rajasthan (1964), Bongarwar Committee of Maharashtra (1971), Zeenabhai Darji Committee of Gujarat (1967), Narsimham Committee (1973), and Vengal Rao Committee (1968) of Andhra Pradesh and Girdhari Lal Vyas Committee (1978) of Rajasthan.

World Bank Development Report, 1999-2000. Entering the 21st Century, Oxford: Oxford University Press.